How does identity influence the way adolescents make decisions and cope with stressors? What processes enable the minority adolescent to integrate ethnic identity with other identities into a "meta-identity"? Rooted in the theoretical work of Erikson and Blos, an international team of scholars explores the processes of identity formation, social and behavioral outcomes and management, social contextual factors, and issues of alternative conceptualizations and measurement. Opening with James Marcia's identity status paradigm, the book includes many exciting discussions, including women's identity and Erikson's notions of inner space, Grotevant's process model and how adoptive identity might be studied, the Groningen Identity Development Scale, the question of a unitary self, a multidimensional approach to ethnic identity, how cognitive factors intervene in the process of identity formation, and the influence of cognitive identity styles with the ways in which adolescents cope with stress. Students, researchers, and practitioners interested in the latest work on adolescent identity development and its impact on solving adolescents' problems will find this volume a thought-provoking addition to their studies.

ADOLESCENT IDENTITY FORMATION

ADVANCES IN ADOLESCENT DEVELOPMENT:
AN ANNUAL BOOK SERIES

Series Editors

Gerald R. Adams, *University of Guelph, Ontario, Canada*
Raymond Montemayor, *The Ohio State University*
Thomas P. Gullotta, *Child and Family Agency, Connecticut*

Advances in Adolescent Development is an annual book series designed to analyze, integrate, and critique an abundance of new research and literature in the field of adolescent development. Contributors are selected from numerous disciplines based on their creative, analytical, and influential scholarship in order to provide information pertinent to professionals as well as upper-division and graduate students. The Series Editors' goals are to evaluate the current empirical and theoretical knowledge about adolescence, and to encourage the formulation (or expansion) of new directions in research and theory development.

Volumes in This Series

ADOLESCENT
IDENTITY FORMATION

Edited by
GERALD R. ADAMS
THOMAS P. GULLOTTA
RAYMOND MONTEMAYOR

ADVANCES IN ADOLESCENT DEVELOPMENT
An Annual Book Series Volume 4

SAGE PUBLICATIONS
International Educational and Professional Publisher
Newbury Park   London   New Delhi

For information address:

SAGE Publications, Inc.
2455 Teller Road
Newbury Park, California 91320

SAGE Publications Ltd.
6 Bonhill Street
London EC2A 4PU
United Kingdom

SAGE Publications India Pvt. Ltd.
M-32 Market
Greater Kailash I
New Delhi 110 048 India

Printed in the United States of America

ISBN 0-8039-4615-5
ISBN 0-8039-4616-3   (pbk.)
ISSN 1050-8589

92   93   94   95   96   10   9   8   7   6   5   4   3   2   1

Sage Production Editor: Judith L. Hunter

Contents

Preface

Advances in Adolescent Development is a serial publication designed to either bring together an integrative review of existing knowledge or introduce new developments in theory, research, and practice. This volume focuses on contemporary issues associated with the conceptualization, measurement, and empirical investigation of identity development during adolescence. Each chapter is written by an individual (or individuals) who has an authoritative line of research on the theme. Contributors were selected to include scholars who represent differing perspectives. Likewise, both highly eminent and emerging scholars were invited, based on their visible impact or clear promise for making a substantive contribution to the field of adolescent development. And contributions reach beyond North America to introduce an international dimension to the series. The theme was selected by the senior editor, in consultation with the other editors, based on his longstanding interest in the topic. Readers with ideas for future themes can contact any of the editors with suggestions for consideration.

Throughout the early and continuing development of this series the editors at Sage have been most supportive. We are particularly thankful at Terry Hendrix and C. Deborah Laughton for their support and advice.

The senior editor of this volume has undertaken the preparation of this book while being employed at two universities. He is thankful to his colleagues at Utah State University and the institutional support he received to operate the Laboratory for Research on Adolescence. Currently, he is employed at the University of Guelph in Ontario, Canada.

Finally, as one of three editors of this series I am thankful for the advice and counsel I receive from my associates. While each of us assumes primary responsibility for developing a specific volume, we provide one another with varying, and sometimes contrasting, perspectives on how this series should be developed and managed. That dialectic process, nonetheless, provides each of us with a certain form of synergistic energy and creative potential.

— Gerald R. Adams
Senior Series Editor

Acknowledgments

Edited books require substantial assistance. In addition to the authors of the chapters in this volume, who graciously provided one another with constructive feedback, we are appreciative of several peer reviewers for their thoughtful comments on early drafts of chapter manuscripts: Robert Enright, Ruthellen Josselson, George Kawash, Harry Kitano, Daniel Lapsley, Joseph LaVoie, Jacob Orlofsky, Derald Wing Sue, and Ronald L. Taylor.

As a professor and chair of a large multidisciplinary program, I need the assistance of several individuals to protect some time for scholarship. I am appreciative of the extensive assistance from my administrative secretary, Barbara Aldridge, and my administrative assistant, Margo Shoemaker. Without their dedication and willingness to cover several aspects of administrative duties, I would be unable to serve as senior editor of this volume.

— Gerald R. Adams
Senior Series Editor

1. Introduction and Overview

Gerald R. Adams
University of Guelph

Adolescence is widely recognized as a stage associated with substantial change in the self. Perhaps the two most widely recognized frameworks for conceptualizing the transformation of the self during adolescence have been provided by Erik Erikson (1968) and Peter Blos (1962, 1979).

Both theorists recognize adolescence as a major life stage for identity formation. Identity is conceptualized as an internalized, self-selected regulatory system that represents an organized and integrated psychic structure that requires the developmental distinction between the inner self and outer social world. Identity formation is seen as an evolutionary process of differentiation and integration, synthesis and resynthesis, and increasing cognitive complexity. Early stages of identity development involve indiscriminate use of introjection and identification mechanisms and reflect unstable or immature internal self-images. With the onset of puberty, ego maturation in role-taking and cognitive operations enhances the ability to deal with the dialectic of psychological life (e.g., good versus evil; my perspective versus your perspective) and facilitates the capacity for an integrated and self-selected psychic character that is based on self-mastery and accurate perceptions of talent, skills, and abilities.

Erikson and Blos make substantive distinctions between a passive versus active identity formation process. For Erikson, a passive identity is reflected in either a foreclosing process where an adolescent accepts, without evaluation, the roles and self-images provided by others, or a diffused identity associated with role confusion. Blos portrays passivity of identity in his description of prolonged adolescence, where arrested movement is observed through the resistance to make final choices. For both theorists, passive identity youths are thought to harbor self-doubt and uncertainty, and are hypothesized to lose one's self when removed from the foreclosed and structured environment in which they live. In contrast, active identity formation is based on a searching and self-selection process, where self-chosen commitments are integrated into an organized psychic structure. This form of identity is hypothesized to be associated with self-assurance, self-certainty, and a sense of mastery.

At the extreme opposite of the active identity formation process is a passive form of identity diffusion. Both theorists portray this youth as manifesting pathological symptoms. Severe identity diffusion is seen as a defensive, ego dystonic state, reflecting the absence of both an organized psychic structure and corresponding appropriate ego strengths.

Erikson and Blos view identity formation and development within a social context. Erikson views individual development as occurring within a social context where societal expectations require a selection from available choices, with the individual, in turn, needing confirmation of choices and community acceptance. Erikson speaks of the role of intergenerational socialization where society must provide for a mutual trustworthiness to assure self-chosen values and interests, experience with ego autonomy so that the individual can independently select a future, and encouraged initiative to assure a sense of purpose and promise of fulfillment. This same society must allow for experimentation, acceptance, and support of commitments made, and provide a fidelity for self-selected choices.

Blos, in contrast, argues that while the individual must be supported by unceasing interactions with others, increasing separation of self from caregivers and emotional disengagement are critical to ego maturity and identity development. Generational differences and corresponding tension and conflict between parent(s) and adolescent are thought to be necessary to facilitate psychological differentiation. Therefore, regressive behaviors during adolescence are hypothesized to be necessary to resolve early childhood emotional relationships with parents. Essentially, Blos argues that progressive differentiation in ego-identity requires a supportive environment that provides foundational emotional support but allows for an expression of the natural tensions and conflicts that occur due to generational differences.

Although much credit must be given to these two psychoanalytic theorists for their powerful and insightful descriptions of the nature and process of identity formation during adolescence, the actual broadening of empirical investigations on identity formation is most appropriately credited to James Marcia. Utilizing aspects of Erikson's theoretical writings, Marcia (1966) devised an innovative conceptualization and measurement of ego identity formation. This perspective is most commonly referred to as the Ego Identity Status Paradigm. This important strategy for the empirical investigation of identity formation and development has provided the foundation for not only more than 20 years of systematic research (see Marcia, 1980, for a review), but also the catalyst for the creation of many new and emerging perspectives (some of which are provided in this volume) as well as debates about the usefulness and/or appropriateness of the Ego Identity Status Paradigm (e. g., Cote & Levine, 1988; Waterman, 1988).

Therefore, it is most fitting that the first substantive chapter in this volume has been written by Marcia and his colleagues. This chapter offers a general description of his conceptualization and addresses a highly controversial issue of women's identity and Erikson's notions of inner space. In this chapter Serena Patterson, Ingrid Sochting, and James Marcia discuss issues regarding the assessment of women's identity, timing of identity development, confluence of psychosocial stages, adaptiveness of the identity statuses, and the meaning of identity for women. With brevity and precision these authors provide considerable food for thought while reflecting the currently popular theme that the conceptualization and measurement of identity must include interpersonal content and context.

Chapter 3 also focuses on women's identity. Sally Archer examines feminist concerns about identity research. She highlights the invisibility of women, class, and race in theories of normal healthy development. Focusing on the definitional framework of identity, Archer discusses issues of exclusivity, subjectivity, and related dimensions of measurement and methodology. In this chapter Archer discusses the use of global versus domain status scoring in the study of identity formation. Further, she shares her troubling thoughts on the intrapersonal and interpersonal distinctions that have emerged, in part, to the response of feminist criticisms of the identity status methodology. In this chapter she offers a feminist methodology to address the male-biased measurement issues of the past. Archer clarifies her views through examples from her own research program. Writing as an advocate for change, in the remainder of the chapter she examines the cost of politicizing methodologies through a discussion of the implications of invisibility and ignoring social context.

Chapter 4, written by Alan Waterman, offers one of the many emerging perspectives in the study of personal identity. (His perspective, like that of many of the remaining authors in this text, appears to be moving away from the earlier traditional ego psychoanalytic frameworks to a more social-cognitive perspective.) Waterman begins with a definition of criteria for assessing optimal psychological functioning. Next, he reviews Erikson's psychosocial theory of stage development and analyzes it within his criteria for optimal psychological functioning. This is followed by a discussion of Marcia's identity statuses based on a reflective self-structure. Waterman argues that in addition to the dimensions of exploration and commitment, the assessment of identity statuses should include a third dimension of personal expressiveness. Much of the remainder of this chapter reviews research on identity as an aspect of optimal psychological functioning. In his conclusion, Waterman gives a clear rationale for the development of intervention strategies that promote a reflective personal identity. In addition to his own theoretical perspectives, around which this chapter is written, the material provides an excellent selective review of much of the recent research on identity formation utilizing Marcia's identity status paradigm.

In Chapter 5 Harold Grotevant expands upon his proposed process model for the study of identity formation. His model is developmental, contextual, and life-span in scope. This emerging process model focuses on the processes that are foundational to identity development, contextual in its recognition of interdependent influences, and life-span in that it considers continuities form childhood through adulthood. In this chapter Grotevant makes a major substantive distinction between chosen and assigned identity using occupational identity to illustrate the chosen identity and the case of adopted children as an example of an assigned identity. In the remainder of this chapter Grotevant explores and examines the interaction of assigned and chosen components of identity. The chapter provides insights on the manner in which an adoptive identity might be studied. Issues of compartmentalization, organizational principles of identity integration, embeddedness of the self, and identity as narrative are introduced as meaningful dimensions of research on identity formation.

Chapter 6 brings to this series the added dimension of an international perspective beyond North America. Harke Bosma summarizes some of his ongoing research in the development of the Groningen Identity Development Scale (GIDS). This contribution reflects a wave of new scale and measurement development to assess identity formation using self-report instruments. Bosma summarizes several studies using the GIDS and demonstrates the foundational role that the management of commitment assumes in identity formation. His efforts represent a strong and growing interest in the study of identity formation beyond North America.

Chapter 7 provides another international contribution to this volume. Jane Kroger offers an examination of three models of ego development and their potential use in understanding normative intrapsychic development. Each model uses a structural conception of the ego. She begins with an analysis of the ego psychoanalytic theories of Erikson and Marcia. This is followed by the analysis of object relations theories of Mahler and Blos. The third model involves the constructive-developmental theories of Kegan and Noam. Within each of these theoretical perspectives, Kroger examines various conceptual and methodological issues in the study of identity development. This chapter offers an excellent analysis of varying ego development paradigms that are in current use in the study of intrapsychic development during adolescence. Likewise, Kroger concludes with an interesting discussion regarding the question of a unitary self. Throughout this and other chapters in this volume the issue of consistency, organizational structure, and structural unity can be seen as an unsettled and challenging question to contemporary researchers and their conceptual and theory building.

Chapter 8 includes the cooperative writing of Jean Phinney and Doreen Rosenthal. It represents a growing trend toward international cooperative scholarship in the study of identity. The authors examine the process, context, and outcome of ethnic identity in adolescence. Phinney and Rosenthal offer a conceptualization of ethnic identity that is dynamic and multidimensional. They suggest that an adequate understanding of ethnic identity requires the inclusion of developmental and contextual dimensions. To illustrate their points they examine the interaction of development and context through an analysis of published research on family influences, the ethnic community, and the ethnic group in the larger society. In the remainder of this chapter the authors explore the assumption that achieving a positive sense of ethnic identity is a healthy outcome for minority adolescents through the examination of evidence that links ethnic identity and feelings of self-worth. The authors draw upon their own research programs to build their case. They conclude that the proposed association is both complex and mediated by numerous social, cultural, environmental, and possibly historical factors. Like Grotevant's writings on adoptive identity, Phinney and Rosenthal demonstrate the need for understanding the contextual nature of identity formation.

Following the general theme on contextual factors, Carol Markstrom-Adams provides a useful delineation of many intervening factors in adolescent identity formation. In Chapter 9 Markstrom-Adams selectively examines social contextual, cognitive, and psychopathological factors that facilitate or constrain adolescent identity formation. She explores the social contexts of family relationships, ethnic and racial group membership, and religiosity; the potential cognitive barriers associated with formal operations, assimilation and accommodation, perspective-taking and egocentrism, cognitive complexity, and continuity of the self; and psychopathological disturbances of abandonment depression, narcissism, and related dysfunctionality. As Waterman has suggested, the evidence supporting the need for social intervention is apparent, and Markstrom-Adams provides an analysis of numerous dimensions around which social intervention programs might be constructed.

Chapter 10, by Michael Berzonsky, offers another process perspective on identity and elaborates upon how this perspective might be used to understand stress management. Berzonsky's work bridges that of developmental and social psychological paradigms. As a self-construction theorist, Berzonsky studies the social-cognitive processes that underlie the identity statuses. He refers to these processes as identity styles that an individual characteristically uses and prefers to deploy. In this chapter he outlines and discusses the identity styles reflective of an information-oriented, normative-oriented, and avoidant-oriented social-cognitive process. He reviews the literature to demonstrate how the identity statuses are associated with varying social cognitions. Then Berzonsky examines the Identity Style Inventory and provides information on the reliability and validity of this self-report instrument. As suggested in the Markstrom-Adams chapter that cognitive factors intervene in the identity formation process, Berzonsky demonstrates how the cognitive factors underlying identity styles have ramifications for the ways in which adolescents cope with stress. His findings indicate considerable promise that further understanding of identity formation can be obtained by examining identity style by environmental context interactions.

Chapter 11 is perhaps the most directly applied chapter in this volume. Randall Jones summarizes his work in the study of ego identity status and adolescent problem behavior. Drawing largely on Richard Jessor's conceptualizations of psychosocial explanations for substance use and abuse, Jones has connected this paradigm with that of Erikson and Marcia in the study of adolescent problem behaviors. Using large data sets from public and private schools in Arizona, Jones demonstrates how diffused adolescents are at great risk for substance use/abuse. Among his many reported findings he reports that preadolescent behaviors and psychosocial development may create a heightened state of risk for adolescent drug abuse. Jones concludes that fostering psychosocial development, perhaps in the form of social interventions designed to enhance ego identity, may be an effective alternative to traditional prevention or intervention approaches to drug abuse.

An overview of this text might be summarized in this manner: We owe much to the clinical writings of Erikson and Blos. Their ego psychoanalytic perspectives have provided us with the view that identity formation is dynamic, developmental, and contextual. This heritage is readily seen in contemporary empirically focused scholars' writings and research. With the creation of the identity status paradigm, Marcia provided an initial framework for studying adolescent identity formation. This framework has influenced every contributor to this text—in one or more ways. It has created a method of conceptualization and measurement, a paradigm for empirical investigation, a framework for communication and sharing of ideas, and it has also created controversy, discussion, and innovation. This text is as much a reflection of the use and influence of the Ego Identity Status Paradigm as it is one of evolution from it.

The chapters in this text illustrate the evolution of research perspectives on adolescent identity formation. Issues of alternative conceptualizations and measurement, identity formation processes, social and behavioral outcomes and management, and social contextual factors are salient features in these chapters. As these authors continue their work we shall see many differing and viable alternatives to the study of adolescent identity formation and development that began with the theoretical foundations of Erikson and Blos, followed by the conceptualization and measurement of ego-identity statuses as constructed by Marcia, which are now being deconstructed, reconstructed, and modified by a different generation of scholars interested in the study of adolescent identity. It is an exciting time with an ever-expanding interest in the study of adolescent identity development. It is my hope that you will find the chapters in this text descriptive of the new wave and forthcoming directions of scholarship on this topic.

REFERENCES

Blos, P. (1962). *On adolescence*. New York: Free Press.

Blos, P. (1979). *The adolescent passage*. New York: International Universities Press.

Cote, J. E., & Levine, C. (1988). A critical examination of the ego identity status paradigm. *Developmental Review, 8*, 147-184.

Erikson, E. H. (1968). *Identity: Youth and crisis*. New York: Norton.

Marcia, J. E. (1980). Identity in adolescence. In J. Adelson (Ed.), *Handbook of adolescent psychology* (pp. 149-173). New York: John Wiley.

Waterman, A. S. (1988). Identity status theory and Erikson's theory: Communalities and differences. *Developmental Review, 8*, 185-208.

2. The Inner Space and Beyond: Women and Identity

Serena J. Patterson
Ingrid Sochting
James E. Marcia
Simon Fraser University

THE CONCEPT OF IDENTITY

Identity as a Psychosocial Stage: Erik Erikson

Erik Erikson saw the formation of a personal sense of identity (versus identity diffusion) as one of the cornerstones of ego development (Erikson, 1982). Defined as "the accrued confidence [in] the inner sameness and continuity of one's meaning for others" (Erikson, 1950, p. 235), identity is considered to be of central concern during late adolescence. In Erikson's definition, three elements emerge as necessary for a sense of identity. First, the person must experience inner sameness, or integrity, so that actions and decisions are not random. Defined values, principles, and expectations order one's behavior, and a deviation is perceived as "not me." Second, the sense of inner sameness is continuous over time. Actions in the past and hopes for the future are experienced as related to the self of today. Third, identity is experienced within a community of important others. Relationships and roles serve, ideally, to support and validate an integrated, continuous identity.

This sense of inner continuity and purpose is predicated on the resolution of previous developmental stages, each dominated by a central, organizing theme. In infancy, the central issue is trust versus mistrust, with its corresponding ego strength of hope.

AUTHORS' NOTE: *This work was presented to the Canadian Psychological Association Annual Convention in Halifax, Nova Scotia, in June 1989. The authors gratefully acknowledge Lynne Robinson for her thoughtful editing of the manuscript. Reprint requests should be sent to Dr. Serena J. Patterson, North Island College, 1480 Elm Street, Campbell River, B.C., Canada, V9W 3A6.*

Between basic trust and identity, the child passes through stages of development in which the ego strengths of will, purpose, and competence emerge from the struggles of autonomy versus shame and doubt, initiative versus guilt, and industry versus inferiority (Erikson, 1982). According to Erikson, stages progress in a definite order that is linked to social expectations and bodily maturation. The psychosocial crisis, or central issue of each stage, rests upon and may modify the outcome of all preceding stages. At the same time, each crisis incorporates the forerunners of issues and stages to come. Erikson places the task of intimacy versus isolation after that of identity, indicating that the sense of continuity and fidelity to one's values at a personal level is a prerequisite to true intimacy (see Figure 2.1).

According to Erikson, the life stage of adolescence provides young people with the optimal situation for defining a sense of identity. Not yet firmly tied by adult commitments, the adolescent may try out a variety of possible commitments in occupation and ideology, eventually adopting a more or less permanent sense of who he or she is.

Identity as a Personality Construct:
Marcia's Identity Status Model

Building upon Erikson's work, James Marcia (1966, 1980) developed the identity status approach to studying the process of identity formation. Marcia's four identity statuses occupy unique positions along the dimensions of exploration and commitment. Identity statuses are both outcomes of the process of identity formation and structural properties of the personality, and each portrays a dominant mode of experiencing the world. Identity status at late adolescence should thus affect and shape future identity formation as well as the person's passage through subsequent life stages (Marcia, Waterman, Matteson, Archer, & Orlofsky, in preparation) (see Figure 2.2).

The four identity statuses are as follows:

(a) *Identity diffusion* is the least developmentally advanced status, although, like all of the statuses, it has adaptive aspects, and may be the most adaptive mode of functioning under certain con-

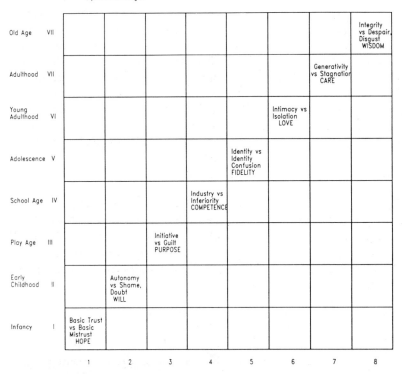

Figure 2.1. Erikson's Psychological Stages of Development

ditions. Commitment to an internally consistent set of values and goals is absent, and exploration is either missing or shallow. People in identity diffusion tend to follow the path of least resistance, and may present as having a carefree, cosmopolitan lifestyle, and/or as being empty and dissatisfied.

(b) *Identity foreclosure* represents a high level of commitment following little or no exploration. For some, identity foreclosure is a developmental starting point, from which a period of exploration will ensue. However, as an identity resolution, foreclosure is considered by Marcia to represent a less developed state than that of *moratorium* or *identity achievement*. People who follow

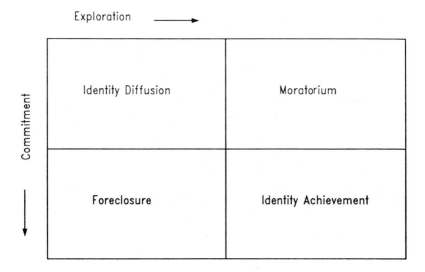

Figure 2.2. Marcia's Identity Statuses

the foreclosure pattern adopt a single set of values and goals, usually those of their parents.

(c) *Moratorium* is arguably considered a stage, rather than a resolution of the identity formation process, although some people
apparently remain in moratorium over many years. Marcia's moratorium status refers to the process of forging an identity—occupational, interpersonal, and ideological commitments—from the
myriad of possibilities available. The person in moratorium is intensely preoccupied with exploring options and working toward
commitment.

(d) *Identity achievement* represents an autonomous resolution of
identity, incorporating a set of commitments adopted during a period of exploration (moratorium). It is the exploration of the moratorium period that distinguishes the flexible strength of identity
achievement from the rigid strength of identity foreclosure.

Eriksonian Perspectives on Women and Identity

From the beginning, the construct of identity was arguably descriptive of male development. Its generalization to women has

not been straightforward. Erikson first addressed women's identity in his controversial article "Women and the Inner Space" (1968). Apparently taken aback by feminist criticism, he returned to the topic in the early 1970s with a rebuttal and an attempt to state more clearly his original principles regarding the development of girls and women (Erikson, 1975).

Although Erikson saw identity as developing within the context of anatomy, history, and personality, he appeared ambivalent about whether to distance himself from Freud's concept of anatomy and destiny. Rather than deny penis envy as an anatomical fact (as opposed to a social experience), Erikson referred to the "inner space," or womb, as the basis for a positive (anatomically based) potential for the girl's identity. Although some feminists may have been impressed by the addition of a positive pole to women's identity, Erikson's insistence on defining women's identity in anatomical terms was troubling. Erikson's argument seemed to imply that women were anatomically destined to be nurturant and accommodating, and were thus uniquely suited to service roles.

Paradoxically, Erikson conceptualized women's identity as the individual's construction of the experience of womanhood, of living in a woman's body and of living with the gender-based role prescriptions and proscriptions of her culture. This conceptualization was sympathetic to women's struggles to define and control their reproductive power within a patriarchal culture. In retrospect, Erikson seems far-seeing in his insistence that if feminists ignored the reproductive power of women's bodies, they would be in danger of contributing to the further devaluation of women and of the values of care and nurturance in Western culture.

At least three testable hypotheses concerning women's identity can be drawn from the inner space articles. First, Erikson believed that interpersonal issues formed the core of women's identity, and vocational and ideological issues were of peripheral importance. Second, a women's resolution of identity was expected to be left partially open and flexible at adolescence, in order to accommodate the man she would marry and the children she would nurture. The girl's first, temporary resolution of identity in adolescence consisted of a sense of her own attractiveness, an image of the mate she would seek, and a decision about the use she would make (or not make) of her body and its reproductive capacity. Her identity was thus to be completed in marriage and motherhood. Third, the sequence of women's development appeared to be less stage specific than that of men. Issues of identity, intimacy, and generativity could be resolved almost concurrently, rather than in a clearly sequential manner.

These three issues of identity content, timing, and confluence with other stages have been investigated over the two and a half decades since "Women and the Inner Space" was written. In addition, researchers have questioned the appropriateness of applying the identity construct to women, and whether the construct of identity itself is biased toward the Western, masculine ideal of individualism over relatedness.

RESEARCH ON WOMEN'S IDENTITY

Content Domains in Assessing Women's Identity

In 1970 Marcia and Friedman employed the Identity Status Interview, which had been developed using male samples only, in the study of female development. Hypothesizing that the content areas of occupation, religion, and politics were not necessarily the most salient areas for women's identity development, and taking a cue from Erikson's 1968 article, Marcia and Friedman added the content area of "attitudes toward premarital sexual intercourse" to the interview format. Schenkel and Marcia (1972) found that identity achievement in the area of sexuality was associated with higher self-esteem and lower anxiety among women, but identity achievement solely in the areas of occupation, religion, and politics (ORP) was not. Two studies from the 1970s indicated that more women than men were identity achieved in the area of sexuality (Poppen, 1974; Waterman & Nevid, 1977). Matteson (1977) added the area of sex roles to the interview, and suggested that interpersonal content areas (now represented as attitudes toward sexuality and sex roles) were important to both men and women. However, Hodgeson and Fisher (1979) noted that men tended to be more advanced in the ORP, or male pathway identity issues, while women were more advanced in the interpersonal, or female pathway issues of sexuality and sex roles. The general impression left by research on gender and content domains of identity through the 1970s was that a neat split existed between predominantly male identity issues of occupation, religion, and politics, and predominantly female issues of sexuality and sex roles.

This neat split appeared to break down in the 1980s. Although gender differences in identity development continued to be found, they were defined in a different and more complex manner. Hopkins (1982) constructed an "inner space" interview emphasizing interpersonal issues, but found it to have no predictive advantage over the ORP or "outer space" interview for women. Bilsker, Schiedel, and Marcia (1988) found that both men and women claimed that the interpersonal area was the most important to them. When identity ratings within content areas were compared with overall ratings for each subject, no gender differences in occupation as a predictor of overall identity status were found. However, the interpersonal area (sexuality and sex roles) was most predictive for women, and ideology (religion and politics) was most predictive for men.

The unique task of women defining their sense of identity in the 1980s seemed to be balancing identity issues and interpersonal concerns. Thorbecke and Grotevant (1982) noted that although men negotiated occupation and interpersonal concerns as separate and independent identity concerns, it was important for young women to negotiate interpersonal issues in order for occupational identity formation to proceed. Kroger (1987) noted that identity concerns among women involved not simple decisions within content areas, but meta-decisions about how to balance competing commitments, while considering the implications of these commitments for significant others. Archer (1985a) found that although adolescent girls and boys were equally concerned about occupation, the career/marriage issue was of greater salience for girls than for boys. She concluded that women face a more complex task in identity formation than do men, because of the number of content domains within which they define themselves, and the relative lack of societal support for their position.

Timing of Identity Development for Women

Most studies of identity formation have focused on the college years (ages 18-22). Early research suggested that men progressed in identity development during these years, while women did not (Constantinople, 1969). Reanalysis of Constantinople's data (Whitbourne, Jelsma, & Waterman, 1982) suggests that the women's apparent lack of progress was due to a cohort effect. Schiedel and Marcia (1985) found that the proportion of high identity males in their sample of university students increased with age, while the proportion of high identity females did not. They suggested that either women reach a ceiling on identity development before men do, or women have a diphasic developmental pattern, with one group achieving an initial identity before age 20, and the other forming a self-constructed identity after fulfilling the socially pre-scribed roles of wife and mother.

Examining the effects of marriage and motherhood on identity, O'Connell (1976) found it useful to distinguish between a per-sonal and a reflected sense of identity. Personal identity was char-acterized by introspection and self-knowledge, which we might equate with Marcia's moratorium and achievement statuses. Re-flected identity referred to knowing and valuing oneself primarily through the eyes of others, (i.e., as mothers, daughters, partners, and such). O'Connell found that women with continuous careers conceived of their identities as strong and personally defined at all stages of the life cycle. Nonemployed mothers, and mothers who postponed employment to care for young children, de-scribed their identities primarily in reflected terms until their chil-dren reached school age. Once children reached school age, the women in every group studied tended to claim a strong, personal sense of identity. These results appear to support the notion of diphasic identity development. They refute Erikson's claim that women's sense of identity was strengthened by the arrival of chil-dren (unless, of course, one considers the reflected identity to represent the true nature of women's identity. This notion prob-ably seemed less absurd in the early part of the century than it does now).

Archer (1985b) found that early nonreflective role choices tended to predispose women to subsequent disruptive life expe-riences. The tendency of women to approach the task of personal identity formation in response to changes in role expectancies might explain the otherwise somewhat curious finding of Kroger (1987) that moratorium was the predominant identity status among women of all ages studied (ages 17-47).

To summarize, the task of identity formation appears to begin in adolescence for women as it does for men. For some women (notably those who will follow nontraditional lifestyles of continuous employment), late adolescence is expected to be the optimal time of life for resolution of the identity versus identity confusion task. For other women, the task of defining a personal sense of identity may wait, not, as Erikson supposed, for the arrival of a mate and children, but for the partial departure of children, which allows the time for these women to identify and pursue identity commitments of their own choosing.

Confluence of Psychosocial Stages

For men, the evidence indicates that the resolution of developmental issues is stepwise, as described by Erikson (1950, 1968, 1982). The resolution of intimacy is contingent upon identity (Hodgeson & Fischer, 1979; Kacerguis & Adams, 1980; Orlofsky, Marcia, & Lesser, 1973; Schiedel & Marcia, 1985). However, findings with women suggest that the sequence of identity preceding intimacy is not inviolable. Some women are successful in resolving the intimacy issue without successful identity achievement (Marcia, 1976; Prager, 1977; Schiedel & Marcia, 1985; Tesch & Whitbourne, 1982; Zampich, 1980). Schiedel and Marcia suggest that intimacy and identity concerns tend to merge for women, rather than to be resolved in a stepwise manner.

Relative Adaptiveness of the Identity Statuses in Women

Research findings have consistently indicated advantages of moratorium over foreclosure status among men, in terms of both psychological strength and well-being (see Marcia et al., in preparation, for a review). Men in moratorium appear to be more advanced in psychological maturity than those who remain in foreclosure, and this advance is reflected in higher self-esteem and a greater sense of personal control in their lives. Although moratorium may be disruptive and characterized by anxiety, this does not seem to be overwhelming for men and is outweighed by the psychological and social gains that the crisis engenders.

For women, the experience of moratorium may hold a different configuration of threat and promise than it does for men. Whether women in moratorium are seen as more similar to those in identity achievement or to those in identity diffusion seems to depend largely upon two aspects of the research itself: when the research was conducted; and the depth of the dependent variable. Research conducted prior to 1976 focused primarily on self-report measures of self-esteem, and on conformity and field independence as surface features of autonomy. Research using female subjects in the late 1970s and the 1980s tended to focus on constructs such as moral reasoning, psychosocial development, and ego strength, all of which presumably tapped deeper levels of psychological structure and maturity.

The dominant pattern of earlier studies was that women in identity foreclosure looked more similar to those in identity achievement than did moratorium women, who were similar to those in identity diffusion. This grouping of achievement and foreclosure, moratorium and diffusion, reflects an ordering of the statuses along the dimension of commitment. On the basis of these early studies Marcia (1980) suggested that the foreclosure status was adaptive for women, possibly because girls and women were not supported in the process of exploration necessary to form self-chosen commitments. Marcia's reasoning implied that social changes which brought about equal support for women following the moratorium route to identity achievement would also reverse the ordering of foreclosure and moratorium statuses along dependent variables reflecting self-esteem and well-being. Under these conditions women, like men, would show an association between identity exploration, greater ego strength, and self-esteem.

The pattern among studies of females after 1976 was for moratoriums to resemble achievements, and for foreclosures to resemble diffusions. Women higher along the dimension of exploration showed more favorable psychological characteristics. This ordering of the statuses along the dimension of exploration was identical for women and men, seeming to suggest that Marcia's predictions had come about: Society was encouraging choices and nontraditional roles for women, and women appeared to negotiate moratorium without the negative consequences suggested by earlier data. But the newer studies were not replications of the older ones. Not only the times, but the measures had changed.

Because the effects of cohort and type of measure are confounded, it is not possible to tell why the later pattern (which found moratoriums similar to achievements and foreclosures similar to diffusions) differs from the earlier pattern of findings. Changes in women's roles resulting from the women's movement may have allowed women to experience moratorium similarly to men in a context of support and mastery. On the other hand, ego strength and maturity do not necessarily bring about higher self-esteem, resistance to conformity, or greater personal happiness. There is simply no evidence to contradict earlier conclusions regarding identity exploration and well-being in women. The process of moratorium may, in women (and some men), presuppose sufficient ego strength to embrace and tolerate conflict, which was as painful in the 1980s as it was in the 1970s.

Our position is that both cohort and measurement effects are operating. Whether the moratorium stage appears advantageous or disadvantageous to women is likely to be a function of age cohort, the historical moment which the study reflects, and the particular construct measured. In addition, the ordering of identity statuses along measures that reflect well-being and confidence in one's position may vary according to the content area or issue being discussed. In the early 1970s foreclosures seemed to exhibit an advantage over moratoriums in self-esteem and resisting peer pressure. In the late 1970s the foreclosure position seemed to protect women from the conflict between achievement motivation and fear of success (Orlofsky, 1978). In the 1980s there may have been more support than in previous years for women having their own opinion, valuing themselves, and/or pursuing high academic and professional goals. However, in areas such as career and family goals, where traditional values and expectations as well as social and structural support systems continue to conflict with expectations of achievement and self-actualization, the safety and assurance of foreclosure may offer a certain comfort in contrast to the pain of choice, exploration, and social pressure inherent in the moratorium process.

The Meaning of Identity for Women

Josselson (1988) conducted a descriptive study of women interviewed in college and recontacted in their mid-30s. Her study was influenced by recent developments in ego psychoanalytic and object relations theory (Chodorow, 1978; Gilligan, 1982; Kaplan & Klein, 1985; Miller, 1976, 1984; Surrey, 1984), which suggest that women construct identity not as an elaboration of individual autonomy, but within a context of connection to others. For Erikson, the construction of identity led to a position that can be characterized by the phrase: "Here I stand." For women, the construction of identity takes place in the context of relationships and important connections. It is characterized by a complex set of statements of the form: "I stand here, in relation to another person who is there." The self-in-relation operates and is defined in terms of important interpersonal relationships. The issues with which women struggle in defining who they are concern what is dear to them, and involve issues of care and relatedness as well as individually defined goals and principles[1].

Josselson's descriptions of women suggest that a third dimension of connectedness be added to the dimensions of exploration and commitment in determining identity status for women. From this perspective, women in diffusion appear to be not only without commitments and without a sense of directed exploration, but also isolated. They are distant or estranged from their parents, and have not found a long-term, stable, and positive relationship to function in their stead. Their position in relation to their parents (or parental figures) can be characterized as: "I don't know where I stand, but you stand far away from me." Women in foreclosure maintain strong commitments that are a reflection of their parents: "Here I stand, loyally at your side." In moratorium, women are caught in the struggle between their own need to be self-guided and loyalty to their parents: "If I stand here, will you still be there for me?" In identity achievement, women can afford to state, in Erikson style, "Here I stand," because they are strongly rooted in relationships that they have trusted to weather the storms of their explorations.

CONCLUSIONS

Josselson's conceptualization of women's identity as being in connection with others offers an integrative framework from which to view several previously puzzling aspects of women's identity.

First, interpersonal content areas are more prominent identity concerns for women than they are for men, at least in the adolescent years. Although a shift in concerns has occurred in recent years, the central importance of interpersonal connectedness remains apparent in women's struggle to integrate personally defined aspects of their identity with their interpersonal relationships and responsibilities.

Second, although women may approach the task of identity formation during adolescence, there are other times in women's lives when they can be expected to be involved in the moratorium process, either for the first time or in a reevaluation of earlier identity choices. In general, it seems that transitions in important interpersonal relationships often precipitate a reformulation of identity. This is particularly apparent when relationship changes result in a lessening of the woman's responsibility for others.

Third, issues of identity and intimacy seem to blend and merge for women. It appears that women's experiences of loving and being loved are integral to their sense of themselves.

Finally, a conceptualization of identity as occurring within the context of relationships allows us to predict, to some degree, the benefits and losses associated with the moratorium process across historical times and content areas. Issues that threaten relationships will be both crucial and difficult for women to resolve through the moratorium pathway.

It must be emphasized that the redefinition of identity we are suggesting is not simply the addition of interpersonal content into the construct as it stands. What is suggested here is that interpersonal relatedness is central to the process of identity formation, and therefore to the meaning of identity itself.

From the inner space perspective, Erikson believed that women's sense of identity would be strongest when the ties and responsibilities of marriage and children were greatest; that is, when young children were at home. Instead, women's identity seems to strengthen as those ties loosen, that is, as children gradually grow up and leave home. Yet an outer space perspective seems equally misleading, because identity does not thrive in the absence of meaningful ties. In the balancing of separation and attachment, autonomy and connection, identity emerges as a commitment to a set of values and ways of being in relation to important others.

FUTURE DIRECTIONS

A logical next step in identity research is to operationalize the dimension of interpersonal connection in identity formation. Several important questions could be addressed using this dimension. To what degree do interpersonal concerns in identity formation reflect common processes and personality characteristics versus gender-related phenomena? What are the characteristics of men and women who articulate the interpersonal perspective in identity formation? What social and economic conditions are supportive of identity exploration? What are the adaptive costs of identity exploration for women and men in varying personal, political, and economic situations?

Moving identity research farther out of the university and into the broader world may ultimately challenge the values and assumptions that underlie the research itself. How might the relatively impersonal context and methodology of identity research affect the articulation of interpersonal processes in identity formation?

There is a parallel between recognizing the interpersonal nature of identity formation in the subjects of our observation, and recognizing the interpersonal nature of our observations themselves. It seems obvious that scientific exploration, like identity exploration, is an interpersonal event. The next challenge may be to write theory that is conscious of its own social origins and utility, and to employ a methodology that illuminates the context of observation.

NOTE

1. It is important here that the reader distinguish between the self-in-relation, which places personally defined identity in the context of connection, and O'Connell's category of reflected identity. Similarly, the ties that connect women to others include more dimensions than the burden of responsibility for the well-being of the others. If they did not, the distinction between the connected and reflected self would not be meaningful, and autonomy and connection would truly be dichotomous experience (which, of course, they are not).

REFERENCES

Archer, S. L. (1985a). Career or family: The identity process for adolescent girls. *Youth and Society, 16*, 289-314.

Archer, S. L. (1985b). Reflections on earlier life decisions: Implications for adult functioning. In G. R. Adams (Ed.), *Identity development from adolescence to adulthood: Advances in conceptualization and methodology.* Symposium presented at the meeting of the Society for Research in Child Development, Toronto.

Bilsker, D., Schiedel, D., & Marcia, J. E. (1988). Sex differences in identity status. *Sex Roles, 18*, 231-236.

Chodorow, N. (1978). *The reproduction of mothering: Psychoanalysis and the sociology of gender.* Berkeley: University of California Press.

Constantinople, A. (1969). An Eriksonian measure of personality development in college students. *Developmental Psychology, 1*, 357-372.

Erikson, E. H. (1950). *Childhood and society.* New York: Norton.

Erikson, E. H. (1968). Womanhood and the inner space. In *Identity, youth and crisis.* New York: Norton.

Erikson, E. H. (1975). Once more the inner space. In *Life history and the historical moment.* New York: Norton.

Erikson, E. H. (1982). *The life cycle completed: A review.* New York: Norton.

Gilligan, C. (1982). *In a different voice: Psychological theory and women's development.* Cambridge, MA: Harvard University Press.

Hodgeson, J. W., & Fischer, J. L. (1979). Sex differences in identity and intimacy development in college women. *Journal of Youth and Adolescence, 8*, 37-50.

Hopkins, L. B. (1982). Assessment of identity status in college women using outer space and inner space interviews. *Sex Roles, 8*, 557-566.

Josselson, R. L. (1988). *Finding herself: Pathways of identity development in women.* New York: Jossey-Bass.

Kacerguis, M. A., & Adams, G. R. (1980). Erikson stage resolution: The relationship between identity and intimacy. *Journal of Youth and Adolescence, 9*, 117-126.

Kaplan, A., & Klein, R. (1985). *The relational self in late adolescent women.* Works in Progress. Wellesley: Stone Center Working Papers Series.

Kroger, J. (1987). *Sex differences in the relative importance of ego identity status content areas.* Unpublished manuscript, University of Wellington, New Zealand.

Marcia, J. E. (1966). Development and validation of ego identity status. *Journal of Personality and Social Psychology, 3*, 551-558.

Marcia, J. E. (1976). *Studies in ego identity.* Unpublished research monograph. Simon Fraser University, Burnaby, B.C., Canada.

Marcia, J. E. (1980). Identity in adolescence. In J. Adelson (Ed.), *Handbook of adolescent psychology* (pp. 159-187). New York: John Wiley.

Marcia, J. E., & Friedman, M. (1970). Ego identity status in college women. *Journal of Personality, 38*, 249-262.

Marcia, J. E., Waterman, A. S., Matteson, D. R., Archer, S. L., & Orlofsky, J. L. (in preparation). *Ego identity: A handbook for psychosocial research.* Simon Fraser University, Burnaby, B.C., Canada.

Matteson, D. R. (1977). Exploration and commitment: Sex differences and methodological problems in the use of the identity status categories. *Journal of Youth and Adolescence, 6*, 353-379.

Miller, J. B. (1976). *Toward a new psychology of women.* Boston: Beacon.

Miller, J. B. (1984). *The development of women's sense of self.* Works in Progress. Wellesley, MA: Stone Center Working Papers Series.

O'Connell, A. N. (1976). The relationship between life style and identity synthesis and re-synthesis in traditional, neotraditional and nontraditional women. *Journal of Personality, 44,* 675-688.

Orlofsky, J. L. (1978). Identity formation, achievement, and fear of success in college men and women. *Journal of Youth and Adolescence, 7,* 49-62.

Orlofsky, J. L., Marcia, J. E., & Lesser, I. M. (1973). Ego identity status and the intimacy vs. isolation crisis of young adulthood. *Journal of Personality and Social Psychology, 2,* 211-219.

Poppen, P. J. (1974). *The development of sex differences in moral judgment for college males and females.* Unpublished doctoral dissertation, Cornell University.

Prager, K. J. (1977). The relationship between identity status, intimacy status, self-esteem, and psychological androgyny in college women. *Dissertation Abstracts International, 38,* 2347-2348. (University Microfilms No. 7723020)

Schenkel, S., & Marcia, J. E. (1972). Attitudes toward pre-marital intercourse in determining ego identity status in college women. *Journal of Personality, 3,* 472-482.

Schiedel, D. G., & Marcia, J. E. (1985). Ego identity, intimacy, sex role orientation, and gender. *Developmental Psychology, 18,* 149-160.

Surrey, J. (1984). *The self-in-relation.* Work in Progress. Wellesley: Stone Center Working Papers Series.

Tesch, S. A., & Whitbourne, S. K. (1982). Intimacy and identity status in young adults. *Journal of Personality and Social Psychology, 43,* 1041-1051.

Thorbecke, W., & Grotevant, H. D. (1982). Gender differences in interpersonal identity formation. *Journal of Youth and Adolescence, 11,* 479-492.

Waterman, C. K., & Nevid, J. S. (1977). Sex differences in the resolution of the identity crisis. *Journal of Youth and Adolescence, 6,* 337-342.

Whitbourne, S. K., Jelsma, B. M., & Waterman, A. S. (1982). An Eriksonian measure of personality development in college students: A reexamination of Constantinople's data and a partial replication. *Developmental Psychology, 18,* 369-371.

Zampich, C. L. (1980). *Ego identity status, intimacy status, and self-disclosure in adult men and women.* Unpublished doctoral dissertation. Rosemead Graduate School of Professional Psychology: Rosemead, CA.

3. A Feminist's Approach to Identity Research

Sally L. Archer
Trenton State College

FEMINIST CONCERNS

Although identity researchers over the past 25 years have made tremendous strides toward making meaningful the very complex and exciting construct of identity, I believe that we identity researchers have too narrowly construed the identity process and its content. Feminists (e.g., Harding, 1987; Hubbard, 1989; Keller, 1989) have taken issue with traditional approaches to theory and methodology across the natural and social science disciplines. Their recommendations for change can provide useful guidelines as to how the identity interview could and should be used to counter some of the biases directed toward this research, biases that have culminated to date in the neglect of important directions that need to be pursued.

In particular, feminists (e.g., Maccoby, 1988; O'Leary, Unger, & Wallston, 1985; Rothenberg, 1988; Sherif, 1987) remonstrate about the invisibility of women, class, race, and culture to the development of any theory of "normal" or healthy development. Concomitant with this is a concern for a lack of sensitivity to multiple perspectives. This applies not only to sex, race, and class, but also to the traditional methodology itself where the potential interdynamics of the roles of researcher and participant have been largely ignored, to include their separate interpretations of the

AUTHOR'S NOTE: *"The researcher appears to us not as an invisible, anonymous voice of authority but as a real, historical individual with concrete, specific desires and interests" (Harding, 1987, p. 9). As an identity researcher, I have read, with interest and dismay, the often harsh criticisms directed at the construct of identity and its methodology by feminists. As a feminist, I believe I understand the basic frustrations directed at the identity framework by feminists not engaged in identity research. This chapter is written in the first person deliberately because I choose not to be perceived as an invisible, anonymous voice of authority but a real feminist with many years of identity interview experience. My hope is to convey my concerns and some specific desires and interests pertaining to the linkage of feminist scholarship with the construct of identity.*

research experience and its purpose, their motivations, and the relevance and meaning of questions, and so on. The assumption of objectivity has distorted history and science alike. Just a glance at methodologies reveals a devastating story of political and subjective "choice" of what and who are to be visible, valued, and thus, powerful. In psychology, many of us were trained, unaware, to complacently accept the white male researcher as neutral and objective, with his portrayal of women, lower classes, and non-Europeans as deviant if not invisible. Psychologists have fit these people to our a priori theories of good health (Gilligan, 1982), based fairly consistently on studies conducted with white males who were college bound, in college, and/or professionally successful by male standards (e.g., Erikson, 1963, 1968; Freud, 1925; Kohlberg, 1969, Levinson, 1978; Piaget, 1932).

This chapter is divided into three major sections. The first section is devoted to the definitional framework for identity and addresses issues of exclusivity and subjectivity. Have theoreticians and researchers of identity narrowly construed its definition such that feminists are justified in criticizing us for having developed a model designed exclusively for well-educated males? Do women, people of color, members of the lower social economic classes, and such, not have identities or at most have deviant identities? Is there an objectively correct definition of identity? Many feminists think not. Is it not more useful to acknowledge subjective preferences in choice of operational definitions, given one's specified research purposes? Would stipulating one's ideological framework not contribute to a better understanding and appreciation of each other's endeavors?

The second section of the chapter is focused on the identity methodology, which will be examined in light of whether we have been constrictive in its development, such that we have contributed to such problems as biases of normality and the invisibility of groups and issues. Proposed are recommendations for how researchers might expand our methodology to attempt to enrich our understanding of the meaning and role of identity for humankind in line with feminist concerns. These include reexamining: (a) the purpose and usefulness of the global process and specific domains approaches (How might we best know who engages in what activity at what point in life about what areas of one's life?); (b) the intrapersonal-interpersonal dichotomy of domains (Is there consistency between our a priori categories and what the narratives tell us?); and (c) the connection or separation of domains (Might we be distorting reality by not examining the interrelationship between the domains?).

The third section of the chapter is directed to the costs of politicizing methodologies. The social context has been largely ignored as a factor in our growing body of knowledge about identity development. By focusing primarily on a select population, college students in their college environment, we have disregarded much of the life-span and much of the real-life interactive phenomena that are probably influencing identity formation and its refinement. We must more globally examine the impact of stereotypic gender/culture/socioeconomic status expectations and the lack of social and economic support systems. What has been omitted from consideration to date and what can be done about it?

THE DEFINITIONAL FRAMEWORK FOR IDENTITY

The Issue of Exclusivity

One of the feminist criticisms of traditional epistemology focuses on the destructiveness of the artificial construction of dichotomies (e.g., Code, 1989; Hare-Mustin & Maracek, 1990). Identity has often been portrayed in very narrow terms that convey a negative connotation (by the theorist's standards of value)—rugged individualism, isolation, separateness, a turning away from community, selfishness, maleness (e.g., Carlson, 1971; Chodorow, 1974; Gilligan, 1982; Lykes, 1985; Sampson, 1985). The artificially constructed dichotomy refers to the assumption that if one is not an individual with a distinct sense of identity, then one is intimate, connected, communal, caring, and probably female. Over the past decade and a half the above-mentioned authors and others have presented an argument focusing our attention on identities (for males) versus intimacy (for females). Exclusivity by sex has thus been conveyed. By the same token, identity researchers historically established a dichotomy by speaking of the identity interview focused on vocation, religious and political ideologies as the men's interview (e.g., Marcia, 1980) and introduced "interpersonal" subject areas to the interview (e.g., Marcia & Friedman, 1970; Schenkel & Marcia, 1972) in order to provide meaningful areas of identity for women, such as sexuality and family roles (as though males are not sexual, or husbands or fathers). Furthermore, social constructionists and others of similar perspective also dichotomize by co-relating individualism, identity, internal locus of control, and so on, as opposed to communal living to enrich "care" and escape the "empty self" (Cushman, 1990; Shotter & Gergen, 1989).

The dichotomizing of identity versus intimacy parallels the historical dichotomizing of masculinity and femininity. Being excluded from a category is the consequence of a basic premise underlying the gender literature that personal qualities are unidimensional (e.g., if one is masculine, one cannot be feminine). Thus, demonstrating one set of characteristics precludes the expression of the other. The findings on androgyny have revealed the limitations of this orientation and have precipitated movement in the direction of perceiving qualities in light of orthogonal dimensions (e.g., that one can express both masculine and feminine characteristics) (Bem, 1975; Spence & Helmreich, 1980). The unidimensional orientation, however, continues to pervade much of our thinking about personal qualities, attitudes, and behaviors (Archer & Waterman, 1988). When one applies this unidimensional orientation to the constructs of identity and intimacy, then exclusivity can emerge here as well. The argument that follows is that one cannot be both self-defined and intimate. Although authors have spoken of connection and care as typically female attributes (e.g., Gilligan, 1982) and agency and identity as typically characteristic of males (Bakan, 1966; Lykes, 1985), those who have conducted research in these areas usually find that one sex places more emphasis or gives higher priority to particular qualities, attitudes, or behaviors than does the other sex on average (e.g., Lyons, 1983).

Unfortunately, the qualifiers are often lost and the sense of dichotomy is retained by the general readership. I have not encountered research findings to suggest that the aforementioned dichotomy is supportable, at least within the confines of studies conducted to date, to include males and females as respondents within the same studies (e.g., Archer, 1989a, Archer & Waterman, 1988; Ryff, 1989; Waterman, 1984). Class, race, and culture variables, however, need far more investigation. At least with regard to issues of sex, I find the dichotomy inappropriate. Indeed, feminists have fought long and hard to define themselves as unique individuals, and that has not disconnected them from community, at least from some communities. So why this persistent separation?

I suspect that one of the problems is the association of identity with Erik Erikson's name. Erikson has probably given more in-depth clinical thought to the concept of identity than anyone else. It is not surprising, given Erikson's long history of writing on the subject of identity, that empiricists would turn to his works for the foundation or even framework for an operational definition of the construct of identity. One of the joys and frustrations of Erikson's work is the fact that he provides many dimensions to identity, as demonstrated by Waterman (1988) when he easily filled a page simply by listing descriptors of identity from Erikson's *Prologue to Identity: Youth and Crisis* (1968). Not being a research methodologist, Erikson is not attempting to find the operational definition of identity. As a clinician he does an exquisite job of conveying the complexity and richness of a concept that perhaps defies a single definition.

A major feminist criticism of Erikson's work is that it portrays a primarily Eurocentric male model of normality. Indeed, it is regrettable that the models through which his points are demonstrated are virtually all male (e.g., George Bernard Shaw, Sigmund Freud, William James, Martin Luther, Gandhi). Does his model portray normality for males only? That is an important question eloquently challenged by Gilligan (1982), who questions how one can assume a "normal" model when one sex has been essentially invisible in the development of the theoretical postulates.

A scanning of Erikson's writings reveals that female psychosocial development is presented at the latter end of his books and chapters and consistently focuses on biology, "the inner space," as a primary determinant of female goals, values, and beliefs. Erikson did not choose to weave women through his writings. He did not include distinct female exemplars as factors in his empirical formulation of psychosocial development. As a consequence, many feminist readers feel that they have been written about as an afterthought, portrayed as deviant rather than normal, biologically driven (far beyond the dictates of male biology) and thus controlled by their biology.

Additionally, without multiple exemplars, it would appear that Erikson perceives of women as clones of one another, to be lumped together as valuing the same things, believing the same things, and needing/seeking very similar goals. How very different from the real men he analyzes as exemplars of his theory, each man's distinctiveness carefully portrayed. Does his theory of normality apply only to males? It is difficult to feel otherwise, given the above. Is psychosocial normality something else or something more when we are inclusive in our thinking of humankind? This is an important question that requires extensive empirical investigation, which is only just beginning. The fact that Erikson demonstrates identity through male models does not necessarily negate females from having identities. What are identities for women? For men and women of color? For our adolescents and our adults? For the rich and the poor? We must not feel compelled to abide by Erikson's historically and societally situated context. We should not assume that his demonstrations equate for all people at all times. In fact, I don't believe he would want us to assume that.

There is an additional point I would like to make about the criticism surrounding the association of identity research with Erikson's work. Because Erikson speaks of multiple facets of identity, one can find phrases to pull out of context to argue in support of many theoretical and empirical orientations, signifying everything from rugged individualism to the essentialness of community. In reality, he does not even choose to clearly specify boundaries of the term. My earlier remark about the inappropriateness of the dichotomy of identity versus intimacy pertains to an expenditure of energy on an issue that I think prevents us from getting on with an understanding of human development. Very few people live without community, and very few people are comfortable having no inner sense of self. Selecting one of Erikson's many descriptions of identity demonstrates an inclusivity I think we may all be able to resonate with if we drop out the "his" and speak to our individual and multiple group identities. Consequent to making remarks about the lives of James and Freud, Erikson (1968) notes that their statements and lives "serve to establish a few dimensions of identity . . . for we deal with a process 'located' *in the core of the individual* and yet also *in the core of his communal culture.*" (p. 22). He goes on to say:

We cannot separate personal growth and communal change, nor can we separate . . . the identity crisis in individual life and contemporary crisis in historical development because the two help to define each other and are truly relative to each other. In fact, the whole interplay between the psychological and the social, the developmental and the historical, for which identity formation is of prototypal significance, could be conceptualized only as a kind of psychosocial relativity. (p. 23)

Those of us trained as identity researchers using the interview format employ numerous questions that tap individual development in the context of significant others (Marcia, Waterman, Matteson, Archer, & Orlofsky, in press). Those interpersonal psychosocial dynamics, or the lack thereof, are essential factors in the operational definitions of the processes of identity with which we work.

The Issue of Subjectivity in the Choice of Definition

An important issue for feminists is that theoreticians and researchers recognize that they operate out of ideological frameworks, that they are influenced by their values and hence are subjective (e.g., Harding, 1987). Stipulating one's framework is thus preferred to the pretense of objectivity. Empiricists have been trained to think that we objectively operationalize definitions of constructs. However, in recent years we have become sufficiently sophisticated to recognize the subjectivity inherent in our attempts to be objective (e.g., Gergen, 1982; Sherif, 1987). Subjectivity immediately enters the picture for identity researchers—first for choosing Erikson as a theoretical guide, and second because in operationalizing the concept of identity, we must choose those dimensions that we rationally and intuitively *feel* are documentable and meaningful. Rather than expend energy arguing over whose position is most true to Erikson's theory (e.g., Bourne 1987a, 1987b; Cote & Levine, 1988), it would appear far more fruitful to draw upon this bounty and enthusiastically embrace learning about identity formation from multiple perspectives (e.g., Waterman, 1988; Waterman & Archer, 1990). It is a subjective preference to choose to either ignore Erikson's theory or select components of it as a foundation or as a framework for one's understanding of the concept. Indeed it might be very fruitful if we listened to life stories to get a panoply of "senses" of identity, as people share not only their own ways of constructing their self-definitions but also their struggles, or ease in explaining, what identity is to them, unfettered by our choice of questions. Even at that, their individual stories will still be colored by our perceptions of the patterns we hear. The meshing and contrasts of theories, findings, and applications over time should result in our learning the robustness of the phenomenon.

In a section of a chapter focused on the definitional framework of identity, one might by now have expected the author to have led up to *the* all-inclusive definition. But that would defeat my purpose. Alas, there is no definitive definition of identity. With regard to *a* definition of identity, one subjectively chooses those dimensions that intuit well and appear justifiable, given one's specified research purposes. Waterman and Archer (1990) provided three mutually compatible but progressively narrowing definitions of the construct of identity by Erikson, Marcia and Waterman, respectively, and discussed the benefits and costs of empirical clarity and rich clinical associations inherent in one's choice of definition. Their definitions are offered as an example of how one might choose to proceed.

CONSTRICTIVE CHOICES IN THE
METHODOLOGIES TO STUDY IDENTITY

Feminists in the social sciences are calling for a "broadening of available methods, more intensive descriptive research, more attention to understudied issues . . . and awareness of the political and cultural context for research" (Wallston & Grady, 1985, p. 7). The remainder of this chapter is an attempt to highlight these concerns within the identity methodology framework.

An Examination of the Process Approach

James Marcia (1966) carefully studied Eriksonian theory and singled out for empirical investigation several dimensions of identity that so strongly resonated with researchers interested in this construct that 25 years of intensive study has ensued. This fascination with the construct and its methodology has culminated in hundreds of studies, multiple measures, national and international conference presentations, and numerous books. The primary focus has been on the identity process and, in particular, how it takes place in adolescents.

In Marcia's (1966) early research devoted to this area, two primary dimensions of self-definition were chosen for examination: exploration and commitment. Four identity statuses were derived from combinations of these two dimensions. Simply put, *diffusion* is characterized by lack of exploration and lack of commitment; *foreclosure,* by commitment without exploration; *moratorium* as exploration in progress; and *identity achievement* as commitment subsequent to serious exploration of alternatives.

In-depth manuals (e.g., Grotevant & Cooper, 1981; Marcia, Waterman, Matteson, Archer, & Orlofsky, in press) have been created that demonstrate the complexity of meaning that is attributed to the identity statuses. Criteria of knowledgeability, activity, interdynamics with significant others, projection into the future, and so on, are delineated with exquisite care such that a common language and understanding prevail among identity researchers. Thus, when identity researchers speak of an individual who is foreclosed, a complicated set of images emerges for us with certain expectations and hypotheses about the individual's past and present experiences and approach to life. One of our major tasks is to convey this information to our general readership.

At a symposium in Tucson, Arizona (Archer, 1984), I asked the questions: "Why do we expend all this energy conducting these interviews, listen to these people share life stories, and then walk away with only these four little letters—'A' for identity achievement, 'M' for moratorium, 'F' for foreclosure, and 'D' for identity diffusion—that we statistically report in relationship to other variables? Why are we not attending to and sharing the actual content of these interviews, which are rich with stories about the context and motivation surrounding identity development?" At that time, I sensed that we were not getting across to others the incredible richness that we understood. Indeed, only in the past few years have several identity researchers begun to focus on reporting patterns in the narratives that might enrich our understanding of the content that might coincide with the identity statuses (Archer, 1985a, 1990a; Josselson, 1987; Kroger, 1989; McAdams, 1985).

The Global Versus Domain Process Approaches

Initially, identity was represented with a global status score. The individuals would be given identity status scorings in each content area (domain) in which they had been interviewed. An overall or most characteristic status then would be determined. This has been a particularly valuable approach for the investigation of the individual's ability or choice to engage in the process of identity via exploration and commitment. It has also allowed for an extensive assessment of the relationship between identity and many other psychological variables, to include personality characteristics and social behaviors (Archer, 1989b; Marcia, 1980).

An additional approach to the assessment of identity has focused on the use of the identity processes specific to each content area addressed (e.g., Archer, 1985a, 1985b; Grotevant, Thorbecke, & Meyer, 1982; Meilman, 1979; Waterman, 1985). Identity decisions can be made specific to any area of one's life in which values, beliefs, and goals are important. Erikson (1968) focused on vocation, ideology, and family. The identity interviews have now included the domains of vocational plans, avocation, religious beliefs, political ideologies, sex-role orientation, sexuality, values, friendship, dating, marriage, parenting, family and career prioritizing, and ethnicity. I believe that this is, to date, an exhaustive list of what has been attempted. An important finding in studies conducted, typically using between three and seven of these domains, is that a majority of individuals do not use the same decision-making identity mode in all domains (Archer, 1989b). Finding a most characteristic or *global* mode can limit our understanding of the task of forming one's identity if it is the only approach used. Examining identity activity separately by domain allows us to document the areas of salience to individuals differing in sex, age, ethnicity, class, and so on. We can identify domains in which energy is expended in establishing values, goals, and beliefs as well as the areas in which activity does not take place. Knowing whether and where the potential for the "examined life" is being realized could be important information for the developmentalist, the counselor, and those of us concerned with social policy regarding vocational preparation or sexual activity, as examples. Further, listening to the narratives themselves, within domains of concern, provides the opportunity to hear the issues that the group(s)/individuals center on as the dynamic factors contributing to their activity or lack thereof. Motivation and barriers become increasingly apparent as patterns of issues emerge and become meaningful through repetition, as well as from hearing approaches to core dilemmas from different perspectives.

EXPANSIVE CHOICES IN THE METHODOLOGIES TO STUDY IDENTITY

A Dilemma of Dichotomy

Paralleling the feminist issue of definitional exclusivity that results from dichotomizing identity and intimacy is the methodological dichotomy of separating the domains of identity into intrapersonal versus interpersonal categories (Dyk & Adams, 1987; Grotevant, Thorbecke, & Meyer, 1982; Rogow, Marcia, & Slugoski, 1983). Those domains that focus on development that is primarily due to an internalized process that impacts on the individual's purpose and direction in a rather singularized fashion are subsumed under the *intrapersonal* label. This would include vocational choice, religious beliefs, and political ideology, sometimes labeled the men's identity interview areas. Those domains focused on development that are primarily perceived as belief about self concerning connection with others, due to both an internalized and externalized interactive process that is initiated by and/or impacts on self and other(s), are subsumed under an *interpersonal* label. This has typically included sexuality, family roles, dating and friendship, and sex roles, content areas introduced to provide meaningful identity areas for those individuals focused on connection, typically women.

Initially it was thought that the introduction of interpersonal areas would contribute to an understanding of identity formation for college women (Marcia & Friedman, 1970; Schenkel & Marcia, 1972). By the early 1980s researchers who were introducing the domains that took us beyond the men's interview areas clearly stated expectations that interpersonal areas could be of relevance to both sexes (Grotevant, Thorbecke, & Meyer, 1982; Kroger, 1986; Matteson, 1977; Rogow, Marcia, & Slugoski, 1983). In the vast majority of studies, sex differences have been the exception rather than the rule. Sex differences have been found in the domains of sexuality (C. Waterman & Nevid, 1977), family/career prioritizing (Archer, 1985a), and friendship (Thorbecke & Grotevant, 1982), but not vocation, religious beliefs, sex roles, values, dating, and such. Some sex differences have emerged during the past two decades on correlations between identity statuses in some of the intrapersonal as well as interpersonal domains and personality and social behavioral characteristics (Archer, 1989b: Grotevant & Thorbecke, 1982; Marcia, 1980; Thorbecke & Grotevant, 1982). Some have not been consistently replicated (Marcia, this volume). However, the theoretical distinction of intrapersonal and interpersonal as male versus female, perhaps reinforced by the correlational findings, has persisted in adolescent psychology textbooks and numerous articles.

For epistemological reasons I am troubled by this intrapersonal-interpersonal methodology. Granting the historically strong theoretical dichotomies generated by theorists and researchers of both sexes that males have identities and females are intimate, it is understandable that there was an attempt to modify research orientations to rectify one of the grave errors that has historically been made in psychology, that of making women invisible or deficient. I believe the intrapersonal-interpersonal methodology has been a sincere effort at inclusivity. However, the approach is grounded in a traditional Eurocentric perspective. Labels have been generated to which data is forced to fit. Are the terms *intrapersonal* and *interpersonal* useful and meaningful? How does one determine this? What determines which domains belong in each category? And without answers to these questions, what meaning can be attributed to the correlational studies?

A Feminist Methodology
to Address the Issue of Dichotomy

From a feminist approach the order of methodological activities would be reversed. In an attempt to address the reality of multiple perspectives, one would first listen to the narratives of the many respondents to hear them tell us how they perceive their experiences within each of these domains and the relationship of one domain to another. The researcher would try to sketch schemas— discover, recognize, and create meaningful patterns instead of assuming that there is only one schema to which all data must be fit (Frye, 1990).

Assumption: Religious beliefs are, of course, intrapersonal. Perhaps religious beliefs are not necessarily an area of self-definition that is intrapersonal. Some males and females of adolescent age, at least, expend a considerable amount of time during this segment of the interview discussing the importance of their personal relationship with their God. How do we value this connection on an individual level with one's God? In process terms, how is this communication and pouring out of one's fears, hurts, hopes, and quests for guidance different from one's needs expressed with dates or in intimate connections of other forms categorized as interpersonal? This is one pattern. Another pattern is that of focusing on one's comfort with an organized religion, the majority of its belief structures and maintaining an expected lifestyle. Still a third pattern is that of emphasizing the essentialness of sharing spiritualism with others and the strength it provides to help others in one's community (however broadly or specifically the community is defined). Which of these are intrapersonal and which are interpersonal? Whether the researcher acknowledges these different perspectives; and if he or she does, how they are valued; and what further questions are pursued can result in vastly different explanations of identity in the realm of religious beliefs between and within the sexes, ethnicities, races, classes, and such.

If perhaps the domain of religious beliefs has been assessed too narrowly, isn't vocational choice assuredly intrapersonal? Again, recalling patterns within interviews, or considering your own experiences with adolescents engaged in decision making about career choices, how many of these youths make their initial decisions more in light of what significant others want and expect of them than in terms of what might be personally expressive? How many times have you heard the same story that "my dad insists that jobs can only be found in the area of _____ and so I've got to major in _____." Connection is strongly involved in this decision-making process. Is it therefore intrapersonal or interpersonal? How many females find that connections directly impact upon their choice of career if, for example, they want to have children? "I want to be a teacher, in part because the hours are flexible and I can be home with my children during their school vacations." Or "I chose this career because I love to work with people and cannot bear to feel alone." The weighing of connection factors does not negate the desire or plan for a career. By labeling vocational choice or religious beliefs as a priori intrapersonal, one simplifies all the respondents' experiences to one factor and negates the very inclusivity that had been intended. Without listening to the patterns in the narratives, we do not know whether the focus is intrapersonal or interpersonal. Indeed, poor quality "friendships" might be very intrapersonal.

Questions for an Expansive Methodology

Working with domains of self-definition is exciting and can be extremely informative. It is imperative that we be far more sophisticated in our conceptual and methodological approaches to this potentially rich way of further understanding identity development and its refinement. There are many variations to be pursued, dependent upon one's research questions. Some of the factors to keep in mind include: Who chooses which domains to interview in and what are the implications of respondent-chosen domains, as opposed to or in combination with researcher-chosen domains? Do we listen to the narratives for other than just identity statuses, and if so, how do we discover or develop meaningful patterns, and how are they to be labeled? Are dichotomies and recognition of multiple perspectives and experiences incompatible? As one begins to address the areas that have been invisible for so long, is the use of domains appropriate? And if domains are used, what domains would allow us to understand the effects of race, class, ethnicity, age, sex, and gender on identity formation and its refinement? How we answer these kinds of questions will determine to a very large extent whether the domain approach is conceptually constrictive or expansive in understanding the quest for a sense of self in context.

To date there have been several attempts to expand the use of domains. A domain of ethnicity has been introduced and is being studied with numerous ethnic groups at high school and college ages. Ethnic/racial groups studied to date have included Native Americans, blacks, Hispanics, Asians, and whites (e.g., Phinney &

Rosenthal, this volume; Rotheram, 1989; Spencer & Markstrom-Adams, 1990). A second attempt to expand the use of domains has been to examine the interrelationship of decision making between domains. This approach will be addressed in the next section.

A Further Expansion:
Interrelationships Among the Domains

Traditionally, the interviews as well as the paper and pencil instruments have been divided into separate domains. As noted before, scores are obtained for each domain. Data are analyzed, either by domain or by using a specific formula, and the domains are averaged to obtain a global identity score for analyses. Because we define identity as a process by which one may ultimately *synthesize* the component parts, arriving at a unique individual, it is interesting that an interactive assessment of domains has not been undertaken. Does one's self-definition regarding religious beliefs impact upon one's self-definition with regard to sex-role or family choices? Do one's vocational ambitions alter one's family role expectations, or vice versa? It would appear productive to assess the parts and their relationship to one another.

In my own research I have begun to ask the following: (a) Is identity decision making about one's values, beliefs, and goals conducted in a single-channeled, isolated manner? (b) Have we artificially constructed an identity process by using separate domains? (c) Have we disconnected or severed real connections? (d) Do males and females approach the identity task differently, one decision making in linear fashion, the other through connections among domains? (e) As well, do different ethnic groups or classes keep the components of identity separate or connected? (f) Is there a developmental process involved in connecting the separate parts of one's identity, perhaps at some crucial point when one is cognitively able? (g) Are these possibilities underlined by a social or historical contextual condition?

In my own work (Archer, 1985a, 1985b, 1989b; Waterman & Archer, 1990) I have made a mere dent in this series of questions. It had fascinated me to listen to adolescents' interviews regarding fairly intricate vocational plans. When I then asked about family plans, typically marriage and children were desired and by such-and-such an age. No spontaneous connections were made between the two sets of goals during the interviews. It was as though adolescents had tunnel vision with regard to future plans—there was no integration of their goals. One of the few connections among any of the domains that I would hear pertained to conflicts between some females' religious beliefs and those of their potential partners. If they married, what would be the family (i.e., the children's) religion?

In a first attempt to empirically investigate whether identity decision making was made in isolation by domain or might be integrated (Archer, 1985a), I used two domains that the majority of males and females expressed plans for, vocation and family, and focused direct questions on their interrelationship—as family/career prioritizing. The vast majority of males from 6th, 8th, 10th, and 12th grade didn't see a relationship between vocational choices and plans to marry and have children. Even when they acknowledged that their future life partner would probably want a career as well, they saw no potential conflicts for themselves. Economic impact of children and the need for childcare were not connected to their identities, even though they perceived of self as "father" in their projections into the future. Nor was facilitating their life partner's growth and development perceived as part of their spouse image. Any difficulties that emerged pertaining to the children *he* wants and plans to have are *his spouse's* problem and do not affect *his* future. A substantial minority of females also were unable to connect the two life goals and perceive their potential interdynamics for future self-definition. However, a significant number of females, especially at the senior grade level, were both able to and desirous of integrating their stories. They saw the interconnections between career goals and family goals and, for the most part, were quite concerned about integrating both into daily life and maintaining responsibility to all without losing an important component of their sense of self. Development and sex appear to be interacting variables for this meta-decision making process, at least between these domains. With regard to the social and historical context, these were youths of the late 1970s and early 1980s, many of whose mothers worked outside the home as well as within. Some of the girls were the children of divorce; others spoke with animosity about their fathers, who worked outside the home and then expected to be waited on at home. The boys, whether of divorced or intact families, rarely made note of these circumstances. In subsequent work with college students (Archer, 1990b), this pattern appears to be continuing.

Work with divorced women (Archer, 1985b; Waterman & Archer, 1990) has shed further light on the possibility of developmental and/or social contextual questions here. When asked to retrospectively share the development and refinement of their self-definitions, from the time of high school, to marriage, to divorce, to the present, a significant number of these women revealed multiple, interactive changes in self-definition at the time of marital dissolution. For example, through reexamining what it meant to be a female, they might have made changes with regard to sex role, religious beliefs, and political ideology. Much more work needs to be initiated with regard to the interrelationship among domains. Kroger (1989) provides demonstrations of integration in her recent book focused on adolescent identity development. Meta-analytic (or integrated) versus channeled decision making could provide us with a much more sophisticated appreciation of the identity process, beginning with our adolescents.

SOCIAL CONTEXT: THE COSTS OF POLITICIZING METHODOLOGIES

To this point, I have addressed methodological issues about process and domain that have underlying implications as to what knowledge is most essential to our understanding of the task of identity formation. Perhaps my most important concern is that we now begin to expand our theory building and empirical studies to become more inclusive—focusing on external factors that interrelate extensively with one's ability to approach the identity task in a healthy manner.

Costs of Invisibility

Let us return to the theoretical positions that have rendered identity and community as dichotomous, excluding one from the other. When this is perceived in a political light, theory and methodology have had detrimental effects on our understanding of females' self-definitions. Paralleling the assumption that girls didn't have identities was the assumption that the Erikson-Marcia framework was designed only for investigating male identity formation. Early research in this area, focused on vocational plans and religious and political ideologies, did not typically include female respondents, enhancing their invisibility with regard to self-development. Writers who have focused on community have taken the earliest identity research findings on women out of their historical context and have used them to justify the position that the Erikson-Marcia framework is race-, class-, and sex-bound. Slugoski and Ginsburg (1989) provide an excellent example. They reference only the earliest identity research conducted with women (e.g., Marcia & Friedman, 1970; Shenkel & Marcia, 1972) and contrast those findings with findings obtained with men in studies focused only on male identity formation. They conclude that there are sex differences because some personality correlates (e.g., self-esteem) of the statuses differed by sex. They do not reference years of data compiled since these early studies in which it has been found that female within-sex correlates differ from those early female findings. They do not reference the extensive number of studies in which sex similarity is found with regard to identity activity (see Waterman, 1982, for review). They announced in 1989 that, in their opinion, there is a sex bias to the identity construct, making it "sex-bound," ergo inappropriate to women. For all their insistence on the importance of social context, they seem unaware of the sensitivity of the construct and methodology to societal change. In these 25 years of research, wherein at least some women have been made visible as respondents in identity studies, we have captured aspects of the impact of the women's movement on self-development—women fighting oppression caused by "required connection" in the society that denied women a sense of self, with self-chosen connections. Critiques such as that of Slugoski and Ginsburg (1989) deter investigations of identity formation in females. It is interesting to note that they offer no substantive directions to take in order to understand females, as well as race and class, thus enhancing the likelihood of invisibility and misleading the reader due to their omission of the aforementioned data.

Textbooks are also rife with theory that has tremendous political implications for human rights. Textbooks that perpetuate a myth that males have identities, while females are intimate, enhance the likelihood of continued oppression for females. Why encourage females to pursue their education and careers if there are inadequate childcare support systems in this society? Why improve childcare support systems when we all know that females only want connection in the form of marriage and children? In 1982, 1985, and again in 1989, I published articles demonstrating that females have approached identity formation either comparable to or in a more sophisticated manner than that of males. Numerous articles (e.g., Adams & Fitch, 1982; Grotevant & Thorbecke, 1982; C. Waterman & Nevid, 1977; Whitbourne & Tesch, 1985) have been referenced in reviews (e.g., Archer, 1989a; Marcia, 1980; Waterman, 1982) demonstrating minimal sex differences. Yet these findings of sex similarity are infrequently referenced in identity chapters of textbooks. Working within the "intrapersonal male domains of identity," females and males approach the task of identity formation comparably. Working in the "interpersonal female domains of connection," females have either comparable processing or significantly more sophisticated identity activity than do males. The sense of self and the desire for connection are intertwined, not incompatible, at least for some females. Perhaps this is the case for many of us (male and female) when domains essential to our self-definition are heard for the context of connection. Unfortunately, our a priori definition of "appropriate domains" for connection has placed artificial constraints on our examination of this empirical question. Listening to identity in connection does convey a complexity of the identity process that had previously been rendered invisible.

Ironically, the assumption of connection and care has been costly to our understanding of female psychosocial development. By denying identity development in adolescent girls, and thus not hearing the complexity with which they are faced, we have not taken the crucial next steps to assess their efforts at development in a historically social context that does not support or recognize their self-definitional process. Rather than perpetuating this notion of dichotomous exclusivity of self versus community, it is time that we integrate these essential ingredients in our research endeavors.

Costs of Ignoring Social Context

There are many potential barriers to healthy psychosocial development that could result in dystonic resolutions of stages, phases, and so forth, of development and thus render futile a person's ability to establish a personally expressive sense of self. There have been some theoretical and research questions focused on the importance of social and historical context for healthy development (Archer, 1989b; Baumeister, 1986; Kroger, 1989), but there is a need for much more. Although significant increases in the use of moratorium and identity achievement have been documented with increase in age, in terms of frequency, male and female adolescents and youth are more likely to be identity diffuse or foreclosed in the domains investigated to date (Archer, 1989b). Questions as to the "health" of expressing one identity status as opposed to another and the need for intervention are now being initiated (Archer, 1989c).

In a recent conference (Archer, 1990a), an attempt was made to identify a number of social facts that may render identity formation difficult or painful for females. Such social experiences may cause or enhance the likelihood of "rigid" stability with regard to diffusion or foreclosure, or precipitate a stressful moratorium. A comparable set of facts and issues should be developed as appropriate for both sexes, and made more meaningful by incorporating age, culture, race, and class as essential variables. What impact do the following potential experiences have upon a female's developmental attempts to define herself with values, beliefs, and goals about careers, family, religion, politics, and so on? Citing from that conference presentation[1]:

1. In the United States there are approximately 1.2 million pregnancies per year to individuals in the teen years with 500,000 infants being born annually to teenage mothers; 34,000 of those are births to teens 15 or younger.

2. One girl in every four in the United States will be sexually abused in some way before she reaches the age of 18.

3. Females are severely penalized in the work world—on average, they have lower paying jobs than males; their jobs have been defined as inferior to the work of men and are thus paid less; single-headed households that are primarily run by females are much more likely to be at or below poverty level than are male-headed households; the average working woman spends 23% of her potential work years out of the work force, primarily due to having or caring for children, as compared to 2% for men.

4. Adults continue to report preferring boy babies to girl babies.

5. Working mothers continue to maintain primary responsibility for home tasks of parenting and housekeeping; and many of our adolescents have been reared by parents and media that continue to reinforce sex-typed behaviors of aggression and autonomy for boys; nurturant, emotional, and passive behavior for girls.

In addition, if part of the adolescent female's task of establishing a personally expressive identity includes the areas of career and family, the several ideal images of these options may appear incompatible. To attain the educational level necessary to enhance the likelihood of a career, the female adolescent must override societal sex-role stereotypes. These stereotypes cover areas such as "appropriate" vocational choices, psychological characteristics and behaviors pertaining to passivity, the timing of marriage and parenting, filial duty to remain attached to parental values, and the fear of losing popularity and date-ability with the adolescent boys and hence risk becoming an "old maid."

To maintain her female identity of nurturant, supportive helpmate and parent, she must forego her preparation and/or implementation of a career (as opposed to a job one takes to pass the time while awaiting a mate and pregnancy). Or she may attempt dual priorities, trying to cope with the complexity of career and family, with little or no hope for support systems (as noted, more often than not, by her own mother's predicament). Ergo, the identity process for the female adolescent can easily be described as potentially confusing and complex.

How do such experiences impact upon identity formation? We don't know. We have not as yet made the social and historical context a central factor in our research endeavors. With some modifications in our interview questions, the narratives of our interviewees could lead us toward such an understanding.

CONCLUSIONS

Erikson envisioned a need that continues to exist. We must work together, appreciate each other's theories and expand our methods if we are to learn about this complex construct of identity:

Teamwork methods are, at the moment, the best approach in this general area. What these approaches as yet lack, however, is a theory of human development which attempts to come closer to something by finding out wherefrom and whereto it develops. (Erikson, 1968, pp. 23, 24).

We need to use multiple operational definitions of identity. We must become inclusive, eliminating issues of invisibility of peoples by sex, class, and race. We should be clear about our subjective choices of definition, theoretical foundations, and frameworks, explaining their relationship to our well-specified research purposes. We need to use a variety of methods. Even within the traditional methodology of identity, utilizing numerous expansive procedures and forms of assessment could greatly enrich our understanding of identity formation for humankind. Perhaps most neglected has been the environmental contexts that impact on one's opportunities for, and style of, addressing self-development. As well, what implications does that have for everyone's life story of who they have been, who they are, and who they can become?

NOTE

1. Full citations for each of these facts can be found in S. L. Archer (1990a).

REFERENCES

Adams, G. R., & Fitch, S. A. (1982). Ego stage and identity status development: A cross-sequential analysis. *Journal of Personality and Social Psychology, 43*, 574-583.

Archer, S. L. (1984, March). Rudiments of identity formation among early and mid-adolescents: An examination of process and content. In C. Cooper (Chair), *An assessment of adolescent identity research: An update with commentary on implications for future research*. Symposium conducted at the Meetings of the Second Biennial Conference on Adolescent Research, Tucson, AZ.

Archer, S. L. (1985a). Career and/or family: The identity process for adolescent girls. *Youth and Society, 16*, 289-314.

Archer, S. L. (1985b, April). Reflections on earlier life decisions: Implications for adult functioning. In G. R. Adams (Ed.), *Identity development from adolescence to adulthood: Advances in conceptualization and methodology*. Symposium conducted at the meeting of the Society for Research in Child Development, Toronto.

Archer, S. L. (1989a). Gender differences in identity development. *Journal of Adolescence, 12*, 117-138.

Archer, S. L. (1989b). The status of identity: Reflections on the need for intervention. *Journal of Adolescence, 12*, 345-359.

Archer, S. L. (Ed.). (1989c). Adolescent identity: An appraisal of health and intervention [Special Issue]. *Journal of Adolescence, 12*(4).

Archer, S. L. (1990a). Females at risk: Identity issues for adolescents and divorced women. In C. Vandenplas-Holper & B. P. Campos (Eds.), *Interpersonal and identity development: New research directions.* ICPFD; Porto and Academia: Louvain-La-Neuve, 75-90.

Archer, S. L. (1990b, May). Knowing myself, loving my partner: Is there a gender dilemma? Paper presented at Distinguished Research Award Colloquium. Trenton State College, Trenton, NJ.

Archer, S. L., & Waterman, A. S. (1988). Psychological individualism: Gender differences or gender neutrality? *Human Development, 31*, 65-81.

Bakan, D. (1966). *The duality of human existence.* Chicago: Rand McNally.

Baumeister, R. F. (1986). *Identity: Cultural change and the struggle for self.* New York: Oxford University Press.

Bem, S. L. (1975). Sex role adaptability: One consequence of psychological androgyny. *Journal of Personality and Social Psychology, 31*, 634-643.

Bourne, E. (1978a). The state of research on ego identity: A review and appraisal. Part I. *Journal of Youth and Adolescence, 7*, 223-251.

Bourne, E. (1978b). The state of research on ego identity: A review and appraisal. Part II. *Journal of Youth and Adolescence, 7*, 371-392.

Carlson, R. (1971). Sex differences in ego functioning: Exploratory studies of agency and communion. *Journal of Consulting and Clinical Psychology, 37*, 267-277.

Chodorow, N. (1974). Family structure and feminine personality. In M. Z. Rosaldo & L. Lamphere (Eds.), *Woman, culture, and society* (pp. 43-66). Palo Alto, CA: Stanford University Press.

Code, L. (1989, March). The impact of feminism on epistemology. *American Philosophical Association, 88*(2), 25-29.

Cote, J. E., & Levine, C. (1988). A critical examination of the ego identity status paradigm. *Developmental Review, 8*, 147-184.

Cushman, P. (1990). Why the self is empty: Toward a historically situated psychology. *American Psychologist, 45*, 599-611.

Dyk, P.A.H., & Adams, G. R. (1987). The association between identity development and intimacy during adolescence: A theoretical treatise. *Journal of Adolescent Research, 2*, 223-235.

Erikson, E. H. (1963). *Childhood and society* (2nd ed). New York: Norton.

Erikson, E. H. (1968). *Identity: Youth and crisis.* New York: Norton.

Freud, S. (1925). Some psychical consequences of the anatomical distinction between the sexes. Vol. XIX.

Frye, M. (1990). The possibility of feminist theory. In D. L. Bindo (Ed.), *Theoretical perspectives on sexual difference.* New Haven: Yale University Press.

Gergen, K. J. (1982). *Toward transformation in social knowledge.* New York: Springer-Verlag.

Gilligan, C. (1982). *In a different voice.* Cambridge, MA: Harvard University Press.

Grotevant, H. D., & Cooper, C. R. (1981). Assessing adolescent identity in the areas of occupation, religion, politics, friendships, dating, and sex roles: Manual for administration and coding of the interview. JSAS Cat. Select. Documents Psychol. 11: 52 (Ms. No. 2295).

Grotevant, H. D., & Thorbecke, W. (1982). Sex differences in styles of occupational identity formation in late adolescence. *Developmental Psychology, 18*, 396-405.

Grotevant, H. D., Thorbecke, W., and Meyer, M. L. (1982). An extension of Marcia's Identity Status Interview into the interpersonal domain. *Journal of Youth and Adolescence, 11*, 33-47.

Harding, S. (1987). Introduction: Is there a feminist method? In S. Harding (Ed.), *Feminism and methodology* (pp. 1-14). Indianapolis: Indiana University Press.

Hare-Mustin, R. T., & Maracek, J. (1990). *Making a difference: Psychology and the construction of gender*. New Haven: Yale University Press.

Hubbard, R. (1989). Science, facts, and feminism. In N. Tuana (Ed.), *Feminism and science* (pp. 119-131). Indianapolis: Indiana University Press.

Josselson, R. (1987). *Finding herself: Pathways to identity development in women*. San Francisco: Jossey-Bass.

Keller, E. F. (1989). The gender/science system: Or, is sex to gender as nature is to science? In N. Tuana (Ed.), *Feminism and science* (pp. 33-44). Indianapolis: Indiana University Press.

Kohlberg, L. (1969). Stage and sequence: The cognitive-developmental approach to socialization. In D. A. Goslin (Ed.), *Handbook of socialization theory and research* (pp. 347-480). Chicago: Rand McNally.

Kroger, J. (1986). The relative importance of identity status interview components: Replication and extension. *Journal of Youth and Adolescence, 9*, 337-354.

Kroger, J. (1989). *Identity in adolescence*. New York: Routledge.

Levinson, D. J. (1978). *The seasons of a man's life*. New York: Knopf.

Lykes, M. B. (1985). Gender and individualistic vs. collectivist bases for notions about the self. *Journal of Personality, 53*, 356-383.

Lyons, N. P. (1983). Two perspectives: On self, relationships, and morality. *Harvard Educational Review, 53*, 125-145.

Maccoby, E. E. (1988). Gender as a social category. *Developmental Psychology, 24*, 755-765.

Marcia, J. E. (1966). Development and validation of ego identity status. *Journal of Personality and Social Psychology, 3*, 551-558.

Marcia, J. E. (1980). Identity in adolescence. In J. Adelson (Ed.), *Handbook of Adolescent Psychology* (pp. 159-187). New York: John Wiley.

Marcia, J. E., & Friedman, M. L. (1970). Ego identity status in college women. *Journal of Personality, 38*, 249-263.

Marcia, J. E., Waterman, A. S., Matteson, D. R., Archer, S. L., & Orlofsky, J. L. (in press). *Ego identity: A handbook for psychosocial research*. New York: Springer-Verlag.

Matteson, D. R. (1977). Exploration and commitment: Sex differences and methodological problems in the use of identity status categories. *Journal of Youth and Adolescence, 6*, 353-374.

McAdams, D. P. (1985). *Power, intimacy and the life story*. Homewood, IL: Dorsey.

Meilman, P. W. (1979). Cross-sectional age changes in ego identity status during adolescence. *Developmental Psychology, 15*, 230-231.

O'Leary, V. E., Unger, R. K., & Wallston, B. S. (Eds.), (1985). *Women, gender, and social psychology*. Hillsdale, NJ: Lawrence Erlbaum.

Piaget, J. (1983). *The moral judgment of the child*. New York: Free Press.

Rogow, A. M., Marcia, J. E., & Slugoski, B. R. (1983). The relative importance of identity status interview components. *Journal of Youth and Adolescence, 12*, 387-400.

Rothenberg, P. S. (1988). *Racism and sexism*. New York: St. Martin's Press.

Rotheram, J. J. (1989). Ethnic differences in adolescents' identity status and associated behavior problems. *Journal of Adolescence, 12*, 361-374.

Ryff, C. D. (1989). Happiness is everything, or is it? Explorations on the meaning of psychological well-being. *Journal of Personality and Social Psychology, 57*, 1069-1081.

Sampson, E. E. (1985). The decentralization of identity: Toward a revised concept of personal and social order. *American Psychologist, 40*, 1203-1211.

Schenkel, S., & Marcia, J. E. (1972). Attitudes toward premarital intercourse in determining ego identity status in college women. *Journal of Personality, 3*, 472-482.

Sherif, C. W. (1987). Bias in psychology. In S. Harding (Ed.), *Feminism and methodology* (pp. 37-56). Indianapolis: Indiana University Press.

Shotter, J., & Gergen, K. J. (Eds.). (1989). *Texts of identity.* Newbury Park, CA: Sage.

Slugoski, B. R., & Ginsburg, G. P. (1989). Ego identity and explanatory speech. In J. Shotter and K. J. Gergen (Eds.), *Texts of identity* (pp. 36-55). Newbury Park, CA: Sage.

Spence, J. T., & Helmreich, R. L. (1980). Masculine instrumentality and feminine expressiveness: Their relationships with sex role attitudes and behaviors. *Psychology of Women Quarterly, 5*, 147-163.

Spencer, M. B., & Markstrom-Adams, C. (1990). Identity processes among racial and ethnic minority children in America. *Child Development, 61*, 290-310.

Thorbecke, W., & Grotevant, H. D. (1982). Gender differences in adolescent interpersonal identity formation. *Journal of Youth and Adolescence, 11*, 479-492.

Wallston, B. S., & Grady, K. E. (1985). Integrating the feminist critique and the crisis in social psychology: Another look at research methods. In V. E. O'Leary, R. K. Unger, & B. S. Wallston (Eds.), *Women, gender, and social psychology* (pp. 7-33). Hillsdale, NJ: Lawrence Erlbaum.

Waterman, A. S. (1982). Identity development from adolescence to adulthood: An extension of theory and a review of research. *Developmental Psychology, 18*, 341-358.

Waterman, A. S. (1984). *The psychology of individualism.* New York: Praeger.

Waterman, A. S. (1985). Identity in the context of adolescent psychology. In A. S. Waterman (Ed.), *Identity in adolescence: Processes and contents* (New Directions for Child Development, No. 30). San Francisco: Jossey-Bass.

Waterman, A. S. (1988). Identity status theory and Erikson's theory: Commonalities and differences. *Developmental Review, 8*, 185-208.

Waterman, A. S., & Archer, S. L. (1990). A life-span perspective on identity formation: Developments in form, function, and process. In B. P. Baltes, D. L. Featherman, & R. M. Lerner (Eds.), *Life-span development and behavior, 10*, Hillsdale, NJ: Lawrence Erlbaum.

Waterman, C. K., & Nevid, J. S. (1977). Sex differences in the resolution of the identity crisis. *Journal of Youth and Adolescence, 6*, 337-342.

Whitbourne, S. K., & Tesch, S. A. (1985). A comparison of identity and intimacy statuses in college students and alumni. *Developmental Psychology, 21*, 1039-1044.

4. Identity as an Aspect of Optimal Psychological Functioning

Alan S. Waterman
Trenton State College

INTRODUCTION

In this chapter, I will advance the claim that a clear sense of personal identity constitutes an aspect of optimal psychological functioning, and that this proposition is itself empirically testable. In making such a claim, I am returning to a line of theorizing in psychology begun in the 1950s. At that time much of the discussion on optimal functioning was carried out under the term *positive mental health* (J. M. Erikson & E. H. Erikson, 1950; Jahoda, 1958; Shoben, 1957). It was believed that psychopathology might best be understood in terms of the ways in which abnormality differed from normal or healthy functioning. Perhaps because these early theorists were concerned with forming a global picture of positive mental health, interest in their work dwindled when it seemed that few people were able, in their day-to-day activities, to live up to the standards advanced. A more productive approach to considering optimal psychological functioning may be to analyze possible components singly, focusing on how each is expressed in day-to-day living.

Given the theme of this volume, the personality quality on which I will focus is a sense of personal identity. This construct is discussed by Erikson (1963, 1968) as part of his eight-stage theory of psychosocial development across the life cycle. Erikson's theory is an outgrowth of his concern with understanding mentally healthy functioning. Each of the eight-stage components, and the corresponding virtues of each stage, are discussed in the context of what represents healthy, or optimal, psychological functioning. Whereas Erikson reasoned his case about identity on the basis of clinical experiences, and a psychoanalytic understanding of human nature, there is now an extensive body of empirical research literature on which to draw when assessing whether a sense of personal identity constitutes an aspect of optimal psychological functioning. In this chapter, both the theoretical and the empirical research records will be examined.

Criteria for Assessing
Optimal Psychological Functioning

In advancing any claim regarding what constitutes optimal psychological functioning, it is necessary to examine the criteria against which the claim is to be evaluated. I have proposed that there are four criteria against which such claims can be evaluated (Waterman, 1990b).

1. To be deemed optimal, psychological qualities should contribute to a sense of personal well-being. Personal well-being can be defined as a overall favorable ratio of positive to negative affects, where both the positive and negative affects experienced are situationally appropriate. The more favorable this ratio, the stronger is the support for a claim regarding optimal functioning.

2. To be deemed optimal, psychological qualities should contribute to the realization of goals held by individuals. The concern here is not with particular qualities, narrowly defined, that may be essential to the realization of some specific goal. Rather, claims regarding optimal functioning pertain to qualities that can contribute to the advancing of the broad range of goals a person may pursue.

3. To be deemed optimal, psychological qualities should contribute to social acceptance, that is, the qualities should be viewed as positive ones to enact within the person's social context.

4. To be deemed optimal, psychological qualities should contribute to the realization of goals deemed to be valuable within the societal context within which individuals function. In other words, optimal psychological qualities serve socially constructive ends.

I have contended that the more of these criteria that are satisfied, and the stronger the evidence that can be demonstrated in support of each criterion, the more sustainable is a claim regarding optimal functioning (Waterman, 1990b). However, the demonstration of evidence consistent with any particular criterion, considered in isolation, cannot be viewed as sufficient to support a claim of optimal functioning. Correspondingly, the failure to find support with respect to a particular criterion does not automatically defeat a claim of optimal functioning.

I will mention here only a few of the complexities that can arise in considering the possible relationships among the criteria advanced as standards against which to evaluate claims of optimal functioning. It is possible that psychological qualities that are associated with the psychological well-being of individuals will be neutral, or even negative, with respect to any of the other three criteria. What leads to a subjective positive cognitive-affective state need not contribute to the advancement of a person's goals, nor to ends deemed positive within one's society. Conversely, psychological qualities that are socially constructive and socially attractive do not necessarily contribute to a person's subjective experience of well-being.

It is also true that the personal goals an individual is pursuing may be incompatible with the goals deemed valuable within the larger societal context. Whether personal or societal goals should take precedence has been a perennial subject for debate among philosophers (Bentham, 1948; Marx, 1972; Rand, 1964; Smith, 1981). Ironically, those philosophers giving precedence to individual goals have generally concluded that what is good for individuals is good for society, while those philosophers giving precedence to societal goals typically conclude that what is good for the society is good for individuals. Fortunately, it is not necessary to resolve this philosophical debate, or even to take a stand on it, in order to evaluate claims regarding optimal psychological functioning. It is sufficient to observe what the same set of psychological qualities may plausibly contribute to the advancement of both personal and socially constructive goals.

THEORETICAL PERSPECTIVES ON IDENTITY AS AN ASPECT OF OPTIMAL PSYCHOLOGICAL FUNCTIONING

Erik Erikson: The Construct of Ego Identity

Erikson (1963, 1968) developed the construct of ego identity within the broad framework of psychoanalysis. His theorizing reflected the influences of Anna Freud and Heinz Hartmann, with an emphasis placed on the adaptive functions of the ego. For Erikson, the concept of ego identity reflects the range of possible ways one comes to construct one's view of oneself. These processes involve a combination of conscious and unconscious mechanisms. The outcomes developed may be more or less serviceable in terms of the manner in which one makes one's way through the world. At its best, the process of identity formation involves achieving a resolution of the identity crisis in which the emerging sense of identity integrates one's biological capabilities and one's personal inclinations with the opportunities for expression available within one's societal context.

Within the context of Erikson's psychosocial theory of stage development, a sense of ego identity can be considered an aspect of optimal psychological functioning in that it constitutes the syntonic outcome of the normative crisis of identity formation. An outcome is considered syntonic if it is experienced positively by a person—the type of outcome that he or she strives to attain and, if attained, then maintain. In contrast, a dystonic outcome to a normative crisis is one that is experienced negatively—the type of outcome a person strives to avoid, or if experienced, then rectify. According to Erikson (1982), individuals inevitably emerge from each normative developmental crisis with outcomes that incorporate both syntonic and dystonic elements. Thus, healthy psychological development for Erikson entails resolutions of the successive normative crises with favorable ratios of syntonic to dystonic elements, where both types of elements can be considered situationally appropriate. According to the epigenetic principle (Erikson, 1968), each developmental stage builds upon the foundation provided by preceding stages, such that an outcome with an unfavorable ratio will compromise the likelihood of healthy development at all subsequent stages in the life cycle.

For Erikson (1968) the construct of ego identity is very broad, as reflected in the following definition:

> The wholeness to be achieved at this stage [adolescence] I have called a sense of inner identity. The young person, in order to experience wholeness, must feel a progressive continuity between that which he has come to be during the long years of childhood and that which he promises to become in the anticipated future; between that which he

conceives himself to be and that which he perceives others to see in him and to expect of him. Individually speaking identity includes, but is more than, the sum of all successive identifications of those earlier years when the child wanted to be, and often was forced to become, like the people he depended on. Identity is a unique product, which now meets a crisis to be solved only in new identifications with age mates and with leader figures outside the family. (p. 87)

With respect to the content of an individual's sense of identity, Erikson (1968) identifies a broad array of domains in which the person develops a self-reflective perspective. Identity elements develop around the choice of one's vocation; one's ideologies (e.g., religious, political, and economic beliefs); one's philosophy of life; one's ethical capacities; one's sexuality; the personal meaning of one's gender, ethnicity, culture, and nationality; and one's relationship to "an all-inclusive human identity" (Erikson, 1968, p. 42). By creating a construct with such breadth, Erikson has created problems for those of us concerned with operationally defining identity for research purposes (Waterman, 1988).

In terms of the criteria for optimal psychological functioning advanced at the beginning of this chapter, Erikson's theorizing appears to incorporate each of the four criteria. To be considered successful, the resolution of an identity crisis must reflect a favorable ratio of syntonic to dystonic elements, by definition incorporating a sense of personal well-being. A predominantly dystonic outcome, one not characterized by personal well-being, cannot be considered successful.

With respect to the realization of goals held by individuals, having a clearly delineated perspective of oneself, knowing who one is and what one wishes to do in life, would appear essential for the realization of goals in virtually any sphere of endeavor. This is reflected in the very broad range of domains that Erikson (1968) discusses as pertinent to the task of identity formation. To choose a goal, to identify activities by which to seek the attainment of that goal, and to implement those activities are all expressions of a person's sense of ego identity.

As a psychosocial theorist, Erikson (1968) emphasizes the importance of the sociocultural context as a determining factor in the process of ego identity formation. Given the array of identity-related goals compatible with one's biological capacities and psychological inclinations, the range of those for which support and encouragement are available within one's social context will be considerably narrower. Societies differ widely with respect to the content and diversity of identity-related goals deemed acceptable for a person to adopt, with acceptable options typically based on considerations of gender, race, class, ethnicity, family, and age. While Erikson's writings in this regard might be interpreted as emphasizing the importance of adapting to one's society, of conforming to social expectations, as indicative of optimal functioning, in his psychohistorical writings it is clear he puts the priority elsewhere. In both *Young Man Luther* (Erikson, 1958) and *Ghandi's Truth* (Erikson, 1969), he focused on individuals who sought to expand the range of identity-related goals beyond those sanctioned by the particular societies in which they lived. The hallmark of socially constructive activities for Erikson (1964) is the compatibility of individual and community interests. Erikson (1964) has written: "Truly worthwhile acts enhance a mutuality between the doer and the other—a mutuality which strengthens the doer even as it strengthens the other" (p. 233). While this may be more frequently found in actions carried out in line with societal norms, norm-breaking may itself be socially constructive.

James Marcia: The Identity Statuses

Marcia (1966, 1980) construes identity as a reflective self-structure:

> [A]n internal, self-constructed organization of drives, abilities, beliefs, and individual history. The better developed this structure is, the more aware individuals appear to be of their own uniqueness and similarity to others and their own strengths and weaknesses in making their way in the world. The less developed this structure is, the more confused individuals seem about their own distinctiveness from others and the more they have to rely on external sources to evaluate themselves. (1980, p. 159)

In attempting to establish an operational definition of ego identity, Marcia (1966) focused attention on the processes by which identity structures are formed. On theoretical grounds, he identified two dimensions, exploration and commitment, that in combination define four identity statuses, or alternative positions regarding the task of identity formation. *Exploration* refers to a period of struggle or active questioning in arriving at various aspects of personal identity, such as vocational choice, religious beliefs, or attitudes about the role of a spouse or parenting in one's life. *Commitment* involves making a firm, unwavering decision in such areas and engaging in appropriate implementing activities. Persons in the *identity diffusion* category do not have firm commitments and are not actively trying to form them. They may never have had a period of exploration in the past, or they may have been in an identity crisis but were unable to resolve it successfully. The category of *foreclosure* applies to individuals who have not undergone a period of exploration but who are, nevertheless, committed to particular goals, values, and beliefs. The commitments made by foreclosures generally reflect the wishes of parents or other authority figures. The term *moratorium* is used to refer to persons who are currently exploring alternatives in an attempt to arrive at a choice. *Identity achievers* are people who have gone through a period of exploration and have emerged from it with relatively firm commitments.

Marcia (1980) draws a relatively complex relationship between the identity statuses and the concept of optimal functioning:

> There are *both* healthy and pathological aspects of each of the styles, save perhaps the Identity Achievement status. For example, Foreclosures may be seen either as steadfast or rigid, committed or dogmatic, cooperative or conforming; Moratoriums may be viewed either as sensitive or anxiety-ridden, highly ethical or self-righteous, flexible or vacillating; Identity Diffusions may be considered either carefree or careless, charming or psychopathic, independent or schizoid. Identity Achievements, for the most part, are seen as strong, self-directed, and highly adaptive. Even here, however, there is a kind of premature identity achievement that may limit one's ultimate adaptiveness by fixing too early on occupational and ideological commitments. (p. 161-162)

Since Marcia (1966, 1980; Marcia et al., in press) has been most concerned with demonstrating the affective, cognitive, and behavioral consequences associated with use of the various approaches to the task of identity formation, an assessment of the relative strengths and limitations of each of the identity statuses is best derived from a review of the empirical research record established over the past 25 years. Variables related to each of the four criteria for evaluating claims regarding optimal psychological functioning have been employed in various research studies, and this research will be reviewed later in this chapter.

Personal Perspectives on Identity: Personal Expressiveness as a Third Defining Dimension for the Identity Statuses

In my own efforts to study identity, I (Waterman, 1984a) have defined the construct in terms of:

> [H]aving a clearly delineated self-definition comprised of those goals, values, and beliefs to which the person is unequivocally committed. These commitments evolve over time and are made because the chosen goals, values, and beliefs are judged worthy of giving a direction, purpose, and meaning to life. (p. 331)

I submit that the definitions of identity offered by Erikson (1968), Marcia (1980), and Waterman (1984a) have the same referent, yet each theorist has chosen to focus on different descriptive elements of the construct and on different functions that a sense of identity can serve. In developing the definition I put forth, I have chosen to emphasize, to a greater degree than either Erikson or Marcia, the strength of a person's investment in particular identity elements and the centrality of that identity to the manner in which she or he chooses to live.

While it might be assumed that an individual in Marcia's identity achievement status, who has explored alternatives and has committed to a particular goal, value, or belief, would care deeply about the chosen identity element, my experiences in more than two decades of research on identity formation have led me to the conclusion that often this is not the case. I have observed individuals in identity crises who are instrumentally seeking the most practical option to which to commit. If an identity commitment emerges from such an exploration process, the person seldom feels fully engaged in what he or she is doing, although there is no apparent desire to reopen the questioning and seek an alternative identity resolution. If one wishes to view a sense of personal identity as reflecting not just commitments, but commitments experienced as fully engaging, commitments passionately held, then there is something missing from the criteria for the identity statuses originally provided by Marcia (1966). I propose that the missing element is feelings of personal expressiveness, and that it can appropriately be utilized as a third defining dimension of the identity statuses.

Experiences of an activity as personally expressive for an individual occur when there is: (a) an unusually intense involvement in an undertaking, (b) a feeling of special fit or meshing with an activity that is not characteristic of most daily tasks, (c) a feeling of intensely being alive, (d) a feeling of being complete or fulfilled while engaged in an activity, (e) an impression that this is what the person was meant to do, and (f) a feeling that this is who one really is (Waterman, 1990a). Such experiences of personal expressiveness appear conceptually linked with the feelings associated with intrinsic motivation (Deci & Ryan, 1985), flow (M. Csikszentmihalyi, 1975; M. Csikszentmihalyi & I. S. Csikszentmihalyi, 1988), and peak experiences (Maslow, 1964, 1968). (See Waterman, 1990a, for a discussion of the links among these concepts.)

The concept of personal expressiveness has it roots in the classical Greek philosophy of *eudaimonism*. Eudaimonism is an ethical theory that calls upon people to recognize and live in accordance with the *daimon* or "true self." It received its most notable treatment in Aristotle's (1985) *Nicomachean Ethics*, and contemporary presentations of eudaimonistic ethics are provided by May (1969) and Norton (1976).

As I use the term, the daimon refers to those potentialities of each person, the realization of which represents the greatest fulfillment in living of which each is capable. These include both the potentialities that are shared by all humans by virtue of our common specieshood and those unique potentials that distinguish each individual from all others. The daimon is an ideal, in the sense of being an excellence, a perfection toward which one strives, and hence, it can give meaning and direction to one's life. A person's sense of identity is an approximation of the daimon, a set of goals, values, and beliefs that to a greater or lesser extent correspond to the actual potentialities of the individual.

When an individual is succeeding in living in truth to his or her daimon, it gives rise to a condition the Greeks called *eudaimonia*. While the usual translation of eudaimonia in Aristotle's (1985)

Nicomachean Ethics is as "happiness," there is a controversy within philosophy over whether this is indeed a proper translation (Cooper, 1975; Kraut, 1979; Telfer, 1980). Aristotle clearly rejected the view that "hedonic happiness" was an appropriate ethical goal. The term "eudaimonia" carries an implication that one has "what is *worth* desiring and worth having in life" (Telfer, 1980, p. 37). Norton (1976) writes of eudaimonia as a feeling of "being where one wants to be, doing what one wants to do" (p. 216), where what is wanted is taken as being worth having. In psychological terms, eudaimonia may be understood as feelings of personal expressiveness. Identity-related activities consistent with one's potentials are characterized by intense involvement, feelings of special fit or meshing with the activities, feelings of completeness and fulfillment, and so on.

From a eudaimonistic perspective, a person's search for identity is an effort to identify those potentials that correspond to the "true self." The metaphor for identity development used here is one of discovery (Waterman, 1984a), rather than one of construction (Berzonsky, 1986; Marcia et al., in press). According to the discovery metaphor, for each person there are potentials, already present though unrecognized, that need to become manifest and acted upon if the person is to live a fulfilled life. For many people, the task of recognizing and acting upon these potentials is not an easy one, as evidenced by the stresses associated with an identity crisis. Feelings of eudaimonia or personal expressiveness can serve as a basis for assessing whether identity elements are well-chosen. The presence of such feelings can be used as a sign that identity choices are consistent with an individual's potentials and thus can provide a basis for self-fulfillment (Waterman, 1990a).

This is not the place for an extended discussion of eudaimonistic philosophy and its implications for an understanding of personal identity. I have written on these themes in greater depth elsewhere (Waterman, 1984b, 1990a, 1990c). What is most relevant for my present purposes are the conclusions that (a) feelings of personal expressiveness can serve as a third defining dimension of identity, and (b) such feelings are themselves related to each of the four criteria against which claims regarding optimal psychological functioning can be evaluated.

It should be noted that feelings of personal expressiveness as a defining dimension of the identity statuses cut across the dimensions of exploration and commitment. Not all identity commitments are personally expressive, and this is the case regardless of whether a period of active questioning was involved in their development. Further, individuals in the moratorium status may or may not make an effort to reach a decision on the basis of personal expressiveness. For some, the task of exploration is directed primarily toward pragmatic ends, whether of a material or social nature. Other moratoriums are engaged in a process of self-discovery, seeking that which will be personally expressive.

The result of adding feelings of personal expressiveness as a third defining dimension of identity is an expansion of the number of identity statuses from four to seven:

1. Expressive identity achievers who, after exploration, are committed to goals, values, and beliefs that they experience as consistent with their aptitudes and talents and that are perceived as furthering their purpose in living;

2. nonexpressive identity achievers who, after exploration, establish commitments perceived as primarily instrumental, that is, associated with ends that are not integral either to their aptitudes and talents and/or their purposes in living;

3. moratoriums seeking an expressive resolution to their identity concerns;

4. moratoriums for whom expressiveness is not a criteria for the resolution of their identity crises;

5. expressive foreclosures who have committed to the first alternative they seriously considered, where the specific identity elements involved are experienced as furthering the person's aptitudes and talents and purposes in living;

6. nonexpressive foreclosures who have also formed identity commitments without the consideration of alternatives, and for whom the commitments serve functions not primarily associated with aptitudes and talents or purposes in living; and

7. identity diffusions. (Since identity diffusions have not formed commitments, nor are they engaged in the task of identity formation, I am conjecturing that the concept of personal expressiveness does not apply. I have received, however, personal communications from several colleagues describing how individuals might experience the identity diffusion status in an expressive manner. Hence, whether there are both expressive and nonexpressive identity diffusions may best be treated as an empirical question.)

In a study of the relationship between the identity statuses, as defined in terms of exploration and commitment, and experiences of personal expressiveness, Gordon (1989) found a strong, significant, positive correlation between scores on the Identity Achievement scale of the Extended Objective Measure of Ego Identity Status (Grotevant & Adams, 1984) and reports of personally expressive activities. The correlations of personal expressiveness with the Moratorium, Foreclosure, and Identity Diffusion scales were all statistically significant in the negative direction. As would be expected on the basis of advantages presumed to be associated with the flexible, reflective consideration of identity alternatives, commitment following exploration appears more likely to result in expressive outcomes than is the forming of identity commitments through nonreflective identification with significant others. The negative correlation between scores on the Moratorium scale and personal expressiveness may be a reflection of the stresses associated with an identity crisis, and the lack of satisfaction experienced with alternatives under consideration.

RESEARCH ON IDENTITY AS AN ASPECT OF OPTIMAL PSYCHOLOGICAL FUNCTIONING

In evaluating the claim that a sense of personal identity represents an aspect of optimal psychological functioning, the presence of three defining dimensions introduces some complexities into the analysis. Most of the studies to be reviewed here were conducted using the identity status paradigm developed by Marcia (1966). This involves the simultaneous applications of the dimensions of exploration and commitment. While the identity achievement status would be expected to be strongly associated with each of the criterion variables of optimal functioning, it would not necessarily be expected that either moratoriums or foreclosures will fare poorly on these variables. If what is important for optimal functioning on a particular criterion is the dimension of exploration, then identity achievers and moratoriums may look quite similar. Correspondingly, if what is important is the dimension of commitment, then identity achievers and foreclosures may look quite similar. It should also be noted that research on the dimension of feelings of personal expressiveness has begun only recently. As yet, studies of its relationship to the criteria for optimal functioning have been carried out independently of the dimensions of exploration and commitment.

Research on Identity and Personal Well-Being

Self-Esteem. A series of studies has been conducted relating identity to self-esteem and self-acceptance. Individuals scoring high on measures of identity have been found to report higher levels of self-esteem than those whose sense of identity is not, as yet, well formed (Adams et al., 1979; Breuer, 1973; Bunt, 1968; Cabin, 1966; Marcia & Friedman, 1970; O'Connell, 1976; Prager, 1982; Rasmussen, 1964; Read et al., 1984; Rosenfeld, 1972; Schenkel & Marcia, 1972; Simmons, 1970), though in several studies no differences have been found (Fannin, 1979; Marcia, 1967; Orlofsky, 1977). In terms of the identity status paradigm, it is identity commitment that appears to be the salient dimension, with identity achievers and, in some studies, foreclosures showing higher self-esteem than individuals lacking in identity commitments. The findings for the commitment dimension appear more consistent for females than for males. With respect to feelings of personal expressiveness, Waterman (1989) found significant positive correlations between reports of such feelings and items indicative of high self-esteem.

Happiness. Waterman (1989) reported a very strong positive correlation between a measure of feelings of personal expressiveness associated with activities and a measure of hedonic enjoyment. Feelings of personal expressiveness and hedonic enjoyment were shown not to be equivalent conditions, however, since extensive discriminant validity for the two scales was demonstrated with respect to hypotheses drawn from eudaimonistic theory.

Debilitating Emotional States, e.g., Anxiety, Depression. Across a series of studies, individuals with a strong sense of identity have generally been found to report lower levels of a variety of debilitating emotional states (Bronson, 1959; Constantinople, 1970; Howard & Kubis, 1964; Marcia, 1967; Marcia & Friedman, 1970; Oshman & Manosevitz, 1974; Reimanis, 1974; Schenkel & Marcia, 1972; Stark & Traxler, 1974; Wessman & Ricks, 1966). Null findings have also been reported in a number of studies (Cross & Allen, 1970; Orlofsky, 1978; Tobacyk, 1981). With respect to the identity statuses, individuals in the moratorium status consistently report the highest levels of anxiety, while those in the committed identity statuses, particularly foreclosures, report the least. Somewhat surprisingly, Waterman (1989) found that reported levels of personal expressiveness associated with activities were unrelated to the presence of negative emotional states when engaged in those activities.

Research on Identity and Goal-Directed Activity

Goal Setting. Rothman (1984) observed individuals with identity commitments, identity achievers and foreclosures, to be goal-oriented, while identity diffusions had problems in that regard. Among college women, Marcia and Friedman (1970) found identity achievers to choose the most challenging college majors, while moratoriums and identity diffusions chose the least challenging majors. With regard to feelings of personal expressiveness, Waterman (1989) found significant positive relationships between such feelings and having clear goals, feeling challenged, and investing a great deal of effort in activities.

Sophistication of Cognitive Functioning. Among the aspects of psychological functioning that can be expected to be strongly related to success in goal-realization is the quality of cognitive functioning. Positive relationships between identity functioning and stage scores on Loevinger's scheme for ego development have been found by Adams and Fitch (1981, 1982), Adams and Shea (1979), Ginsburg and Orlofsky (1981), and Newman (1986). Identity achievers, in particular, were most likely to be in the post-conformist (integrated) level. Positive relationships between identity functioning and formal operational thought have been reported by Leadbetter and Dionne (1981), Rowe and Marcia (1980), and Wagner (1987), but null findings for these variables were reported by Afrifah (1980), Berzonsky, et al. (1975), Cauble (1976), and Leiper (1981). Positive relationships between identity functioning and Kohlberg's levels of moral reasoning have been reported by Hult (1979), Leiper (1981), Podd (1972), Poppen (1974), and Rowe and Marcia (1980). Only Cauble (1975) has failed to replicate this relationship. Two other variables that have been studied in this regard are integrative complexity and conceptual impulsivity. Slugoski et al. (1984), using integrative complexity as a measure of cognitive sophistication with a sample of college males, found moratoriums and identity achievers to be more cognitively advanced than were foreclosures and identity diffusions. C. K. Waterman and Waterman (1974) found foreclosure and identity diffusion males were more often impulsive on the Matching Familiar Figures Test (responding quickly and making errors), while identity achievers and moratoriums were more often found to be reflective.

Beliefs About Personal Responsibility. Success in goal-directed activity may also be assumed to be related to feelings of personal responsibility, for example as operationalized in terms of an internal locus of control. Having a strong sense of personal identity, particularly as an identity achiever, has been found linked to internality by Adams and Shea (1979), Dellas and Jernigan (1987), Howard (1975), and C. K. Waterman et al. (1970). Null findings have been reported by Ginsburg and Orlofsky (1981) and Matteson (1974). Neuber and Genthner (1977) found moratoriums and identity achievers to take greater personal responsibility for their actions than foreclosures and identity diffusions. In addition, Orlofsky et al. (1973) and Matteson (1974) found individuals in the foreclosure or identity diffusion statuses to score lower on measures of autonomy in comparison to identity achievers and moratoriums.

Research on Identity and Social Attractiveness

The only direct test of the hypothesis that a sense of personal identity is viewed as a positive quality to enact was provided by Goldman et al. (1980). College student respondents who had been classified into the various identity statuses were provided with one-page descriptions of fictional college students constructed to represent each of the four identity statuses. Target individuals in the identity achievement and moratorium statuses were rated as more likable by the respondents than were foreclosure or identity diffuse targets, and this was the case irrespective of the identity status of the respondents.

Research on Identity and Socially Constructive Behavior

Social Attitudes. At a minimum, the pursuit of socially constructive goals would appear predicated on the holding of social attitudes of tolerance and acceptance of others. The relationship between the identity statuses and the holding of authoritarian attitudes has been assessed in a series of studies (Adams et al., 1979;

Marcia, 1966, 1967; Marcia & Friedman, 1970; Matteson, 1974; Schenkel & Marcia, 1972; Streitmatter & Pate, 1989). Foreclosures have consistently been found to hold the most authoritarian attitudes, while identity achievers and moratoriums were usually the least willing to endorse authoritarian attitudes. In addition, Tzuriel and Klein (1977) found high scores on an identity measure to be negatively associated with ethnocentricity.

Cooperation and Helping. In two studies, functioning in the identity achievement status was found to be linked to individuals' effectiveness in generating a helping atmosphere in a face-to-face interaction, while foreclosures and identity diffusions were least effective (Genthner & Neuber, 1975; Neuber & Genthner, 1977). Walter and Stivers (1977) found undergraduate student teachers with a clearly defined sense of identity to be more accepting of student ideas. Similarly, Slugoski et al. (1984) demonstrated that in social interactions, the behavior of identity achievers was most cooperative and reflected an interest in listening to the ideas of others. With respect to the dimension of feelings of personal expressiveness, Waterman (1989) found that activities involving helping others received the second highest ratings for personal expressiveness, based on a content coding for 14 different types of activities. (The highest ratings for personal expressiveness were found for social activities, i.e., activities carried out with family and friends.)

Capacity for Intimacy. A large body of research has been carried out relating a personal sense of identity to the capacity for intimacy in relationships. Consistently, individuals in the identity achievement status have been found to be in the highest statuses regarding intimacy as well (Fitch & Adams, 1983; Hodgson & Fischer 1979; Kacerguis & Adams, 1980; Marcia, 1976; Orlofsky et al., 1973; Tesch & Whitbourne, 1982). In general, individuals in the foreclosure status tend to approach relationships in a stereotyped, role-bound manner, while identity diffusions have the most difficulties with intimacy.

CONCLUSIONS

I began this chapter by advancing the claim that the quality of a sense of personal identity constitutes one aspect of optimal psychological functioning and I proposed four criteria against which to evaluate this claim. The review of the empirical research literature on identity provides support for the claims made for identity with respect to each of the four criteria. A clear sense of personal identity, based on the exploration of various possible identity elements followed by the formation of identity commitments, appears to have a number of very notable strengths:

1. A clear sense of identity is associated with a sense of personal well-being in the form of self-esteem and self-acceptance and the relative absence of debilitating emotional states such as anxiety and depression.

2. A clear sense of identity is associated with goal-directed activity both in terms of goal setting and in the sophistication of cognitive functioning necessary for success in achieving the goals set.

3. A clear sense of identity is perceived as a positive quality to enact (though additional research on this criteria is needed).

4. A clear sense of identity is associated with the pursuit of socially constructive ends in terms of the attitudes of tolerance and social acceptance, cooperation and helping, and the seeking of intimate personal relationships.

While feelings of personal expressiveness, as a defining dimension of identity, have only recently begun to receive research attention, the findings available strengthen the case that can be made for identity as an aspect of optimal psychological functioning. Feelings of personal expressiveness were found to be associated with personal well-being, probability of success in goal-related behaviors, and the pursuit of socially constructive ends.

A careful reader will have identified a difference between the phrasing of the criteria for evaluating claims of optimal functioning advanced in the beginning of this chapter and the way in which the criteria have been applied in the review of the literature. At the beginning of the chapter, the criteria were phrased in terms of a causal contribution of the psychological quality to be evaluated to the criterion outcomes. In the review of the research literature, what was assessed were correlational associations of identity, the psychological quality evaluated, with the criterion outcomes. It must be recognized that a standard of correlational association, while essential to any claim of causal contribution, is not sufficient for establishing that the association is causal in nature. Given that it is difficult, perhaps impossible, to carry out research that might establish claims of causal contributions to the criteria employed here, we must reconcile ourselves that claims regarding what qualities constitute aspects of optimal psychological functioning are not ultimately provable. Rather, we are left in a position of judging candidates for optimal qualities as either viable, if the research record supports hypotheses of correlational associations between the qualities and the criterion outcomes, or nonviable, if such hypotheses are not sustainable. Given this standard, and the existing research record, the quality of a sense of personal identity clearly constitutes a viable candidate for continuing consideration as an aspect of optimal psychological functioning.

Given the analysis provided here, it is appropriate that we seriously consider the development of intervention strategies designed to promote the reflective consideration of identity alternatives and the formation of identity commitments, particularly to goals, values, and beliefs experienced as personally expressive. Archer (1989, this volume) has directed our attention to the various groups that might benefit from interventions and to the range of venues in which intervention strategies may be applied, including counseling and clinical settings, schools, out-of-school programs, and the media. If improvements in the quality of the lives of participants in intervention activities promoting identity formation can be demonstrated, this will provide still further support for the viability of the candidacy of a sense of personal identity for consideration as an aspect of optimal psychological functioning.

REFERENCES

Adams, G. R., & Fitch, S. A. (1981). Ego stage and identity status development: A cross-lag analysis. *Journal of Adolescence, 4*, 163-171.

Adams, G. R., & Fitch, S. A. (1982). Ego stage and identity status development: A cross-sequential analysis. *Journal of Personality and Social Psychology, 43*, 574-583.

Adams, G. R., & Shea, J. A. (1979). The relationship between identity status, locus of control, and ego development. *Journal of Youth and Adolescence, 8*, 81-89.

Adams, G. R., Shea, J. A., & Fitch, S. A. (1979). Toward the development of an objective assessment of ego identity status. *Journal of Youth and Adolescence, 8*, 223-228.

Afrifah, A. (1980). *The relationship between logical cognition and ego identity: An investigation of Piagetian and Eriksonian hypotheses about adolescence.* Unpublished doctoral dissertation, Columbia University, New York.

Archer, S. L. (Ed.). (1989). Adolescent identity: An appraisal of health and intervention [Special issue]. *Journal of Adolescence, 12*(4).

Aristotle. (1985). *The Nicomachean ethics.* (T. Irwin, Trans.). Indianapolis, IN: Hackett.

Bentham, J. (1948). *An introduction to the principles of morals and legislation.* New York: Hafner. (Original work published 1789).

Berzonsky, M. D. (1986). Discovery versus constructivist interpretations of identity formation: Consideration of additional implications. *Journal of Early Adolescence, 6,* 111-117.

Berzonsky, M. D., Weiner, A. S., & Raphael, D. (1975). Interdependence of formal reasoning. *Developmental Psychology, 11,* 258.

Breuer, H. (1973). *Ego identity status in late-adolescent college males, as measured by a group-administered incomplete sentences blank and related to inferred stance toward authority.* Unpublished doctoral dissertation, New York University.

Bronson, G. W. (1959). Identity diffusion in late adolescents. *Journal of Abnormal and Social Psychology, 59,* 414-417.

Bunt, M. (1968). Ego identity: Its relationship to the discrepancy between how an adolescent views himself and how he perceives that others view him. *Psychology, 5*(3) 14-25.

Cabin, S. (1966). *Ego identity status: A laboratory study of the effects of stress and levels of reinforcement upon self and peer evaluations.* Unpublished doctoral dissertation, The Ohio State University.

Cauble, M. A. (1976). Formal operations, ego identity, and principle morality: Are they related? *Developmental Psychology, 12,* 363-364.

Constantinople, A. (1970). Some correlates of average level of happiness among college students. *Developmental Psychology, 2,* 447.

Cooper, J. (1975). *Reason and human good in Aristotle.* Cambridge, MA: Harvard University Press.

Cross, H., & Allen, J. (1970). Ego identity status, adjustment, and academic achievement. *Journal of Consulting and Clinical Psychology, 34,* 288.

Csikszentmihalyi, M. (1975). *Beyond boredom and anxiety.* San Francisco: Jossey-Bass.

Csikszentmihalyi, M., & Csikszentmihalyi, I. S. (Eds.). (1988). *Optimal experience: Psychological studies of flow in consciousness.* New York: Cambridge University Press.

Deci, E. L., & Ryan, R. M. (1985). *Intrinsic motivation and self-determination in human behavior.* New York: Plenum.

Dellas, M., & Jernigan, L. P. (1987). Occupational identity status development, gender comparisons, and internal-external locus of control in first-year Air Force cadets. *Journal of Youth and Adolescence, 16,* 587-600.

Erikson, E. H. (1958). *Young man Luther: A study in psychoanalysis and history.* New York: Norton.

Erikson, E. H. (1963). *Childhood and society* (2nd ed.). New York: Norton.

Erikson, E. H. (1964). *Insight and responsibility: Lectures on the ethical implications of psychoanalytic insight.* New York: Norton.

Erikson, E. H. (1968). *Identity: Youth and crisis.* New York: Norton.

Erikson, E. H. (1969). *Gandhi's truth: On the origins of militant nonviolence.* New York: Norton.

Erikson, E. H. (1982). *The life cycle completed: A review.* New York: Norton.

Erikson, J. M., & Erikson, E. H. (1950). Growth and crises of the "healthy personality." In M.J.E. Senn (Ed.), *Symposium on the healthy personality* (prepared for the White House Conference, 1950) (pp. 91-146). New York: Josiah Macy, Jr., Foundation.

Fannin, P. N. (1979). The relation between ego identity status and sex role attitude, work role salience, typicality of major, and self-esteem in college women. *Journal of Vocational Behavior, 14*, 12-22.

Fitch, S. A., & Adams, G. R. (1983). Ego identity status and intimacy status: Replication and extension. *Developmental Psychology, 19*, 839-845.

Genthner, R. W., & Neuber, K. (1975). Identity achievers and their rated levels of facilitation. *Psychological Reports, 36*, 754.

Ginsburg, S. D., & Orlofsky, J. L. (1981). Ego identity status, ego development, and locus of control in college women. *Journal of Youth and Adolescence, 10*, 297-307.

Goldman, J. A., Rosenzweig, M., & Lutter, A. D. (1980). Effect of ego identity statuses on interpersonal attraction. *Journal of Youth and Adolescence, 9*, 153-162.

Gordon, L. L. (1989). *Identity development and personal expressiveness*. Unpublished master's thesis, University of Arizona.

Grotevant,. H. D., & Adams, G. R. (1984). Development of an objective measure to assess ego-identity in adolescence: Validation and replication. *Journal of Youth and Adolescence, 3*, 419-438.

Hodgson, J. W., & Fischer, J. L. (1979). Sex differences in identity and intimacy development in college youth. *Journal of Youth and Adolescence, 8*, 37-50.

Howard, M. R. (1975). *Ego identity status in women, fear of success, and performance in a competitive situation*. Unpublished doctoral dissertation, State University of New York at Buffalo.

Howard, S. M., & Kubis, J. F. (1964). Ego identity and some aspects of personal adjustment. *Journal of Psychology, 58*, 459-466.

Hult, R. E. (1979). The relationship between ego identity status and moral reasoning in university women. *Journal of Psychology, 103*, 203-207.

Jahoda, M. (1958). *Current concepts of positive mental health*. New York: Basic Books.

Kacerguis, M. A., & Adams, G. R. (1980). Erikson stage resolution: The relationship between identity and intimacy. *Journal of Youth and Adolescence, 9*, 117-126.

Kraut, R. (1979). Two conceptions of happiness. *Philosophical Review, 87*, 167-196.

Leadbetter, B. J., & Dionne, J. P. (1981). The adolescent's use of formal operational thinking in solving problems related to identity resolution. *Adolescence, 16*, 116-121.

Leiper, R. N. (1981). *The relationship of cognitive developmental structures to the formation of identity in young men*. Unpublished doctoral dissertation, Simon Fraser University.

Marcia, J. E. (1966). Development and validation of ego identity status. *Journal of Personality and Social Psychology, 3*, 551-558.

Marcia, J. E. (1967). Ego identity status: Relationship to change in self-esteem, "general maladjustment," and authoritarianism. *Journal of Personality, 35*, 119-133.

Marcia, J. E. (1976). Identity six years after: A follow-up study. *Journal of Youth and Adolescence, 5*, 145-160.

Marcia, J. E. (1980). Identity in adolescence. In J. Adelson (Ed.), *Handbook of adolescent psychology* (pp. 159-187). New York: John Wiley.

Marcia, J. E., & Friedman, M. L. (1970). Ego identity status in college women. *Journal of Personality, 38*, 249-263.

Marcia, J. E., Waterman, A. S., Matteson, D. R., Archer, S. L., & Orlofsky, J. L. (in press). *Studies in ego identity: A handbook for psychosocial research*. New York: Springer-Verlag.

Marx, K. (1972). *The Marx-Engels reader* (R. Tucker, Ed.). New York: Norton.

Maslow, A. H. (1964). *Religion, values, and peak-experiences.* New York: Viking.

Maslow, A. H. (1968). *Toward a psychology of being* (2nd ed.). Princeton, NJ: Van Nostrand.

Matteson, D. R. (1974). *Alienation vs. exploration and commitment: Personality and family corollaries of adolescent identity statuses.* Report for the Project for Youth Research, Copenhagen Royal Danish School of Education Studies.

May, R. (1969). *Love and will.* New York: Norton.

Neuber, K. A., & Genthner, R. W. (1977). The relationship between ego identity, personal responsibility, and facilitative communication. *Journal of Psychology, 95,* 45-49.

Newman, F. (1986). *Ego development in women in an urban hostel.* Unpublished doctoral dissertation, Simon Fraser University.

Norton, D. L. (1976). *Personal destinies: A philosophy of ethical individualism.* Princeton, NJ: Princeton University Press.

O'Connell, A. N. (1976). The relationship between life style and identity synthesis and re-synthesis in traditional, neo-traditional, and non-traditional women. *Journal of Personality, 44,* 675-688.

Orlofsky, J. L. (1977). Sex role in orientation, identity formation, and self-esteem in college men and women. *Sex Roles, 3,* 561-574.

Orlofsky, J. L. (1978). Identity formation, achievement, and fear of success in college men and women. *Journal of Youth and Adolescence, 7,* 49-62.

Orlofsky, J. L., Marcia, J. E., & Lesser, I. M. (1973). Ego identity status and the intimacy versus isolation crisis of young adulthood. *Journal of Personality and Social Psychology, 27,* 211-219.

Oshman, H. P., & Manosevitz, M. (1974). The impact of the identity crisis on the adjustment of late adolescent males. *Journal of Youth and Adolescence, 3,* 207-216.

Podd, M. H. (1972). Ego identity status and morality: The relationship between two developmental constructs. *Developmental Psychology, 6,* 497-507.

Poppen, P. J. (1974). *The development of sex differences in moral judgment for college males and females.* Unpublished doctoral dissertation, Cornell University.

Prager, K. J. (1982). Identity development and self-esteem in young women. *Journal of Genetic Psychology, 141,* 177-182.

Rand, A. (1984). *The virtue of selfishness: A new concept of egoism.* New York: New American Library.

Rasmussen, J. E. (1964). Relationship of ego identity to psychosocial effectiveness. *Psychological Reports, 15,* 815-825.

Read, D., Adams, G. R., & Dobson, W. R. (1984). Ego identity status, personality, and social influence style. *Journal of Personality and Social Psychology, 46,* 169-177.

Reimanis, G. (1974). Psychosocial development, anomie, and mood. *Journal of Personality and Social Psychology, 29,* 355-357.

Rosenfeld, R. U. (1972). *The relationship of ego identity to similarity among self, ideal self, and probably occupational-role concept among college males.* Unpublished doctoral dissertation, University of Maryland.

Rothman, K. M. (1984). Multivariate analysis of the relationship of personal concerns to adolescent ego identity status. *Adolescence, 19,* 713-727.

Rowe, I., & Marcia, J. E. (1980). Ego identity status, formal operations, and moral development. *Journal of Youth and Adolescence, 9,* 87-99.

Schenkel, S., & Marcia, J. E. (1972). Attitudes toward premarital intercourse in determining ego identity status in college women. *Journal of Personality, 3,* 472-482.

Shoben, E. (1957). Toward a concept of normal personality. *American Psychologist, 12*, 183-189.

Simmons, D. (1970). Development of an objective measure of identity achievement status. *Journal of Projective Techniques and Personality Assessment, 34*, 241-244.

Slugoski, B. R., Marcia, J. E., & Koopman, R. F. (1984). Cognitive and social characteristics of ego identity status in college males. *Journal of Personality and Social Psychology, 47*, 646-661.

Smith, A. (1981). *An inquiry into the nature and causes of the wealth of nations* (R. H. Campbell & A. S. Skinner, Gen. Eds.). Indianapolis, IN: Liberty Classics. (Original work published 1797).

Stark, P. A., & Traxler, A. J. (1974). Empirical validation of Erikson's theory of identity crises in late adolescence. *Journal of Psychology, 86*, 25-33.

Streitmatter, J. L., & Pate, G. (1989). Identity status development and cognitive prejudice in early adolescents. *Journal of Early Adolescence, 9*, 142-152.

Telfer, E. (1980). *Happiness.* New York: St. Martin's Press.

Tesch, S. A., & Whitbourne, S. K. (1982). Intimacy and identity status in young adults. *Journal of Personality and Social Psychology, 43*, 1041-1051.

Tobacyk, J. (1981). Personality differentiation, effectiveness of personality integration, and mood in female college students. *Journal of Personality and Social Psychology, 41*, 348-356.

Tzuriel, D., & Klein, M. M. (1977). Ego identity: Effects of ethnocentrism, ethnic identification, and cognitive complexity in Israeli, Oriental, and Western ethnic groups. *Psychological Reports, 40*, 1099-1110.

Wagner, J. A. (1987). Formal operations and ego identity in adolescence. *Adolescence, 22*, 23-35.

Walter, S. A., & Stivers, E. (1977). The relation of student teachers' classroom behavior and Eriksonian ego identity. *Journal of Teacher Education, 28*(6), 47-50.

Waterman, A. S. (1981). Individualism and interdependence. *American Psychologist, (36)*, 762-773.

Waterman, A. S. (1984a). Identity formation: Discovery or creation? *Journal of Early Adolescence, 4*, 329-341.

Waterman, A. S. (1984b). *The psychology of individualism.* New York: Praeger.

Waterman, A. S. (1988). Identity status theory and Erikson's theory: Commonalities and differences. *Developmental Review, 8*, 185-208.

Waterman, A. S. (1989, August). Two conceptions of happiness: Research on eudaimonia and hedonic enjoyment. In B. Slife (Chair), *Aristotle and contemporary psychology: Empirical investigations.* Symposium presented at the meeting of the American Psychological Association, New Orleans.

Waterman, A. S. (1990a). Personal expressiveness: Philosophical and psychological foundations. *Journal of Mind and Behavior, 11*, 47-74.

Waterman, A. S. (1990b, August). Personally expressive activities and personal potentials: A eudaimonistic analysis. In A. A. Sappington, III (Chair), *Toward an understanding of optimal experiences: Theory and research.* Symposium conducted at the meeting of the American Psychological Association, Boston.

Waterman, A. S. (1990c). The relevance of Aristotle's conception of eudaimonia for the psychological study of happiness. *Theoretical and Philosophical Psychology, 10*, 39-44.

Waterman, C. K., Buebel, M., & Waterman, A. S. (1970). Relationship between resolution of the identity crisis and outcomes of previous psychosocial crises [Summary].

Proceedings of the 78th Annual Convention of the American Psychological Association, 5,
467-486.

Waterman, C. K., & Waterman, A. S. (1974). Ego identity status and decision styles.
Journal of Youth and Adolescence, 3, 1-6.

Wessman, A. E., & Ricks, D. F. (1966). *Mood and personality.* New York: Holt, Rinehart
& Winston.

5. Assigned and Chosen Identity Components: A Process Perspective on Their Integration

Harold D. Grotevant
University of Minnesota

INTRODUCTION

Despite its theoretical complexity, the concept of identity has captured the imagination of researchers, clinicians, and members of the general public alike. At some level, we all know what identity means because it touches on that core sense of self that we associate with a feeling of coherence of personality and continuity over time. The formation of a sense of identity has been widely accepted as a key developmental task for adolescents in Western societies.

The very complexity that makes the construct so appealing, however, has also contributed to a debate over its scientific usefulness. In Erikson's view, individuals construct a sense of identity as they make choices, decisions, and commitments within their societal contexts. In turn, this sense of identity engenders "a sense of psychosocial well-being . . . a feeling of being at home in one's body, a sense of 'knowing where one is going' " (Erikson, 1980, p. 127). A fundamental defining feature of identity is that it addresses issues of self in context. "Identity, then, is a dynamic fitting together of parts of the personality with the realities of the social world so that a person has a sense both of internal coherence and meaningful relatedness to the real world" (Josselson, 1987, pp. 12-13).

AUTHOR'S NOTE: *During the preparation of this chapter, the author was supported by grants from the U.S. Office of Population Affairs, Hogg Foundation for Mental Health, and the Minnesota Agricultural Experiment Station. The author gratefully acknowledges feedback from colleagues Gerald Adams, Michael Berzonsky, David Blustein, William Doherty, Carol Elde, Deborah Fravel, William Goodman, Jane Kroger, Amy Lash, Raymond Montemayor, and Jean Phinney. Address correspondence to the author at Department of Family Social Science, University of Minnesota, 1985 Buford Avenue, St. Paul, MN 55108.*

To date, most of the literature on identity that has grown out of the Eriksonian tradition concerns domains over which individuals have some degree of choice. In Erikson's own writings (e.g., 1968), occupational identity and ideology were highlighted. Studies based on Marcia's (1966, 1980) influential identity status paradigm have focused on adolescents' exploration and commitments to choices in such diverse domains as occupational choice, religious and political ideology, relationships, and values. In these areas, adolescents are faced with the task of making a commitment to one option out of an array of possible choices. Few studies have examined how developments in these different domains might interact with one another across time (Grotevant, 1987).

In the past two decades, as psychologists have had to confront the different realities faced by members of diverse cultural backgrounds and both genders, there has been an emerging interest in aspects of identity relating to personal characteristics over which one has no control (see Phinney & Rosenthal, this volume, for a discussion of ethnic identity). In this chapter, I will contrast the "mainstream" identity literature, concerning domains of identity over which Western adolescents typically have some element of choice, with one aspect over which they have no choice in order to better understand how these components are integrated into one's sense of identity. In this chapter, the child's understanding of self as an adopted individual (hereafter referred to as "adoptive identity") will be used to illustrate an assigned component of identity. Comparison of chosen and assigned components within an identity framework will be used as an opportunity to speculate about the relations between the two and will raise issues that should be addressed in future studies concerning identity development. In addition, the nature of their interdependence in development will be explored. Do assigned and chosen components of identity develop side by side, or are there principles that govern how they affect one another?

"CHOSEN" IDENTITY: STRUCTURE AND PROCESS

In keeping with a constructivist point of view, identity is seen as a structure or framework out of which individuals interact in the world. This identity structure is continually updated as new experiences and information are encountered. Identity is "a theory (or schema) of an individual that describes, interrelates, and explains his or her relevant features, characteristics, and experiences" (Schlenker, 1985, p. 68). For Erikson (1968), this framework ultimately provides a sense of consistency and coherence to the self. It permits the establishment of "a deep sense of unity in the person's perception and experience of himself or herself" (Blasi, 1988, p. 228).

From a research standpoint, the concept of identity as structure is most useful psychologically as an organizational construct. In describing how key aspects of one's sense of self mesh with context, the identity construct has been shown to predict various aspects of concurrent psychological adjustment and subsequent development of intimacy (see Marcia, 1980; Waterman, 1982, for reviews). It specifies the contents of what we are like, and guides and regulates our interpersonal behavior by affecting cognitions, affect, and behavior (Schlenker, 1985).

Recently, several investigators have attempted to push the identity literature beyond a description of statuses or types to specify processes through which identity develops. Grotevant (1987) has proposed a process model that is developmental, contextual, and life-span in scope. It is *developmental* in that it focuses on the process of forming a sense of identity over time. It is *contextual* in its consideration of the interdependent influences of society, school or work environments, and interpersonal relationships on identity. It is *life-span* in scope in that it permits consideration of continuities over time from infancy through adulthood. Berzonsky (1990, this volume) has discussed identity as a "self-constructed theory of the self" and has elaborated a set of processes through which self-relevant experience is encoded, represented, and used.

One of the key processes associated with identity formation has been exploration, which has been defined as "problem-solving behavior aimed at eliciting information about oneself or one's environment in order to make a decision about an important life choice" (Grotevant, 1987, p. 204). For adolescents, the "work" of identity is seen in the exploration process. At the heart of the model is the adolescent's process of engagement in exploration and the cognitive and affective consequences of such behavior. The model also considers individual differences in personality and cognitive abilities that adolescents bring to the identity process, as well as the active brokering between the developing self and the various social contexts in which the process of identity exploration is embedded (e.g., Josselson, 1987).

Identity development in the domain of occupational choice has often served as the prototype for studying identity formation in general. Erikson (1968) mentioned choice of an occupation as a central issue in the identity process, and questions about occupation are included in virtually every identity measure currently in use. Current formulations that take a life-span approach have argued that it is more productive to think of career identity as a lifelong developmental process rather than as a specific stage of adolescence or young adulthood (e.g., Blustein, 1990; Grotevant, 1987; Grotevant & Cooper, 1988).

The process of exploration plays an important role in this aspect of identity development, as the adolescent attempts to find a work environment that fits well with his or her personality, work style, and values. When there is a compatible "match," both job satisfaction (Mount & Muchinsky, 1978) and longevity in the career (Vaitenas & Weiner, 1977) are enhanced.

It is naive to think of this process, however, as one in which all adolescents have identical opportunities and a full range of free choices. As outlined in Grotevant's (1987) process model of identity development, individuals bring their personalities, abilities, and current self-concepts to the identity development process, which in turn influence their ability to explore. Furthermore, their explorations may be constrained or enhanced by developmental contexts at several levels: cultural, family, peer, and school or work environments. In addition, identity development in one domain can affect the identity process in other domains.

Recent attempts to integrate the extensive career development literature with the identity literature (e.g., Blustein, 1990; Grotevant & Cooper, 1988) have led to new insights in both camps. For the identity literature, an important benefit has been clarification of both individual difference and contextual factors related to identity development. For example, Blustein and Phillips (1990) recently tested hypotheses about the relations between career decision-making styles (as conceptualized in the career counseling field) and identity status. Consistent with their predictions, they found that identity achieved college students used planful and logical career decision-making styles, and that foreclosed and diffused students did not use "internal" information-processing strategies. The moratorium status was not consistently associated with variations in decision-making styles. Findings such as these challenge our conceptualizations of identity development. What are the developmental antecedents of decision-making styles? Are the "styles" causally prior to identity development, or are they reflections of different identity resolutions?

Although some existing literature recognizes gender, ethnic, and socioeconomic differences in career development (e.g., Betz & Fitzgerald, 1987), knowledge of how these factors are interwoven with matters of choice is less than adequate. The remainder of this chapter will be devoted to consideration of identity development in domains over which the individual does not have choice, and to the integration of identity development in areas of choice and assignment.

"ASSIGNED" IDENTITY: THE CASE OF ADOPTED CHILDREN

Despite the fact that the identity literature has been dominated by the study of components over which individuals have choices, Baumeister (1986, 1987) has articulated the case that self-definition can be acquired by being assigned as well as by being chosen. In historical periods such as the Middle Ages, during which definition of self was based primarily on assignment, identity formation was not considered problematic. However, historical changes in attitudes about self-knowledge, sources of personal fulfillment, and the relation of the individual to society have made identity formation a modern "problem." In modern times, however, aspects of self that are assigned (e.g., gender, ethnicity, adoptive status) may also pose "problems" for the self in the sense that one must construct meaning around that which cannot be changed (e.g., Kroger, this volume).

Even within the category of assigned components of identity, one can differentiate between components such as gender, which is shared by half the population; ethnicity or group identity, which sets one apart from many people but gives special ties to a particular group; and adoption, which may set the individual apart from most people.[1]

In this section of the chapter, one's understanding of self as an adopted individual (hereafter referred to as "adoptive identity") will be the focus of attention. A working definition of "adoptive identity" would need to include the adoptee's sense of continuity of generations (especially when knowledge of one's past may be unavailable), integration of influence from parents of rearing and parents of birth, and sense of how one fits into a family in which some individuals may be related by blood and others not (see also Goebel & Lott, 1986; Hoopes, 1990). Adoptive identity, then, is the meaning one makes of the fact that he or she is adopted. Compare the voices of three adoptive individuals:

> I seem to have a compelling need to know my own story. It is a story that I should not be excluded from since it is at least partly mine, and it seems vaguely tragic and somehow unjust that it remains unknown to me. (Andersen, 1988, p. 18)

> When I found my natural mother, I felt deep inside me that I had finally found myself. I could fill so many empty pockets: who I looked like; where my ancestors came from; where I got my interests, talents and even allergies. (Baran, Sorosky, & Pannor, 1975, p. 38).

> Common lore and professional opinion agree: We adoptees are missing a crucial piece of ourselves. Not knowing our natural parents, the argument goes, we don't know the sources of our own identity: Whose legacy is the olive skin, the talkative tendency, the curious mind, the unappeasable sweet tooth? But my identity has never really revolved around my genetic roots. I don't believe in the idea that knowing my blood relatives means knowing myself, a notion that seems to trouble many adopted people. Cold as it may sound, I've never felt that I have four parents. In my mind, my adoptive mother and father are my only parents. (Roberts, 1988, p. 50)

These personal accounts reflect strikingly differing views concerning the role of knowledge about adoptees' biological background in their sense of identity. For some, obtaining knowledge of biological heritage is critical, even to the point of being an obsession; for others, this knowledge is irrelevant. Why such differences? How might this special self-knowledge be related to identity development in other domains?

Adoptive identity issues emerge as important for many adolescents and young adults because of the way in which adoption practices in North America have been shrouded in secrecy. Until very recently, adoption practice has emphasized confidentiality. Identities of birth parents and the families who adopt their children have typically been hidden from each other, and children have found it difficult to obtain detailed or identifying information about their birth parents. Although these practices were based on the prevailing "wisdom" about what would be best for all parties concerned, serious challenges to confidentiality have recently emerged in both open records laws and openness in adoption (see McRoy, Grotevant, & White, 1988, for review).

Although clinicians (e.g., Committee on Adoptions, 1971), adoption workers (e.g., Sorosky, Baran, & Pannor, 1975), and adopted individuals (e.g., Fisher, 1973) have spoken extensively about the problematic nature of identity issues for adoptees, relatively little empirical literature on this topic is available. In the studies that do exist, there is a great deal of slippage in the use of terms such as self-concept, self-esteem, and identity.

The findings of several studies comparing aspects of self or identity in adoptees and nonadoptees have been equivocal. In a dissertation comparing 18 adopted versus 18 nonadopted young adults on 19 self-concept and personality scales, Simmons (1980) found that adoptees scored lower on 12 of the scales and concluded that adoptees had identity problems. However, none of the measures assessed identity directly. Norvell and Guy (1977) found no differences between 38 adopted and 38 nonadopted college students on the Berger Self-Concept scale. Goebel and Lott (1986) found no differences between 83 adoptees and 81 nonadoptees (ages 18-35) on the Constantinople identity scale. Despite these findings, none of these studies directly assessed aspects of identity concerning adoption.

One of the more rigorous studies of identity in adoptees was recently completed by Stein and Hoopes (1985), who interviewed 91 high school students (ages 15-18) and their families. They were interested in finding out whether being adopted adversely affected adolescents' consolidation of ego identity, and if there were problems, whether they were related to adoption. "Identity" was assessed by the Tan et al. (1977) identity measure, the Offer Self-Image Questionnaire (Offer, 1973) and an interview. No differences were found between adopted and nonadopted adolescents on the Offer; and on the Tan measure, adoptees scored slightly *higher* than nonadoptees. (Although the mean difference was less than one point, it was statistically significant.) Although these findings appear to dispute the contention that adoptees have identity problems, it should be noted that neither the Tan nor the Offer measure assessed aspects of identity having to do with adoption.

Although approximately two-thirds of the adolescents in the study did not desire to search for their birth parents, the searchers were more likely than the nonsearchers to express dissatisfaction with their adoptive parents and to feel physically dissimilar to them. The perceived "mismatch" might highlight identity questions for them and stimulate the motivation to search. The results of this study are important and provocative, but they do not tell us how adopted adolescents integrate the aspect of self concerning adoption into their overall sense of identity.

The issue of perceived mismatch has been identified as important in other studies as well. Raynor (1980), in a study of 105 young adult adoptees, concluded that "Both adoptive parents and their grown up children have made it clear that a feeling of likeness is part of the feeling of kinship, and that a characteristic of less than happy adoptions is a sense of difference and not belonging" (p. 152). Grotevant, McRoy, and Jenkins (1988), in a study of 50 adolescent adoptees in residential treatment centers for emotional disturbances, found that perceived incompatibility between the behavioral style of the child and that of the adoptive family appeared to play a role in the family's problems in at least 16% of the cases. In contrast, incompatibility was noted in only 2% of the cases of a comparison group of nonadopted adolescents in treatment centers. One adoptive father, whose own style contrasted sharply with that of his son, said it eloquently:

> There needs to be a good match-up between the personality traits with the family traits. But how do you do that with an eighteen-month-old kid? Outside of that, the characteristic you'd look for in an adoptive parent is flexibility. My wife and I come from "walk the straight and narrow path" kinds of backgrounds. Our tolerance range is pretty narrow! If you had somebody whose tolerance range was out to here, it would make them more receptive to a wider range

of kids. . . . The advice I'd give is don't feel obligated to follow through if there is any trait in the kid's personality that seems totally incongruent with your own. Don't feel weird about taking them back and trying somebody else. . . . The blackest part of my whole life is having that kid and everything that it's done to our family. There are times when it's come within a hair's breadth of tearing the whole family apart.

In Kaye and Warren's (1988) detailed study of communication processes in adoptive families, they found that the adolescent's interest in searching for birth parents was associated both with problems in the adoptive family and with low self-esteem. In general, the more problems the families had, the more the adoptive parents attributed them to adoption. "Every indication of problems in the family—reported problems and therapy, lack of communication, a sense that life had been harder due to the adoption—was a predictor of low self-esteem in the adopted adolescent" (p. 45).

From these studies, it is apparent that there is a great deal we need to learn about identity development in adopted adolescents and young adults. Adoptees do not appear to have lower levels of self-esteem or self-concept than their nonadopted peers, on average. For those adoptives who do have lower self-esteem, however, perceived mismatch or poor relationships with parents often are apparent as well.

Research has not systematically addressed adoptees' identity *as an adopted individual*. Identity measures tend either to assess an overall sense of self (e.g., Tan et al., 1977) or identity in various domains (e.g., career choice, ideology, relationships, but not adoption) (e.g., Grotevant & Cooper, 1981). To my knowledge, there is currently no standardized measure available to assess adoptive identity.

In considering the assessment of adoptive identity, one must confront fundamental questions about the nature of identity: Is adoptive identity simply another domain (like career choice) that must be assessed? What kind of interplay occurs among identity formation in different domains? Is there a major difference between identity development in "chosen" domains and "assigned" domains?

INTERACTION OF ASSIGNED
AND CHOSEN COMPONENTS OF IDENTITY

Erikson's notions of identity have always been very global. In attempting to work with the construct empirically, however, researchers have found it necessary to examine identity in a more differentiated sense; one might have a clear sense of political identity but no clue as to an occupational direction. New directions in research have rightfully called for examinations of ethnic identity, gender identity, identity in the domain of work/family priority, and now adoptive identity.

However, one of the defining features of identity is that it gives the individual a sense of coherence and wholeness about the self. Consequently, researchers cannot be satisfied with breaking the individual down into domains; we must find a way to put the person back together. Thus, the identity literature has come full circle.

In an earlier paper (Grotevant, 1987), I discussed the importance of understanding the "interdependencies" among domains of identity and noted that few investigations had been focused on this issue. In this chapter, I would like to develop the idea that understanding the relation between assigned and chosen components of identity can help us move one step closer toward integrating the person and understanding the interdependencies among identity domains more fully.

I propose that assigned components of identity (such as gender, ethnicity, and adoptive status) provide context for the chosen components of identity. In other words, the way in which one has dealt with aspects of the self over which one has no control has ramifications for the types of choices that he or she might make.[2]

One mechanism through which this might take place is that assigned characteristics might place constraints, either real or perceived, on the types of choices considered available to the individual. Visible characteristics such as gender and ethnicity can affect the array of opportunities open for individuals' choice; for example, through racial discrimination or gender stereotyping (Grotevant & Cooper, 1988).

Assigned aspects of identity can also constrain development in other domains through more subtle, internal processes. Despite the fact that adoptive status is typically not known to others without voluntary disclosure, grappling with one's adoptive identity might impose psychological constraints on choice. For example, adoptees who feel that they are "missing a crucial piece of the puzzle" because of lack of knowledge about their birth parents might find the process of identity development more complex and protracted than adolescents who do not have to wonder about or worry about their heritage.

One of the interesting puzzles in this area is to understand why there are differences across individuals and across developmental histories in the tightness of the links between assigned and chosen components of identity. Several explanations are possible, and each suggests a fruitful line of future research. In the section that follows, each issue will be posed as a question.

Is there a relevant interface between the specific assigned and chosen components of identity? Perhaps assigned and chosen components of identity are strongly interdependent only when there is a relevant interface. For example, one's identity as male or female may have a direct impact on occupational choice (because of sextyping of occupations and differential access for women and men in our society). However, gender may be less relevant for one's religious or political affiliation. Ethnic identity may strongly affect aspects of identity that involve access to resources (for example, occupational choices, political affiliations, and so on), but may have less impact on identity in relationship domains. Adoptive status may have little or no impact on occupational, religious, or political identity; however, it may have major impact on relationships, especially in terms of issues dealing with sexuality, childbirth, fertility, or loss. It would be possible to test the hypothesis that confusion about the assigned component would be most likely to impede progress in domains involving choice that have direct conceptual relevance to the assigned component. For example, an adopted adolescent forming values about premarital sexuality might experience conflict stemming from the knowledge that his or her birth parents were unmarried teenagers. On the other hand, his or her career identity development might look no different from that of nonadopted peers.

Are the individual's characteristics in the assigned domain undervalued by society? When assigned characteristics are undervalued by society, both psychological and societal processes can inhibit identity development. Because of a history of prejudice or discrimination, individual adolescents might develop feelings of inferiority, low self-esteem, and external locus of control, which might in turn decrease their likelihood of self-directed identity exploration in other domains. At the same time, external societal processes might restrict the adolescent's actual opportunities for exploration. The consequence of one's assigned (and unchangeable) characteristics being undervalued by society can therefore have a devastating effect on identity development.

The impact of undervaluing is probably strongest when the characteristics in question are highly visible (e.g., one's skin color or one's gender). In the case of adoptive identity (which is not "visible" without voluntary disclosure), its impact on overall identity is likely a more individual matter and may depend on a variety of factors, including how the adolescent's family has handled it.

How has the individual's family handled questions or concerns? Adoptive parents are often surprised by the depth of concern that their adolescents have about their adoptive status. Many families of adolescents hospitalized for emotional disturbance felt that they always dealt openly and honestly with their child's adoptive status and that they were always fully willing to answer questions, despite their children's feeling that the topic of adoption was somehow off-limits (McRoy, Grotevant, & Zurcher, 1988).

However, there may be a gap between the parents' statements about their willingness to discuss adoption and how adoption was actually discussed within the family. The necessary observational work concerning discussions about adoption has not yet been conducted, with the exception of the careful work by Kaye and Warren (1988). Perhaps the key lies not in *how much* adoptive parents discuss adoption with their adolescents, but rather, the nature of *the match* between how parents discuss it and what the adolescents are seeking to understand.

Mismatch can occur along at least two dimensions: (a) amount of information, and (b) cognitive level of information. In terms of amount of information, a mismatch can occur when adoptive parents are unwilling to discuss adoption with an adolescent who is very curious, or when they simply do not have access to the depth of information the adolescent is seeking. Similarly, a mismatch can occur when an adolescent who does not appear very interested in adoptive background issues is bombarded with information from parents who feel he or she needs the information. A good match would be parental disclosure about adoption in a way that is sensitive and responsive to the child's need for information at that particular time.

A mismatch can also occur along the lines of cognitive level of the information. Brodzinsky's (Brodzinsky, Singer, & Braff, 1984) important work has shown that children's cognitive understanding of adoption develops gradually into early adolescence. In order to be in synchrony with the child, parents should match their explanations about adoption with the child's cognitive level of understanding. Explanations that are either far above or far below the child's level of understanding could be perceived as a mismatch and could impede developmental progress in this area. For example, in an earlier study on adolescent adoptees hospitalized in residential treatment centers (McRoy, Grotevant, & Zurcher, 1988), it was not unusual to find large discrepancies in the reports of parents and adolescents about when the child was told about his or her adoption. Parents often reported that their child "always" knew, that they told the child from the very beginning. Adolescents often reported that they did not know they were adopted until they were 7 or 8 years old. In a certain sense, both were reporting truthfully. These parents probably did talk about adoption during the child's infancy and early childhood, but then assumed that the child understood and did not need to be reminded. The children did not comprehend at an adult level what they were being told, typically until some event (such as an unintended disclosure by a relative) raised the issue anew during middle childhood.

To what degree has the adolescent compartmentalized components of identity? Links between assigned and chosen identity components might vary as a function of how strongly the adolescent has compartmentalized identity components. For example, a number of studies have demonstrated that males and females differ in the relation between occupational and interpersonal identity (e.g., Thorbecke & Grotevant, 1982). For males, identity issues tend to be resolved before issues of intimacy are seriously worked on. For females, the processes of occupational and interpersonal identity are more intertwined. It could be that some adolescents compartmentalize other aspects of identity (such as adoptive identity); issues might be held in check or dealt with separately so as not to provide context for chosen components of identity. What kinds of adolescents would do such compartmentalizing? Might their personalities be described in terms of greater rigidity than their peers? What might the developmental antecedents or consequences of such compartmentalization be? Would adolescents who have a less integrated sense of identity be considered less mature psychologically?

The consequence of compartmentalization is addressed in a speculative fashion by Lifton:

> I suggest that the Adoptees who go about their lives seemingly untouched by their adoptive status will not have an easier time in the long run than those who did not have the temperament or inclination to play the Adoption Game. When you stifle curiosity about yourself, you stifle many other things as well. You shrink your area of perception. You live in a smaller space. (1988, p. 53)

The gist of Lifton's argument is that a well-integrated sense of identity is one that does not shrink from exploring all key components of oneself. To the degree that one accepts Erikson's argument that an important aspect of identity is continuity across past, present, and future, it makes sense that coming to terms with one's identity as an adoptee would play an important role in the overall identity development process.

CONCLUSIONS AND ISSUES
FOR FUTURE CONSIDERATION

In this chapter, I have drawn a distinction between (a) components of identity that arise out of choices made available to individuals in their social contexts and (b) components of identity over which individuals have no choice but around which they must construct meaning. In order for the identity literature to address issues such as coherence of personality and continuity over time, it is critical that we identify the similarities and differences in the identity process for assigned and chosen components and that we then understand conceptually how the different components of identity fit together into a whole. Adoptive identity was used as an example of an assigned component, and several avenues by which assigned and chosen components of identity might interact were proposed.

A next step will be to ask how identities are organized. In this chapter, I have taken a preliminary look at this issue by identifying situations in which some aspects of identity constrain development in other domains, specifically in terms of how assigned components of identity might affect development in domains permitting choice.

But what of the more general case, in which different identity components must be assembled into a whole and balanced by some set of processes? Although a full discussion of this issue is beyond the scope of this chapter, at least three directions for future theoretical and empirical work appear fruitful. The *first* takes the study deeper concerning the balance between self and relationship; the *second* considers whether identity might be organized around specific themes or principles for different individuals; the *third* raises the possibility that identity serves as a "narrative" that lends coherence to one's sense of being over time.

In the past several years, many social scientists have recognized the centrality of the balance between self and relationship in understanding individual development and psychosocial functioning. Grotevant and Cooper (1986) have proposed a model of *individuation*, a construct embodying the interplay between individuality and connectedness in relationships, that has implications for the development of identity in individuals. Josselson (1988), in her chapter on the "embedded self," concluded with the statement that "a theory of the self, or of identity, must . . . account for the ways in which the self remains poised between self-expression and relatedness, between the need for self-assertion and social involvement. A theory of the self must, therefore, be interwoven with a theory of relationship" (p. 104). Similarly, Kroger (1989) noted that identity must be defined "as a balance between that which is taken to be self and that considered to be other" (p. 6). These accounts suggest that, for some, identity might be organized around a dynamic tension between self and relationship, between meeting one's own needs and meeting the needs of others. By focusing on one identity domain at a time, most research approaches to date have not fully examined this balancing. A notable exception is the work of Archer (1985) on career/family priorities, because she directly confronts research participants with considering how needs of self and other might be coordinated. The field of interpersonal relationships is currently experiencing rapid growth, as social, developmental, and family psychologists recognize the importance of understanding relational contexts of human development.

A second worthwhile direction concerns the possibility that for certain individuals a particular "leading theme" or "organizing principle" might orchestrate identity development (Bosma, Graafsma, & Grotevant, 1988). In writing this, I am reminded of the chemistry experiment in which crystals grow around a string placed into a solution. Similarly, an individual's sense of identity might coalesce around a particular issue or theme and subordinate other issues to it. The importance of a particular theme might be developmentally transitory (e.g., subordinating all aspects of life to intense but short-lived exploration of a religious cult) or strongly stable over time (e.g., subordinating all identity issues to a strongly held political value).

A third direction of current interest concerns identity as "narrative," as a story that lends coherence to our experience of life over time. McAdams (1987, 1989) suggests that identity is more than commitments to choices, but rather is "a configuration . . . [that] takes the form of narrative" (1987, p. 17). In this emerging field (e.g., Shotter & Gergen, 1989), one's identity is viewed as a story, constructed over time in order to "justify . . . [one's] present stance in the world" (1987, p. 19). This story ties together past, present, and future, thus lending continuity and purpose to life. Identity research examining issues of how the whole is integrated might benefit from pursuing this line of reasoning.

NOTES

1. My thanks to Jean Phinney for drawing this distinction.
2. This linkage is proposed as simply one of the possible ways in which interdependencies among identity domains can develop.

REFERENCES

Andersen, R. S. (1988). Why adoptees search: Motives and more. *Child Welfare, 67*, 15-19.
Archer, S. L. (1985). Career and/or family: The identity process for adolescent girls. *Youth and Society, 16*, 289-314.

Baran, A., Sorosky, A., & Pannor, R. (1975). Secret adoption records: The dilemma of our adoptees. *Psychology Today, 9*(7), 38-42, 96-98.

Baumeister, R. F. (1986). *Identity: Cultural change and the struggle for self.* New York: Oxford University Press.

Baumeister, R. F. (1987). How the self became a problem: A psychological review of historical research. *Journal of Personality and Social Psychology, 52,* 163-176.

Berzonsky, M. D. (1990). Self-construction over the life-span: A process perspective on identity formation. In G. J. Neimeyer & R. A. Neimeyer (Eds.), *Advances in personal construct theory.* (Vol. 1, pp. 155-186). Greenwich, CT: JAI Press.

Betz, N. E., & Fitzgerald, L. F. (Eds.). (1987). *The career psychology of women.* New York: Academic Press.

Blasi, A. (1988). Identity and the development of the self. In D. K. Lapsley & F. C. Power (Eds.), *Self, ego, and identity: Integrative approaches* (pp. 226-242). New York: Springer-Verlag.

Blustein, D. L. (1990, April). Explorations of the career exploration literature: Current status and future directions. Invited address presented at the meeting of the American Educational Research Association, Boston.

Blustein, D. L., & Phillips, S. D. (1990). Relation between ego identity statuses and decision-making styles. *Journal of Counseling Psychology, 37,* 160-168.

Bosma, H., Graafsma, T., & Grotevant, H. D (1988). Unpublished notes from conference on identity development, The University of Texas at Austin.

Brodzinsky, D. M., Singer, L. M., & Braff, A. M. (1984). Children's understanding of adoption. *Child Development, 55,* 869-878.

Committee on Adoptions. (1971). Identity development in adopted children. *American Academy of Pediatrics,* 948-949.

Erikson, E. H. (1968). *Identity: Youth and crisis.* New York: Norton.

Erikson, E. H. (1980). *Identity and the life cycle.* New York: Norton.

Fisher, F. (1973). *The search for Anna Fisher.* New York: Fawcett Crest.

Goebel, B. L., & Lott, S. L. (1986, August). Adoptees' resolution of the adolescent identity crisis: Where are the taproots? Paper presented at the meeting of the American Psychological Association, Washington, DC.

Grotevant, H. D. (1987). Toward a process model of identity formation. *Journal of Adolescent Research, 2,* 203-222.

Grotevant, H. D., & Cooper, C. R. (1981). Assessing adolescent identity in the areas of occupation, religion, politics, friendship, dating, and sex roles: Manual for administration and coding of the interview. *Journal Supplement Abstract Service Catalog of Selected Documents in Psychology, 11,* 52. (Ms. NO. 2295).

Grotevant, H. D., & Cooper, C. R. (1986). Individuation in family relationships: A perspective on individual differences in the development of identity and role taking skill in adolescence. *Human Development, 29,* 82-100.

Grotevant, H. D., & Cooper, C. R. (1988). The role of family experience in career exploration: A life-span perspective. In P. B. Baltes, R. M. Lener, & D. Featherman (Eds.), *Life-span development and behavior* (Vol. 8, pp. 231-258). Hillsdale, NJ: Lawrence Erlbaum.

Grotevant, H. D., McRoy, R. G., & Jenkins, V. Y. (1988). Emotionally disturbed, adopted adolescents: Early patterns of family adaption. *Family Process, 27,* 439-457.

Hoopes, J. L. (1990). Adoption and identity formation. In D. M. Brodzinsky & M. D. Schechter (Eds.), *The psychology of adoption* (pp. 144-166). New York: Oxford University Press.

Josselson, R. (1987). *Finding herself: Pathways to identity development in women.* San Francisco: Jossey-Bass.

Josselson, R. (1988). The embedded self: I and thou revisited. In D. K. Lapsley & F. C. Power (Eds.), *Self, ego, and identity: Integrative approaches* (pp. 91-106). New York: Springer-Verlag.

Kaye, K., & Warren, S. (1988). Discourse about adoption in adoptive families. *Journal of Family Psychology, 4,* 406-433.

Kroger, J. (1989). *Identity in adolescence: The balance between self and other.* London: Routledge.

Lifton, B. J. (1988). *Lost and found: The adoption experience.* New York: Harper & Row.

Marcia, J. E. (1966). Development and validation of ego identity status. *Journal of Personality and Social Psychology, 3,* 551-558.

Marcia, J. E. (1980). Identity in adolescence. In J. Adelson (Ed.), *Handbook of adolescent psychology* (pp. 159-187). New York: John Wiley.

McAdams, D. P. (1987). A life-story model of identity. In R. Hogan & W. H. Jones (Eds.), *Perspectives in personality: A research annual* (Vol. 2). (pp. 15-50) Greenwich, CT: JAI Press.

McAdams, D. P. (1989). The development of a narrative identity. In D. M. Buss & N. Cantor (Eds.), *Personality psychology: Recent trends and emerging directions* (pp. 160-174). New York: Springer-Verlag.

McRoy, R. G., Grotevant, H. D., & White, K. L. (1988). *Openness in adoption: New practices, new issues.* New York: Praeger.

McRoy, R. G., Grotevant, H. D., & Zurcher, L. A., Jr. (1988). *Emotional disturbance in adopted adolescents: Origins and development.* New York: Praeger.

Mount, M. K., & Muchinsky, P. M. (1978). Person-environment congruence and employee job satisfaction: A test of Holland's theory. *Journal of Vocational Behavior, 13,* 84-100.

Norvell, M., & Guy, R. F. (1977). A comparison of self-concept in adopted and non-adopted adolescents. *Adolescence, 12,* 443-448.

Offer, D. (1973). *The Offer Self-Image Questionnaire.* Chicago: Department of Psychiatry, Michael Reese Media Center.

Raynor, L. (1980). *The adopted child comes of age.* London: George Allen.

Roberts, M. (1988, November). My family, myself. *Psychology Today,* p. 50.

Schlenker, B. R. (1985). Identity and self-identification. In B. R. Schlenker (Ed.), *The self and social life* (pp. 65-99). New York: McGraw-Hill.

Shotter, J., & Gergen, K. J. (1989). *Texts of identity.* Newbury Park, CA: Sage.

Simmons, W. V. (1980). A study of identity formation in adoptees. *Dissertation Abstracts International, 40,* (12-B), Part I, 5832.

Sorosky, A. D., Baran, A., & Pannor, R. (1975). Identity conflicts in adoptees. *American Journal of Orthopsychiatry, 45,* 18-27.

Stein, L. M., & Hoopes, J. L. (1985). *Identity formation in the adopted adolescent.* New York: Child Welfare League of America.

Tan, A. L., Kendis, R. F., Fine, J. T., & Porac, J. (1977). A short measure of Eriksonian ego identity. *Journal of Personality Assessment, 41,* 279-284.

Thorbecke, W., & Grotevant, H. D. (1982). Gender differences in adolescent interpersonal identity formation. *Journal of Youth and Adolescence, 11,* 479-492.

Vaitenas, R., & Weiner, Y. (1977). Developmental, emotional, and interest factors in voluntary mid-career change. *Journal of Vocational Behavior, 11,* 291-304.

Waterman, A. S. (1982). Identity development from adolescence to adulthood: An extension of theory and a review of research. *Developmental Psychology, 18,* 341-358.

6. Identity in Adolescence: Managing Commitments

Harke A. Bosma

State University, Groningen, the Netherlands

INTRODUCTION

The identity status approach (Marcia, 1980, in preparation) has proved its value in the study of identity in adolescence. However, it is of limited use for the study of the process of identity development.

A first limitation concerns the choice of areas in the identity status interviews. The procedure was originally used in research on 18- to 25-year-old male university students (Marcia, 1966), and its validity for the study of female identity was questioned since the choice of areas (occupation, politics, and religion) was considered to be male-biased (Schenkel & Marcia, 1972; for a review, see Matteson, in preparation). In general, this controversy concerns the possibility that different areas might be relevant for different populations, such as male and female adolescents; adolescents from different cultural, ethnic, or socioeconomic backgrounds; or those from different age groups. The possibility of an age bias is particularly pertinent in the study of the developmental process.

A second limitation concerns the implicit assumption that adolescence is a period in which only one decision-making period ("crisis") occurs. Coleman (1974), by contrast, found evidence that there are several periods in which the adolescent is confronted with alternatives and in which a commitment is required. Matteson (1975) has suggested that adolescents go through a "multiple-phase identity crisis"—for example, a crisis with regard to the somatic changes in puberty and an ideological crisis in early adulthood.

AUTHOR'S NOTE: *The author wishes to thank all of the students who have helped to run the studies reported here, and Erin Jackson for her careful correction of the English of the manuscript.*

A third limitation lies in the categorical character of the status model. The subject is placed in one out of four possible categories, representing outcomes of the developmental process. This is particularly well suited to the study of inter-individual differences, but less so the study of intra-individual differences, that is, developmental change.

A fourth limitation concerns the status model's psychometric properties. Scoring a status in a reliable way is not an easy task (Bosma & Gerrits, 1985; Raskin, 1984). It is therefore interesting to try to develop a more objective measure (e.g., Adams, Bennion, & Huh, 1989). From a developmental point of view, it is problematic that the assignment of a status is based on a dichotomized rating of commitment and exploration. Such a rating only allows for a very rough estimate of developmental changes in these variables. For a more accurate description of these changes, as Matteson (1977) has already pointed out, they should preferably be assessed as continuous variables.

In this chapter, results will be presented of studies using the Groningen Identity Development Scale (GIDS), which was constructed in an attempt to overcome the above-mentioned limitations. First, however, the results of an empirical study of the importance of psychosocial areas for older and younger adolescents will be presented. This study formed the first phase of the construction of the GIDS.

IDENTITY DEVELOPMENT IN ADOLESCENCE: WHICH AREAS ARE IMPORTANT?

In their study of the "relative importance of identity status interview components," Rogow, Marcia, and Slugoski (1983) suggest that "any personally relevant content could be used in an identity status interview" (p. 398). But which areas are personally relevant for adolescents? And are there differences in this respect between, for example, male and female or younger and older adolescents? Areas may exist that are personally very relevant to a specific group of adolescents (physical handicaps, for example) and not at all relevant to adolescents in general. The following study was designed to explore the relevance of areas in adolescence and their relationship to differences in age, sex, and educational level.

Method

The subjects were sampled from different schools covering the whole range of secondary and tertiary education for adolescents in the age range of 13 to 21 years old in the Netherlands. In each classroom two or three were randomly selected for individual interviews; the other classmates were given a questionnaire to be answered at home and returned by mail. The interview sample, N = 97, is evenly distributed over the whole age range, both sexes, and the higher and lower educational levels. Of the questionnaire group, only 39% returned a questionnaire that could be used for further analyses. In this sample, N = 303, the younger age groups and the higher educated adolescents are overrepresented.

The main instrument was an open interview. First the subjects were invited to write down on cards the topics personally important to them ("things you think about a lot, things you are interested in and/or things you talk about a lot with other people"). Then they were interviewed about each topic: the situation with regard to the topic, why the topic was important to the subject, how he or she was involved in it, and so on. During this conversation new topics (not mentioned on the cards) could emerge. These were explored in a similar way. The whole interview was tape-recorded.

The questionnaire was an adaptation of an interview schedule used by Coleman (1980). In contrast to our interview, most of the items of the questionnaire explicitly referred to topics known to be important for adolescents, for example, leisure-time activities, moral development, peers, sexuality, and individual problems. In other questions the subject was asked to list "things very important in your life" and to describe why these were important. The questionnaire was meant to be used for cross-validation of the interview. The data for this study were gathered in 1981/1982.

The topics were selected from the interview tapes and from the relevant answers to each questionnaire, and the subjects' involvement in them was summarized per topic on a card. A small reliability check on the selection and the summary indicated acceptable agreement. The topics were subsequently categorized into broader areas, similar to the areas in the identity status

Table 6.1 The Popularity of Areas

Areas	Int. 520*	Quest. 731*
School, (future) occupation	20.6**	13.8**
Hobbies, leisure-time	16.0	21.9
Friendship	15.4	16.0
Parents, home	13.7	12.3
Politics, society	9.6	1.5
Intimate relationships	6.2	4.7
Religion	4.8	3.1
Self	4.2	2.5
Social interaction	3.7	4.2
Physical appearance	2.7	1.9
Happiness, health		10.7
Freedom		4.4
Money		2.6
Other areas	3.2	0.4

NOTE: * Number of statements
** Percentages. Column total is 100%.

interview. The resulting lists of areas were studied with a view to identifying differences between males and females, educational levels, and age groups. The summaries were used to give descriptive accounts of the adolescents' involvement in these areas.

Results

With regard to the content (after categorization) and popularity (the number of times mentioned) of each area, the interview and the questionnaire produced highly similar results (Table 6.1). There were four areas with a relatively high popularity: school and (future) occupation, leisure-time activities, friendship, and parents and home. Other areas were reasonably popular: happiness and health (questionnaire), and politics and society (interview). The remaining topics were much less popular.

The differences in respect to age, sex, and educational level have not been statistically analyzed because the aim of this study was to arrive at a complete list of areas relevant for adolescents. As a consequence, differences between subgroups of adolescents were of less importance. Nevertheless, some trends could be observed. With regard to educational level, there were only very small differences. The differences between male and female adolescents were more substantial. Females more often mentioned the interpersonal areas, and males more often mentioned the areas of school and (future) occupation, leisure time, society, and politics. The analysis of differences in popularity in relation to age was difficult because of the small number of subjects interviewed in each age category and because of the uneven distribution of the questionnaires over the age groups. There also appeared to be interactions between age, educational level, sex, and area, so conclusions can only be very tentative. Physical appearance was only mentioned by the younger group (13-16 years of age). When compared to the younger group, the area of school and occupation was less popular, and the area of intimate relationships was more popular in the older group (17-21 years of age). The popularity of friendship increased with age in the higher educated groups, but decreased in the lower educated groups. The same applied for hobbies and leisure-time activities in the male groups; there was an increase with age in the higher educated group and a decrease in the lower educated one. The popularity of parents and home, especially in the male groups, and of self in the female groups, increased with age.

The interviews and the "why" question in the questionnaire also gave a wealth of qualitative information about the areas. This information has been categorized per area into central themes. A detailed description of these themes can be found in Bosma (1985). In the following discussion the most important tendencies in these descriptions will be reported and compared to the empirical findings of other researchers.

Discussion

The main aim of this study was to obtain an empirical overview of areas personally relevant for adolescents. This was done by interviewing a group of randomly sampled adolescents varying in age, sex, and educational level. Cross-validating information came from a questionnaire survey of a second sample. Neither sample is representative for the population of Dutch adolescents in the age group of 13-21: The younger (13-17 years of age), higher educated group is overrepresented. Such a representation was not the aim of this study, though; a random sample representing the

variation in background variables was considered adequate for
our aim and the interview sample meets these criteria to an acceptable degree. However, cultural and ethnic differences were not included as background variables, so the results cannot be generalized
to groups other than Caucasian adolescents living in the northern
parts of the Netherlands. Another limitation is the small sample
size; statements about differences between subgroups are particularly tentative and need replication with larger samples.

The main question is whether the list of areas in Table 6.1 is
exhaustive. Supporting evidence comes from the fact that both
data sets led to highly comparable results. Further evidence may
emerge through a comparison with the findings of other researchers.

In Germany, Dreher and Dreher (1984) investigated how important the developmental tasks suggested by Havighurst (1953)
were considered to be by adolescents (n = 440, 15-18 years of age).
These tasks are related to the following areas: peers, body, sex
role, intimacy, detachment, occupation, future partner/family,
self, values, future goals. All of these tasks were considered to be
important or very important, albeit in varying degrees. Differences in labeling and category definition aside, there is a high correspondence between these tasks and the areas found in our
study. Sex role seems to be missing in our study. Kitwood (1980)
carried out a study in the United Kingdom that is highly comparable to ours. He categorized his results into four broad areas: relationships in the home, social life among peers, experiences of
formal and informal work, and development of the self-image. Only
religion and politics are hardly ever mentioned by the British subjects. In his discussion, Kitwood also refers to missing areas. The
areas of pop music and TV, and sexuality seem to be missing from
both his and our study. They have never been mentioned as important areas per se, although some of our adolescents referred to
the first within the context of leisure-time activities and the second within the context of intimate relationships. The study done
by Douvan and Adelson (1966) in the United States also gives a
wealth of information about areas important to adolescents. The
list of areas that can be derived from their study is comparable
with our results.

The differences found in our study were also found by other
authors. Both Douvan and Adelson (1966) and Offer et al. (1981)
reported that male adolescents are more achievement-oriented

and value autonomy more, while females value interpersonal relationships and sociability more. The stronger political involvement of the higher educated, older male adolescents has also been found in other studies (Matteson, 1975; Waterman, 1982).

The results of this study are supported by other studies, but the sex role area seems to be missing from our list. Although a few girls mentioned the related issue of discrimination in the labor market, none of the adolescents in our study questioned their own sex role. This seems to be contrary to results reported by Douvan and Adelson, who identified groups of female adolescents with anxieties about their femininity and their future role of female and wife. This difference could be due to cultural and economic differences between the Netherlands and the United States. A second area that did not receive much attention was sexuality. However, many studies show that it has a central place in adolescents' fantasies and overt behavior (Conger & Peterson, 1984; Regt, 1982). Perhaps most adolescents did not want to talk about it in our interviews.

Evidence for Coleman's focal theory (1974) was found in several areas. Within the area of school and (future) occupation, for example, there is no single period of exploration of alternatives. At the age of 12, adolescents in the Netherlands have to make a choice among the various types of secondary schools. A few years later they have to make decisions about majors in their curriculum, more or less in preparation for their future occupation. After secondary school new choices have to be made: Look for a job? Attend some form of tertiary schooling? The study even indicated that students who had chosen a career had second thoughts about their choice and felt that they had to make new decisions. This process of educational and occupational choice is a process of permanent decision making—a cyclical process. Similar results were found in other areas. Throughout adolescence, males and females have to make decisions about friends and friendships. Sometimes new friends are chosen, sometimes friendships change. There is clear evidence of age-related changes in friendship patterns and functions (e.g., Coleman, 1974; La Gaipa, 1979; Youniss & Smollar, 1990). A last example comes from studies of sexual behavior. Regt (1982), in his review of Dutch studies on sexual behavior, amply demonstrated the step-by-step character of the development of sexual intimacy. Every step implies decisions; each decision leads to a confrontation with new alternatives.

The list given in Table 6.1 gives a general picture; it does not reveal the great inter-individual and intra-individual variability. Not every subject mentioned every area in the list. Not every area is equally relevant for each individual. For some subjects one area is central in their life (e.g. belonging to a peer group or religion); for others, many areas are important. In some interviews a recent event (a serious quarrel with father, low grades in school, and such) seemed to color the subject's experience in many areas. (Compare the case histories in Josselson, Greenberger, & McConochie, 1977). In this sense, the definition of the separate areas in the list is also arbitrary. For some subjects certain areas can be far apart, while other areas are intermingled. A good example in this study is formed by the areas of school and (future) occupation and leisure-time activities. For most adolescents these areas are connected; commitments with regard to school are strongly related to their commitments to a future occupation and to their leisure-time activities. However, there is much variation in the relative weight given to these different commitments: For some adolescents leisure time comes second to school achievement and future plans, and for other adolescents it is the other way around. (Compare Steinberg's [1985] results related to the interdependence of the respective importance of school and work for adolescents in the United States.) For other adolescents, however, commitments in the area of school can be unrelated to their commitments to a future occupation. Another example lies in the case of fundamentalist religious commitments: Commitments in all of the other areas depend on or are even determined by that single commitment.

THE CONSTRUCTION OF THE
GRONINGEN IDENTITY DEVELOPMENT SCALE

The study of the importance of areas in adolescence only gave very minor indications of an age-related sequence of areas. There is much stronger evidence of individual, age-related changes in exploration and the content of commitments within areas and of variation in the personal relevance of areas and the interdependency of commitments in these areas. Consequently, many areas can be important in adolescence, but any assessment of the process of identity development must deal with intra-individual changes within areas and inter-individual differences in their personal relevance.

The following definition—based on these results and on a theoretical analysis of Erikson's ideas on identity formation in adolescence—was used as a starting point for the construction of the GIDS. Identity development can be defined as the totality of changes in the content and strength of commitments and the amount of exploration involved in the achievement and change of these commitments. Three variables are central in this definition: the content of commitments, the strength of commitments, and the amount of exploration involved in their achievement and change. The latter two variables are also central in the status model. Content refers to the actual content of the subject's commitments rather than the area in which these commitments can be found. It is assumed that developmental changes in identity in adolescence can be described in a valid way in terms of these three variables. The GIDS is constructed to measure these.

With regard to areas in any study of identity development, two essential questions present themselves: "Which areas are personally relevant?" and "Does the subject have commitments in these areas?" In the GIDS these two questions are combined and reformulated as "Does the subject have commitments and what is their content?" The latter part of this question refers to the choice of areas, but also acknowledges the fact that intra- and inter-individual differences can manifest themselves within an area and also between areas. According to this line of reasoning, the choice and definition of areas is subordinate to the content of a subject's commitments. A kind of dragnet procedure is needed to find these commitments, and the areas become places where one could look. A representative sample of a subject's commitments in various areas probably gives a valid indication of the strength and stability of his sense of identity.

Three steps can be distinguished in the GIDS procedure. The first step is a semistructured interview, similar to Marcia's. The interview about an area is directly followed by the second step, in which the subject's commitment(s) in that area are written on a card. In the event of there being more than one commitment, the subject chooses "the one that best expresses himself/herself." In the third step the subject answers a forced-choice questionnaire about the commitment and area in question. This questionnaire assesses the strength of the commitment and the amount of exploration involved. The three-step procedure is repeated for each of the six areas defined for the GIDS.

For practical reasons, the list of areas (places to look for commitments) cannot be too long. In the GIDS a compromise between completeness and practical limitations has been reached through the use of separate and combined areas. The results of the study previously discussed were used for the definition of the following list of areas:

1. *School, (Future) Occupation, and Leisure-Time Activities.* These subareas often overlap. For many adolescents the "boring" school has its only significance in preparing for a future occupation. Leisure-time activities form an escape from the obligations of school and work.

2. *Parents.* There is much variation and developmental change in commitments with regard to parents and the situation at home.

3. *Philosophy of Life.* This area includes religion, politics, and values. These subareas were very closely connected for some subjects in the study of areas. For other subjects religion and politics have nothing to do with each other, or are not important since they are strongly committed to specific values.

4. *Friendship.* The importance of this area to adolescent identity development is widely acknowledged (e.g., Grotevant et al., 1982).

5. *Personal Characteristics.* This composite area includes the subareas of physical appearance, sex role, and personality characteristics. Physical appearance was mentioned as important by a small group of younger adolescents. Sex role has been widely used in identity research, though it was hardly referred to in the study of areas. This is in contrast to the area of personality characteristics—many older female subjects in this study mentioned problems and ambivalence with regard to themselves (being uncertain, and so on) and difficulties in committing themselves to the different aspects of their own personality.

6. Intimate Relationships. This area was also described as important by adolescents of varying ages in the study. In the GIDS it could include sexuality. However, the instrument must also be used with younger adolescents, so this subarea was considered to be less suitable.

The interview in each area is about exploration and commitments and is thus comparable to Marcia's interview. It is, however, aimed at the actual here-and-now situation of the subject, for example, school in the case of 16-year-olds, and not at the future, because their commitments with regard to school can be very strong while commitments with regard to a future occupation do not yet exist. At the end of the interview different questions are used to elicit the subject's commitments: "What do you think about . . . ?" "What is your opinion on . . . ?" "How are you committed to . . . ?" The answers to these questions are summarized by the subject and written down on a card. Each answer indicating a choice, a decision, a point of view, or an attitude is considered to be a commitment. The questionnaire is used to evaluate what the subject has written down. A statement such as "I'm not interested in politics" usually leads to a very low score on the strength of commitment scale (see further), indicating a very weak commitment, or *no commitment* in terms of Marcia's categorization.

The questionnaire comprises two scales, one for the strength of the commitment (18 items, scoring range 0-36) and one for the amount of exploration (14 items, scoring range 0-28). Each question has four possible answers, indicating how strongly a question applies to the subject's commitment or exploration. The questions have been formulated on the basis of qualities ascribed to strong commitments and much exploration in the identity status scoring manuals. The manual of Waterman et al. (1979) has proved particularly helpful. For example, strong commitments give "feelings of confidence, stability and optimism about the future" (Waterman et al., p. 2). Examples of questions are shown in Table 6.2.

GIDS data can be summarized to give a profile for each individual, showing commitments to each area and corresponding scores on both scales (see Table 6.4).

Table 6.2 Examples of Questions from the GIDS Questionnaire

Strength of commitment:				
-Could you easily give up this commitment?	yes	yes, with difficulty	no	don't know
-Does this commitment give you the strong feeling that you can approach the future with optimism and trust?	strongly	to some extent	no	don't know
-Does this commitment give you support in your life?	a lot	sometimes	no	don't know
Amount of exploration:				
-Do you think about . . . (area)?	a lot	sometimes	almost never	don't know
-Do you find it necessary to search for all sorts of different ways of committing yourself to . . . (area)?	yes	to some extent	no	don't know
-Do you talk with others about . . . (area)?	a lot	sometimes	almost never	don't know

A CROSS-SECTIONAL STUDY WITH THE GIDS

The first study with the GIDS involved comparisons of different age groups. It was done to find out whether the instrument was sensitive to differences between groups that could be expected to differ in terms of identity development: younger and older adolescents. The other aim of this study was to gather information about the psychometric qualities of the GIDS.

The study was exploratory, but there were some general expectations: Younger and older adolescents were expected to show strong differences in the content of their commitments; older adolescents would probably have stronger commitments; and, finally, no age-related differences in the amount of exploration were expected. All of the analyses were done per area. A great deal of variation and age-related differences can be found on this level. Perhaps young adolescents have strong commitments in some areas and older adolescents in other areas. We had no expectations about such differences.

Method

In a similar way to the study of areas, the following independent variables were used: age, sex, and educational level. Age and
sex have already proved their relevance (Marcia et al., in preparation; Waterman, 1982). Much less attention in identity research
has been paid to differences in socioeconomic status and the related variable of educational level. Sociological studies, however,
have clearly demonstrated the differences between the life-worlds
of working-class and middle-class adolescents, and it is very
likely that these affect identity development (e.g., Hurrelmann &
Engel, 1989).

The sample consisted of 160 adolescents, evenly distributed
over the conditions: age (14-15 and 19-20 years of age), sex, and
educational level (a low level of general secondary education and
lower vocational training versus a high level of secondary education and university study). In this way, eight groups of 20 subjects
were formed. All subjects came from a total of 15 schools and
other educational institutes in the provinces of Groningen and
Friesland in the Netherlands. Almost all of the subjects were randomly selected and volunteered to participate. The data on the
higher educated adolescents were gathered in 1984 and analyzed and reported by Bosma (1985). The data on the lower educated groups were gathered in 1985 and analyzed and reported
by Andringa et al. (1986).

The GIDS was administered at school, in the subject's home, or
in the psychology department. The interviews were done by a
number of interviewers, including the author. They were undergraduate or graduate psychology students and had some training
in working with the GIDS. The interviews lasted from 1 to 3
hours. Almost all of the subjects enjoyed the experience; some
even expressed gratitude because of the systematic overview of
their situation provided by the interview.

Results

First, some psychometric results. The questionnaire scales are
Likert-type scales. Their internal consistency, computed per scale
and per area, was as follows: alpha for the C-scale ranged from .81
to .85, and for the E-scale from .73 to .84. The correlations between

the C- and E-scales, computed per area, were very small and not significant, indicating that both scales were independent. The C-scales, correlated over areas, showed a pattern of low positive correlations. The correlations between the E-scales were somewhat higher. Factor analysis of the 12 C- and E-scores (one C- and one E-score per area) resulted in a strong general E-factor and three different C-factors. A general E-factor has also been found in other studies using the GIDS. The factorial structure of the C-scales differs per study, however; it is not clear why. Exploration seems to be a general attribute. On the other hand, having strong commitments in one area does not predict the strength of commitments in others.

The dimensionality of the questionnaire has been studied through factor analysis of its 32 items. The results confirmed that the C and E items were unrelated. They also showed that both scales were two-dimensional. The C-scale comprises two subscales: one with items indicating that the commitment gives a sense of support, strength, and direction, and one indicating a sense of involvement and identification with the commitment. The E-scale also comprises two factors: one with items expressing an active orientation to other persons in the process of exploration, and one with items indicating an active attempt to come to a new commitment. Since the multidimensionality of the questionnaire has only been explored in the data of the higher educated subgroups (see Bosma, 1985) and other analyses with these subscales are not yet available, all further results will concern the original C- and E-scale.

The next research questions concern age-, sex-, and educational-level-related differences between the strength and content of commitments and the amount of exploration in the areas of the GIDS. Table 6.3 gives group means per area for the C- and the E-scales, together with the results of statistical tests on the differences. All analyses have been done using SPSS (Nie et al., 1975). Comparisons between groups are considered significant with $p<.05$; comparisons between areas (within groups) require a level of significance of $p<.003$ because these concern dependent measures. Multivariate analysis of variance—separately done for each scale— with group (groups 1-4 are the younger, groups 5-8 the older age groups), sex, educational level, and area as independent variables—resulted for both scales in significant ($p<.05$) main effects for group and area and significant interaction effects between sex and area and between group and area.

With the exception of the area of parents, there are clear differences between the various groups in respect to the strength of commitments. Young adult males and/or females with a higher education have the strongest commitments in all of the other areas. There is one notable exception: In the area of personal characteristics young adult males, both those with a lower and those with a higher educational level, have strong commitments in comparison with the young adult females and the younger age groups. Another difference concerns the weaker philosophy of life commitments of the lower educated adolescents. No age differences can be discerned in the groups of the lower educated adolescents. In the higher educated groups there are clear age differences, except in the areas of parents and personal characteristics.

Except for the higher educated younger and older males, there are differences within all of the groups in respect to the strength of commitments between areas—mostly because of one high or low mean score in a specific area. The young adolescent males with a lower education have relatively strong commitments in the areas of parents and school, and relatively weak commitments in the areas of philosophy of life, friendship, and intimate relationships. The lower educated young female adolescents have much in common with these males, except for the areas of friendship and intimate relationships, in which they have relatively strong commitments. The higher educated young female adolescents have weak commitments in the area of philosophy of life, and strong commitments with regard to friendship. The differences between areas in the group of lower educated young adult males are inherent in their weak commitments in the area of philosophy of life, and their relatively strong commitments in the areas of personal characteristics, school, and parents. In the group of lower educated young adult females the differences are the outcome of the contrast between philosophy of life on the one hand and friendship and school on the other hand. The contrasts in the group of the higher educated young adult females stem from their weak commitments in the area of personal characteristics (personality). In general, the higher educated young adults have the strongest commitments.

Table 6.3 The Strength of Commitments (C) and the Amount of Exploration (E), Mean Scores

Educational level		1 Boys High	2 Boys Low	3 Girls High	4 Girls Low	5 Men High	6 Men Low	7 Women High	8 Women Low	F	p	sign. diff.
I School, etc.	C	24.2	23.9	22.3	25.7	27.5	25.8	29.4	25.2	2.90	.007	3 vs 7
	E	13.2	12.7	13.7	10.7	13.8	14.1	14.9	13.2	1.53	.163	
II Parents	C	25.3	25.7	22.9	25.9	23.5	24.9	28.1	24.5	1.37	.222	
	E	7.7	8.0	11.8	8.3	11.0	9.7	11.4	9.7	2.62	.014	
III Philosophy of life	C	20.2	17.1	18.4	18.5	25.1	20.3	23.8	18.8	3.40	.002	5 vs 2, 3, 4
	E	11.8	9.5	11.7	6.9	14.2	10.2	14.7	9.1	5.14	.000	5 vs 4, 8
IV Friendship	C	24.1	21.1	24.8	23.7	29.2	23.1	29.0	25.4	5.43	.000	5, 7 vs 2, 4, 6
	E	8.5	7.9	10.1	9.9	8.8	8.9	10.6	8.5	.89	.516	
V Pers. characteristics	C	22.1	22.0	20.8	20.4	26.9	27.0	20.7	22.5	3.45	.002	5, 6 vs 4, 7
	E	11.4	8.4	12.5	12.0	11.6	9.5	15.2	10.1	3.33	.003	7 vs 2, 6, 8
VI Intimate relations	C	21.9	21.2	20.0	24.8	24.6	22.1	27.9	23.7	2.91	.007	7 vs 2, 3
	E	10.4	9.4	12.6	11.8	11.8	10.1	14.1	10.3	2.19	.038	7 vs 2
All areas	C	137.3	130.8	129.1	138.1	156.7	143.0	158.8	140.0	4.63	.000	5, 7 vs 2, 3
	E	62.9	55.8	72.3	59.5	70.3	62.5	80.8	60.7	3.21	.003	7 vs 2, 4, 8

Comparisons between the groups

Table 6.3 (cont.)

Commitments

Differences between areas**	F	2.50	5.82	3.53	6.40	3.05	4.25	8.33	4.20
	p	.030	.000	.004	.000	.010	.001	.000	.001
Significant differences			I vs III II vs III, IV, VI	III vs IV	I vs V III vs I, II, IV, VI		III vs I, II, V	V vs I, II, IV, VI, V	III vs I, IV

Exploration

Differences between areas**	F	6.84	5.00	2.24	6.42	6.28	5.49	6.25	4.13
	p	.000	.000	.049	.000	.000	.000	.000	.001
Significant differences		I vs IV II vs I, III, V, VI	I vs II, IV, V, VI	I vs IV	II vs V, VI III vs I, V, VI	IV vs I, III	I vs II, IV, V, VI	IV vs I, III, V	I vs III, IV

*MANOVA; Tukey-HSD procedure, $p \leq .05$
**MANOVA; T-test (related samples), $p \leq .003$

As far as the amount of exploration is concerned, there are also differences between the groups. Except for one, all of these differences are related to the high scores of the higher educated young adult females and the low scores of one or more of the lower educated groups. The only other significant contrast lies in the high score of the higher educated young adult males and the low scores of the lower educated females in the area of philosophy of life. The differences within the groups (between areas) are mainly connected with low exploration scores in the area of friendship, and high scores in the area of school. In general, the youngest groups, with the higher educated young females as an exception, also show less exploration in the area of parents. The exploration score of the lower educated young adolescent females is very low.

The content of the subject's commitments is the third important variable in this approach to identity development in adolescence. The statements written on the cards, one per area, form the relevant qualitative data. This information has been analyzed in a global way. The statements were sorted per area, by the author, into ad hoc categories. The groups were subsequently compared, again per area, through inspection of the categorized information. This method is subjective, but since most statements are rather concrete, it is expected that the procedure allows for a reliable impression both of the content of the commitments and of striking differences between the groups.

In general, there is much variation in content within each area and within each group. The differences in content between the groups are much smaller than the intra-group differences. Because of space limitations, only a very brief account of these differences will be given.

In the areas of school, occupation, and leisure time, commitments tend to refer to each of these sub-areas. Mutual adjustment of the various obligations in these sub-areas is often the main issue involved. School is generally considered to be important for the future, but some adolescents tend to give a higher priority to leisure-time activities. This tendency is more pronounced in the higher educated groups, especially in the group of the young adult females; they want a future job that leaves sufficient opportunity for favorite leisure-time activities. Some of the younger adolescent males express a strong dislike of school.

Commitments in the area of parents mostly concern the relationship with and the qualities of the parents. Qualifications in the commitments range from negative via neutral to positive. A positively valued relationship is characterized by warmth and mutual respect and gives the adolescent enough room to make his own decisions. Most commitments indicate a positive and rewarding relationship. The young adolescent males have no commitments indicating problems. Such problems occur in all of the other groups, however, and as far as the higher educated young male adults are concerned, they occur in as many as one-third of commitments.

There is much variation in the content of commitments in the area of philosophy of life. A few adolescents have strong religious commitments, others are either not interested in religion or express a negative attitude. The same applies for politics. In this area there are some differences between the groups. Lack of interest in religion or politics is evident in each group, except in the group of the higher educated young adult males. Some of these males, however, show skeptical though strong commitments. Such commitments can also be found in the groups of lower educated young adults. A number of adolescents express some sort of principle in their commitment, for example, "Everyone has the right to choose his own religion." Such principled commitments are evident in all of the groups, except for the higher educated young adolescent males and the lower educated young adult females. Commitments indicating doubt with regard to one's religion exist in each group, except in the group of the higher educated young adolescent males.

Most commitments in the area of friendship indicate that friendship is very important for adolescents. In the younger male age groups friendship often indicates belonging to a group of peers; the female groups more often refer to one or two close real friends. Shared activities is a friendship characteristic more often referred to by the younger age groups. A substantial number of commitments held by the higher educated young adult male group, and a few of those held by both older female groups, emphasize the need to maintain one's individuality in a friendship relationship.

Commitments in the area of personal characteristics show substantial differences within groups. Most commitments concern personality characteristics. Sex role is hardly ever mentioned. Physical appearance is referred to by about one-fourth of the younger adolescents and almost none of the older groups. Commitments with regard to one's own personality often express that the person is happy about himself or herself. This is the case with about one-fourth of the commitments of the lower educated groups. The biggest contrast is between the two older female groups: The lower educated female young adults most often show this type of commitment, while almost half of the group of higher educated older females indicated a lack of self-confidence and other problems connected with their personality. Such problematic commitments hardly occur in the male groups.

In the area of intimate relationships, there are differences in the content of commitments within and between groups. In the younger age groups a number of adolescents express a lack of interest in such relationships. Such commitments also occur in the older groups, except for the lower educated females. This group, together with the younger male groups, has no commitments indicating problems either. Some concerns are expressed in the commitments of the higher educated female adolescents, such as: Homework might suffer from such a relationship. References to the more problematic side of intimate relationships are also made in the commitments of the other groups (young adult males and higher educated young adult females): Such a relationship might limit your freedom and hamper other friendships. The higher educated young male adults fairly frequently refer to the problem of losing their own identity in a strong intimate relationship. A number of the young adults (male and female) had had bad experiences with an intimate relationship and had decided not to enter into such a relationship for the time being.

Discussion

The psychometric qualities of the GIDS are quite satisfactory. Both scales give reliable and independent information about exploration and commitment in different areas experienced by adolescents within the age range of 14 to 21 years. There were some indications during the interviews, however, that younger adolescents might not yet have the reflective capacity necessary to answer the interview and questionnaire questions. These questions presuppose some overview of and reflection on one's situation, and a number of late-maturing boys in the youngest age group had difficulties in answering some of them.

Another limitation is that the areas in the GIDS are based on research with Caucasian Dutch adolescents. There is a likelihood that these areas are not fully representative of the life-situation of adolescents from ethnic and cultural minorities, for example adolescents from Turkish families living in the Netherlands. The list of areas would probably need to be adapted in order to represent these adolescents.

With regard to the main variables, the study clearly showed differences related to age, but also to sex and educational level. The study design does not permit conclusions about developmental processes, but an interesting trend is evident. Higher educated older groups have stronger commitments than younger groups. This difference has not been found, however, in the lower educated groups—here the older groups do not show an increase. According to these findings, Waterman's conclusion (1982) that a sense of identity becomes stronger in the course of adolescent development cannot be generalized to adolescents with a lower educational level.

The areas show clear differences in the strength of commitments. For almost all of the groups, the strongest commitments are in the areas of school and parents, and the weakest commitments in the area of philosophy of life. Friendship and intimate relationships are areas in which the female subjects tend to have strong commitments and some of the male groups have weak commitments. The opposite seems to be true for personal characteristics. Here, it is especially the higher educated females who have weak commitments. These trends are also found in other studies (Douvan & Adelson, 1966; Matteson, in preparation; Offer et al., 1981). In general, the relational areas are considered to be more important for females. This might explain their stronger commitments in these areas. Other researchers have also found that female adolescents experience more problems in the intrapersonal sphere (Offer et al., 1981, and, in the Netherlands, Van der Linden & Roeders, 1983). However, both trends must be qualified because of educational background: The higher educated young male adults also have strong friendship commitments, and the lower educated young adult females did not show any problems with regard to their personality. Educational level thus limits the generalizability of conclusions about sex differences in identity research.

Almost all of the group differences in exploration have to do with the high score of the higher educated young adult females in comparison to the lower educated groups. The only other difference is the high exploration score of the higher educated young adult males in the area of philosophy of life. There is a great deal of exploration within all of the groups in the area of school, and a low amount of exploration in the areas of friendship and parents. There are also specific within-group differences between other areas; lower educated males show less exploration in the areas of personal characteristics and intimate relationships, while all of the female subjects and the young male adolescents with a higher educational level show a great deal of exploration in these areas. It is difficult to give a satisfactory explanation for all of these differences in exploration. It is likely that the nature of an area plays an important role; every adolescent is confronted with the need to explore different possibilities in the area of school, future occupation, and leisure time. It is also likely that the relationship with parents does not give room for much exploration. The peer group, on the other hand, is often seen as the preeminent place for exploration and experimentation with interpersonal matters. This is not evident in our data on exploration in the area of friendship commitments. The other differences are probably related to different socializing patterns that result in specific sex and social class differences—both in the individual need and in the societal room for exploring possibilities of choice. In this sense, it could be that the high exploration scores of the female university students, and also those of the higher educated young female adolescents, express their changing social position, a change that has not (yet) affected the position of the lower educated females.

In conclusion, with regard to exploration and commitments, the results indicate that adolescents form a very heterogeneous group. In addition to age and sex, factors like educational level and socioeconomic background have a profound influence on identity in adolescence. The GIDS seems to offer good possibilities for the study of such (and still other) influences because it allows for an objective assessment of both explorations and the strength and content of commitments in a wide range of areas in adolescence.

COMMITMENTS, A COMMON PRINCIPLE?

When GIDS data are used in comparisons between groups, within-group variation in the strength and content of commitments and the amount of exploration is ignored. But this is the information upon which Marcia's identity statuses are based. They represent a psychologically valid way of explaining inter-individual variance. The status model is also a very convenient and useful way of summarizing the data from an individual identity status interview. The GIDS also gives a lot of information about an individual, but is more difficult to use for a short summary statement about someone's identity. If a GIDS profile is homogeneous—for example, all of the commitments are strong and the exploration scores in all of the areas are low—this profile probably represents what Marcia calls "foreclosure." But only a minority of the profiles from the cross-sectional study showed such a neat pattern. Most profiles are heterogeneous in the sense that the C-scores vary widely over the different areas. (The E-scores show less intra-individual variation; the evidence is given for a general E-factor.) What about the interpretation of such profiles?

Table 6.4 presents three individual GIDS profiles. They consist of the subjects' (literal) statements for each area and the corresponding C- and E-scores. *A*'s C-scores are very weak. *B* shows a mixture of weak and strong commitments, and *C* has very strong commitments. *A* and *B* show higher exploration scores in areas where they have weak commitments. On the whole, the exploration scores of all three subjects are fairly high (compare Table 6.3). "General" refers to the common principle (see text).

The profiles originate from a study done by Müllges (1987). She was interested in the relationship between an individual's commitments in different areas and explored whether individuals could formulate some sort of idea, principle, thought, or feeling that was related to all of their commitments. Perhaps adolescents have such (guiding) principles that function as a common base for committing oneself in the different spheres of life. Such principles

Table 6.4 Examples of GIDS Profiles

A. Male, age 20

School, (future) work, leisure time: I have difficulties dividing up my time. I spend a lot of time thinking about what I have to do. When I'm doing nothing, I feel that I should do something. Leisure time is often not really leisure. (E = 14, C = 12)

Parents: My parents play a much larger part in my thoughts than I would like them to. I often have an idea what their opinions of something are, and with that idea or ideal in mind I try to have my "own" point of view. (E = 20, C = 8)

Philosophy of life: I sometimes have certain thoughts which can have a reassuring effect. When this happens, everything seems less threatening and I experience a secure and safe environment. (E = 7, C = 20)

Friendship: I need it very much, but I often feel uncomfortable. It's hard for me to be with somebody then. (E = 17, C = 10)

Personal characteristics: I often experience other people as threatening; I categorize them too quickly as being above or beneath myself. I am preoccupied with the impression I make and I feel as if there are lots of things that I ought to do. (E = 17, C = 10)

Intimate relationships: What is important to me now is that on the one hand I feel very relaxed and at ease and on the other hand I often have doubts whether this is the girl for me. (E = 17, C = 11)

General: With everything I do I have the general feeling that something is expected from me, that I have to live up to certain demands or an ideal. (E = 16, C = 9)

B. Male, age 21

School, (future) work, leisure time: School and occupation (thinking about these) are very closely connected for me. I don't give much time to school, but do lots of things besides. I want to enjoy my work: varied, help other people. (E = 8, C = 28)

Parents: I have never had a good relationship with my parents. Their marriage has been a mess for as long as I can remember. Hopefully all of this will change. (E = 18, C = 10)

Philosophy of life: I have my own way of looking at life. Religion plays no part, politics only a very small part in it. How others look at life is their own business. (E = 4, C = 19)

Friendship: I find the exchanging, sharing of feelings very pleasant and important in friendship. Doing nice things together is less important for me, but of course I enjoy it. This is possible after a change (no friends before). (E = 9, C = 29)

Personal characteristics: I have changed a lot recently. I used to be very shy and had trouble making social contacts. I don't really find that difficult now. (E = 13, C = 33)

Intimate relationships: My thinking about this has changed recently (I've become more self-confident, less shy), but these thoughts have yet to be put into action. (E = 18, C = 7)

General: I have changed a lot during recent months; I am freeing myself from unwanted ties. I stand up for myself more, am more self-confident. (E = 10, C = 32)

C. Female, age 20

School, (future) work, leisure time: I am 100% dedicated as far as school, work and leisure time are concerned, with a view to self-development. (E = 15, C = 36)

Parents: My parents are very important to me, because they accept me unconditionally. Home is a refuge. (E = 12, C = 34)

Table 6.4 Continued

Philosophy of life: Life is a process in which you have to be able to adjust and be open to new things. It is very important to do things with love. (E = 22, C = 34)
Friendship: Feeling comfortable with that person. Trusting him/her and giving each other room for idiosyncrasies. (E = 13, C = 36)
Personal characteristics: Being consciously involved in what you do and are, even if this often leads to conflicts. Daring to live. (E = 19, C = 30)
Intimate relationships: Such a relationship can be fun, but it is not a necessity for being able to function well. (E = 13, C = 30)
General: Live consciously, develop yourself and be open to new, different things. (E = 20, C = 36)

could also be of help in the interpretation of (heterogeneous) GIDS profiles.

Method

This study was done with 25 second-year psychology students (19 females, 6 males, 19-23 years of age). First they were administered the GIDS in the standard way. Then the six cards with commitments were presented to the subjects and they were asked whether there was some sort of common or underlying idea, principle, thought, or feeling with regard to the commitments. When the subjects suggested such a principle, they were then asked to explain how it was related to each commitment. They also answered the GIDS questionnaire about the principle, which resulted in C- and E-scores for it.

Results

Almost all of the subjects could, surprisingly easily, formulate some sort of common principle—14 in immediate response to the question, 10 after a short period (1-3 minutes) and only one after a somewhat longer period. Retrospectively, 17 subjects indicated that they had become aware of it during the last 1 to 4 years; 2 of them were already conscious of it when they were about 16 years of age. For most of them this was a gradual process, though for some it became evident in connection with a specific event (e.g., leaving home, breaking up a steady relationship). Eight subjects formulated it (for some, more or less to their own surprise) in response to the experimenter's question.

The principles were categorized by Müllges to give an analysis of their content. They all concerned the subject's personality and way of life and in most of the cases they indicated a personal wish (striving) to deal with life in a specific way. About two-thirds (17) could be categorized into four groups. The first category concerned (lack of) self-confidence (n = 5), the second category comprised statements indicating (lack of) self-determination (n = 5), the third category indicated a striving for personal growth and development (n = 4) and the fourth category concerned statements indicating that the subject thought it important to be committed. The other principles were mentioned once or twice.

There is a clear relationship between the content of an individual's various commitments and his or her principle. In seven cases the content of the general principle is more or less literally expressed in the commitments in the six areas. In 15 of the 18 other cases there is also a clear relationship, but now in the sense that the principle is expressed in most of the area commitments but not in the others. However, these other commitments (or lack of commitments) in a way contradict that principle, or, alternatively, it has not yet been realized in these deviating areas. Table 6.5 gives an overview of these contrasts. This table also gives the results of a comparison in terms of the respective strengths of the area commitments and of the general principle. In 14 of the 15 cases showing a contrast in terms of content, a similar contrast is also evident in the strength scores (Table 6.5).

Table 6.5 also shows that the contrast can go either way; in the first 11 cases the general principle is not (yet) realized in the deviating areas. In the other three cases the contrasting areas (commitments) form a more or less positive exception to the problems in other areas.

Discussion

This attempt to study the profile of an individual's commitments in terms of a general principle, a meta-commitment, has been successful. Young adults are aware of such principles, and they seem to play a kind of organizing and integrating role in the process of

Table 6.5 Contrasts in Individual GIDS Profiles

Mean C	C princ.	C contr.	Principle	Contrasting areas, motivation
27.8	30	19; 8	need to feel committed	commitment with regard to school and philosophy of life lacks
34.4	36	21	self-determination	most difficult in intimate relationships
37.3	33	18; 20	having personal space, influence	that space is missing in school and intimate relationships
29.2	32	22	self-actualization	unable to realize in the area of parents, they obstruct it
28	29	18	make conscious choices	with intimate relationship more negative choice, not conscious
27.3	32	7; 10	more self-confident	want to leave bond with parents not yet established intimate relationships
23	30	14	self-respect	is threatened by parents
30	34	15	further personal growth	in relationship with parents still a great deal of growth is required
26	30	15	accept things as they happen	not possible to do so at school, school urges planning/decisions
34	34	16	conscious, confronting	still a lot to be done in the area of personality
22.6	21	15	start from an ideal	there is not ideal with regard to school
10	9	20	must meet demands	religious thoughts reduce pressure, form escape
25.6	27	34	doubt, uncertainty	no doubts, not uncertain with friends
10.2	10	26; 28; 28	looking for happiness	less in the case of personal characteristics, philosophy of life and intimate relations

NOTE: Mean C: mean C-score except for contrasting commitments
C princ: C-score general principle
C contr: C-score contrasting area(s)

committing oneself in the different spheres of life. Knowledge of this principle helps one to understand the individual's profile of commitments, especially if it is heterogeneous.

However, these results cannot be generalized. The sample is small and highly selective. It is possible that psychology students, familiar with research on social cognitive development, might have learned to express themselves in terms of principled orientations with regard to themselves. But some of them were already aware of such a principled personal orientation in their life while they were still at high school. There are no psychology courses in secondary education in the Netherlands.

Nevertheless, despite its limitations, the study suggests an interesting and promising area of research, namely, the study of identity development in terms of organizing principles "behind" the commitments in separate areas.

CONCLUSION

The GIDS was constructed in an attempt to come to a more process-oriented measure of identity development in adolescence. The results of the first empirical studies using the GIDS are positive, and the procedure seems to offer promising possibilities for the study of intra-individual change. The next step is a longitudinal study of identity development. However, what exactly would be studied in such a project?

The GIDS can be used to map out changes in the content and strength of commitments and the role of exploration in that process. If adolescents are tested and retested several times in the course of their development, it is indeed possible to see that commitments change over time. Such changes could be preceded by a temporary increase in exploration. In line with Coleman's focal theory (Coleman, 1974; Coleman & Hendry, 1990), it could become evident that such changes are area-specific and that there is some sequence in the occurrence of periods of increased exploration in the different areas. It could also appear that there are stable inter-individual differences in the amount of exploration and change in commitments, different stable styles of committing oneself, for example, an open and flexible style and a more rigid style (compare Berzonsky, 1990, this volume; Raphael & Zelowski,

1980). These are all very interesting perspectives for further research. But we should also be aware of the limitations of such a longitudinal study. These limitations are connected with the validity of the GIDS.

In a sense, the GIDS is as much an outcome measure as the identity status method. The GIDS only allows for a more detailed description of individual patterns of exploration and commitments at the time of measurement than the identity statuses. But the measure does not give insight into the processes underlying the changes between time one and time two. Commitments and their change are the dynamic outcomes of processes, and these processes are not assessed by the GIDS. Even the nature of these processes is far from clear. But here we enter into issues outside the scope of this chapter. The attempt to study the "underlying" or "integrating" principles that "motivate" the choice of commitments in the different areas tackled only one of these issues. Its results demonstrate that there is more to identity development than the mere fact of having changing commitments.

REFERENCES

Adams, G. R., Bennion, L. & Huh, K. (1989). *Objective measure of ego identity status: A reference manual.* Logan: Utah State University, Laboratory for Research on Adolescence.

Andringa, M., Bosma, H. A., Jong, N. de, Martina, M., Meijer, B., Nijholt, M., Nijholt, S., & Otter, P. den. (1986). *Identiteit voor iedereen? Een onderzoek naar de bruikbaarheid van de GIDS bij jongeren met een MAVO-LBO-opleiding* [Identity for everyone? A study of the usefulness of the GIDS for lower educated youth]. Unpublished report, State University, Groningen, the Netherlands.

Berzonsky, M. D (1990). Self-construction over the life-span: A process perspective on identity formation. In G. J. Neimeyer & R. A. Neimeyer (Eds.), *Advances in personal construct theory* (Vol. 1, pp. 155-186). Greenwich, CT: JAI Press.

Bosma, H. A. (1985). *Identity development in adolescence: Coping with commitments.* Unpublished doctoral dissertation, State University, Groningen, the Netherlands.

Bosma, H. A., & Gerrits, R. S. (1985). Family functioning and identity status in adolescence. *Journal of Early Adolescence, 5*, 69-80.

Coleman, J. C. (1974). *Relationships in adolescence.* London: Routledge & Kegan Paul.

Coleman, J. C. (1980). *The nature of adolescence.* London: Methuen.

Coleman, J. C., & Hendry, L. (1990). *The nature of adolescence.* London: Routledge.

Conger, J. J., & Petersen, A. C. (1984). *Adolescence and youth. Psychological development in a changing world.* New York: John Wiley.

Douvan, E., & Adelson, J. (1966). *The adolescent experience.* New York: John Wiley.

Dreher, E., & Dreher, M. (1984, August). Developmental tasks in adolescence. Paper presented at the Inaugural European Conference on Developmental Psychology, Groningen, the Netherlands.

Grotevant, H. D., Thorbecke, W., & Meyer, M. L. (1982). An extension of Marcia's identity status interview into the interpersonal domain. *Journal of Youth and Adolescence, 11*, 33-47.

Havighurst, R. J. (1953). *Human development and education*. New York: Longman.

Hurrelmann, K., & Engel, U. (Eds.) (1989). *The social world of adolescents. International Perspectives*. Berlin: Walter de Gruyter.

Josselson, R., Greenberger, E., & McConochie, D. (1977). Phenomenological aspects of psychosocial maturity in adolescence. Part I. Boys. *Journal of Youth and Adolescence, 6*, 25-55.

Josselson, R., Greenberger, E., & McConochie, D. (1977). Phenomenological aspects of psychosocial maturity in adolescence. Part II. Girls. *Journal of Youth and Adolescence, 6*, 145-167.

Kitwood, T. (1980). *Disclosures to a stranger. Adolescent values in an advanced industrial society*. London: Routledge & Kegan Paul.

La Gaipa, J. J. (1979). A developmental study of the meaning of friendship in adolescence. *Journal of Adolescence, 2*, 201-213.

Marcia, J. E. (1966). Development and validation of ego-identity status. *Journal of Personality and Social Psychology, 3*, 551-558.

Marcia, J. E. (1980). Identity in adolescence. In J. Adelson (Ed.), *Handbook of adolescent psychology* (pp. 159-187). New York: John Wiley.

Marcia, J. E. (in preparation). The ego identity status approach to ego identity. In J. E. Marcia, D. R. Matteson, A. S. Waterman, S. A. Archer, & J. L. Orlofsky. *Ego identity: A handbook for psychosocial research* (Chapter 1). New York: Springer-Verlag.

Marcia, J. E., Matteson, D. R., Waterman, A. S., Archer, S. A., & Orlofsky, J. L. (in preparation). *Ego identity: A handbook for psychosocial research*. New York: Springer-Verlag.

Matteson, D. R. (1975). *Adolescence today: Sex roles and the search for identity*. Homewood, IL: Dorsey Press.

Matteson, D. R. (1977). Exploration and commitment: Sex differences and methodological problems in the use of identity status categories. *Journal of Youth and Adolescence, 6*, 353-374.

Matteson, D. R. (in preparation). Sex differences in identity formation: A challenge to the theory. In J. E. Marcia, D. R. Matteson, A. S. Waterman, S. A. Archer, & J. L. Orlofsky. *Ego identity: A handbook for psychosocial research*. New York: Springer-Verlag.

Müllges, S. (1987). *Identiteitsontwikkeling: Integratie van bindingen in een "algemeen principe"* [Identity development: Integration of commitments in a "general principle"]. Unpublished master's thesis, State University, Groningen, the Netherlands.

Nie, N. H., Hull, C. H., Jenkins, J. C., Steinbrenner, K., & Bent, D. H. (1975). *Statistical package for the social sciences, SPSS*. New York: McGraw-Hill.

Offer, D., Ostrov, E., & Howard, K. I. (1981). *The adolescent: A psychological self-portrait*. New York: Basic Books.

Raphael, D., & Zelowski, H. G. (1980). Identity status in high school students: Critique and a revised paradigm. *Journal of Youth and Adolescence, 9*, 383-389.

Raskin, P. M. (1984). Procedures in research on identity status. Some notes on method. *Psychological Reports, 54*, 719-730.

Regt, W. de. (1982). *Meisjes en jongens en hun sexualiteit* [Boys and girls and their sexuality]. Deventer: Van Loghum Siaterus.

Rogow, A. M., Marcia, J. E., & Slugoski, B. R. (1983). The relative importance of identity status interview components. *Journal of Youth and Adolescence, 12,* 387-400.

Schenkel, S., & Marcia, J. E. (1972). Attitudes toward premarital intercourse in determining ego identity status in college women. *Journal of Personality, 3,* 472-482.

Steinberg, L. (1985). *Adolescence.* New York: Knopf.

Van der Linden, F. J., & Roeders, P.J.B. (1983). *Schoolgaande jongeren, hun leefwreld en zelfbeleving*[Schoolgoing adolescents, their lifeworld and self-experience]. Nijmegen: Hoogveld Instituut.

Waterman, A. S. (1982). Identity development from adolescence to adulthood: An extension of theory and a review of research. *Developmental Psychology, 18,* 341-358.

Waterman, A. S., Besold, B., Crook, W. P., & Manzini, S. (1979). Ego identity status scoring manual for adult women. Unpublished manuscript, Trenton State College.

Youniss, J., & Smollar, J. (1990). Self through relationship development. In H. A. Bosma & A. E. Jackson (Eds.), *Coping and self-concept in adolescence* (pp. 129-148). Berlin: Springer-Verlag.

7. Intrapsychic Dimensions of Identity During Late Adolescence

Jane Kroger
Victoria University at Wellington

The word for universe is Au-Ki. It means heaven and earth. The naming of man cannot take place until the two have separated.

—from a Sumerian creation myth

Just as the universe cannot come into being until heaven and earth have separated, neither can humankind know ultimate relatedness until unique individuals emerge, according to this Sumerian creation myth. Captured in the popular folklore of distant lands, themes of separation and reunion, of "emergence from embeddedness" in order to "stand in relationship to," also pervade existing literature addressing intrapsychic development during late adolescence. In 1978 Bourne (p. 390) noted that "the study of intrapsychic processes mediating late adolescent development remains a relatively untouched domain." Since that time, a small but growing body of theoretical and research effort has begun to explore this intrapsychic territory. The valuable contributions of many individuals to this field are the foundations of this chapter. It is hoped now that through critical review of their ground-breaking efforts we may begin to formulate new questions in refining our existing constructs and research methodologies. This chapter will examine three models of ego development in an attempt to illuminate normative intrapsychic developmental

AUTHOR'S NOTE: *I would like to express my gratitude to Erik and Joan Erikson, Bob Kegan, John Levine, and Gil Noam for many stimulating sessions, both formal and informal, during my year of sabbatical leave at the Erik H. and Joan M. Erikson Center; these exchanges contributed significantly to the preparation of this chapter. I am also grateful for the valuable comments of Gerald Adams, Ruthellen Josselson, and an anonymous reviewer on an earlier version of this manuscript. The present work was supported through a grant from the Internal Research Committee, Victoria University at Wellington.*

processes during adolescence and to identify potentially fruitful areas for theoretical refinement and future research.

THEORETICAL PERSPECTIVES ON
IDENTITY IN LATE ADOLESCENCE

In inquiring more specifically into intrapsychic features of late adolescent ego identity, three theoretical models which utilize a structural conception of the ego will be briefly reviewed. In a manner consistent with the definition offered by Snarey, Kohlberg, and Noam (1983, p. 305), such models understand the ego primarily as an organization (rather than organizer) of experience:

> Ego development, then, may be understood as the overall unity of the ego as it progressively reconstructs itself through a dialectical process in which the person "makes sense" of his or her evolving relationship with others, the world, and life as a whole.

The above structural notion contrasts with the system ego as it is generally understood in classic psychodynamic theory (Kirshner, 1988; Noam, 1988). The latter approach takes ego to mean an organizer, a balancer and regulator having a number of separate functions (e.g., impulse control, stress tolerance). A structural conceptualization, however, regards ego as an intrapsychic organization—an internal structure that develops over time through a hierarchical sequence of qualitatively different stages, which, in turn, give meaning and coherence to both internal and external experience. Ego psychoanalytic psychology, object relations approaches, and constructive-developmental theory all rely, at least to some extent, on such a structural conceptualization of ego; in addition, these models all provide us with ways of empirically investigating that "intrapsychic emergence" so often portrayed in narratives of late adolescence.

Contributions from Ego Psychoanalytic
Theory and Research: Erikson and Marcia

Erikson has conceptualized ego identity in structural terms as a unified organization analogous to the *structure d'ensemble* notion of Piaget (Berzonsky, 1988). Erikson has noted structural features of late adolescent intrapsychic organization in his description of the stages of ego growth: "If we consider introjection, identification, and identity formation to be the steps by which the ego grows in ever more mature interplay with the available models, the following psychosocial schedule suggests itself" (Erikson, 1968, p. 159). He continues by detailing the course of ego development when organized by each of these three principles, concluding with a statement on that structure generally present in late adolescence: "*Identity formation*, finally, begins where the usefulness of identification ends. It arises from the selective repudiation and mutual assimilation of childhood identifications and their absorption in a new configuration . . . " (Erikson, 1968, p. 159). Thus, shift from an intrapsychic structure embedded in significant identifications to a new configuration (now capable of filtering, selectively repudiating, and generally taking some perspective on its earlier ways of being-in-the-world) denote two distinct forms of structural organization. Marcia's (1966) foreclosure and achievement identity statuses, respectively, are derived from these two internal architectures. Erikson himself, however, has not elaborated further on intrapsychic features of ego identity in late adolescence, nor has he detailed the actual *process* by which earlier identifications become synthesized into this new structural form; others have thus inherited the task of detailing structural development in this late adolescent "alteration."

Marcia's innovative expansion of Erikson's "identity versus role confusion" stage in late adolescence has afforded some opportunity for closer scrutiny of ego identity development during life's second decade. Marcia (1980, p. 159) also has defined identity in structural terms:

> I would like to propose another way of construing identity: as a self-structure—an internal, self-constructed, dynamic organization of drives, abilities, beliefs, and individual history. . . . The identity structure is dynamic, not static. . . . Over a period of time, the entire gestalt may shift.

Marcia's achievement, moratorium, foreclosure, and diffusion identity statuses have provided the lenses through which intrapsychic dimensions of late adolescent ego restructuralization might be brought into focus.

For each of the identity statuses, such images have come through measures tapping an adolescent's level of psychosexual development, object relations, and ego development. Josselson (1973, 1982), Donovan (1975a, 1975b), and Orlofsky and Frank (1986) have all found stages of psychosexual development to be linked with ego identity status. Achievement and moratorium subjects have evidenced developmentally more mature psychosexual content in early memory themes than foreclosure and diffusion subjects. An object relations approach has also been employed to examine the adolescent separation-individuation process in relation to the identity statuses; relevant studies will be reviewed in a later section. Loevinger's structural measure of ego development (Loevinger, 1976) has also been used in studies of ego identity status. From Adams and Fitch (1981), Adams and Shea (1979), Ginsberg and Orlofsky (1981), and Hopkins (1982), lower stages of ego development have been associated with diffusion and foreclosure identity statuses, and higher stages have been associated with the moratorium and achievement positions.

On Use of the Identity Status Model for Structural Inference: Conceptual and Methodological Issues

General comments must be made on limitations both of the identity status model and of identity status assessment techniques for accurately inferring forms of underlying structural organization. The identity status model was developed for use with late adolescents to identify particular styles of psychosocial commitment. When applied to late adolescents, the model can do no more than denote one of three general underlying structural configurations: an intrapsychic structure embedded in its identificatory relationships (foreclosure), one able to reflect upon and synthesize such identifications from a more differentiated position (achievement), and a transition between these two forms (moratorium). The model is unable to identify any one structural organization clearly underlying the diffusion status, though there has been some evidence of failure in the process of internalization for some diffusions (Grotevant, 1983; Josselson, 1987; Marcia, 1980). (Similarly, it is unable to identify any specific transitional phases of organization that may underlie the moratorium status.) When the identity status model is applied to other age groups across the life span, the implications of identity status ratings for structural inference are far less clear.

In the last decade, the identity status model has been adapted for use with early adolescents as well as adults. If one's purpose is to gauge structural organization, it is my view that the identity status model is not well suited for research with age groups other than late adolescents. In studies of early adolescence, a diffusion rating does not hold the implications of structural arrest that are present in late adolescence; lack of interest in commitment among early adolescents may, in fact, be a particularly appropriate mode of dealing with psychosocial issues that are not yet salient. In studies of adulthood, an identity achievement rating may denote even more differentiated forms of structural organization than the rating implies for late adolescents (see, for example, Kegan, 1982; Loevinger, 1976). Continuing cycles of moratorium-achievement-moratorium-achievement movement in adulthood are likely to reflect a change of *content* in psychosocial commitment; however, such cycles may or may not reflect change in the underlying *structure* of ego organization. The meanings that identity status ratings hold when applied to age spans other than late adolescence are likely to produce more confusion than enlightenment when one wishes to address matters of structure rather than content.

Different techniques have been employed to assign an ego identity status rating. Marcia (1966) has preferred to assign an identity status based on clinical judgment of the rater rather than on any numerical summation of ratings across domains. Others have preferred to assign an overall rating or numerical score based on the most frequently occurring rating across domains (e.g., Archer, 1982). Some researchers have preferred reporting results by domain only (e.g., Waterman, 1985). If one's goal is an understanding of underlying structure, the best index, in my view, is clinical judgment regarding the mode by which the most salient identity elements are approached. Any strictly numerical summation of domains may not only give an inappropriate diffusion weighing to issues simply not salient for the individual (Marcia, 1989) but also may thereby inaccurately point to structural arrest.

Furthermore, different methods have been used to elicit responses from subjects to identity defining issues. It is my view that questionnaires designed to assess ego identity status are unlikely to provide the best index of underlying structural organization. The scope for allowing a subject to demonstrate the limits of his or her organizational system is simply not possible without the questioning opportunities provided by interview. For example, a subject may respond to a questionnaire item indicating strong agreement that, after much consideration, she has established a very definite view of what her career will be. At face value, strong agreement would be rated as identity achievement. However, it may be that the subject's partner wishes her to deliberate and consider a career; her explorations and subsequent commitment have thus been conducted on his behalf, and her seemingly autonomous stance is a result of embeddedness in this identificatory relationship. Without opportunity for probing, this foreclosed subject may easily be misidentified as identity achieved. Work by Schmid-Kitsikis (1972) has explored methodological differences in standardized questions versus open-ended Piagetian interviews for subjects on a conservation task; use of the different methods yielded evidence of different logical structures within the same children. If one's interest lies in structural organization, questionnaire responses, which allow no opportunity for probing, are likely to be of more limited value than interview data in identity status research.

Finally, many identity status studies have employed statistical procedures involving the untested collapsing of identity statuses into "high" and "low" groupings for the purpose of increasing cell sizes. Not only does this procedure lead to the possibility of either creating or destroying effects, but it also makes it impossible to examine individual identity statuses in relation to dependent variables. With differing structural organizations associated with the identity statuses, it would seem critical to examine dependent variables in relation to each identity grouping. New methods for analyzing sparse contingency tables are now available which avoid problems generated by the untested collapsing of categorical data and should be used in future identity status studies with limited sample sizes (Kroger & Haslett, 1987, 1988).

Contributions from Object Relations
Theory and Research: Mahler and Blos

Through extensive observations of normal infants and their mothers in a naturalistic play setting, Mahler and her associates have chronicled "the psychological birth of the human infant"—a sequence of phases through which the child passes in developing a sense of self as distinct from others (Mahler, Pine, & Bergman, 1975). Mahler's focus, in contrast to other theorists of infant attachment, has been developmental in nature and fixed primarily on the intrapsychic realm of infant experience rather than remaining with the child's observed behavior in relation to the actual caregiver.

Mahler has proposed that initially the infant enters the world unable to differentiate self from other in a "normal autistic phase." (More recently, Mahler modified her view of this initial stage to accommodate findings of infant research and suggested this phrase be renamed "awakening" [Stern, 1985].) From about the second month after birth, "normal symbiosis" ensues; in this stage, the child functions as though fused with the primary caretaker. It is only from satisfactory grounding in these initial stages that the separation-individuation process of infancy can begin. Marked by four subphases, separation-individuation starts with the infant's tentative experiments to distinguish his or her own attributes from those of the primary caretaker. There is a new alertness to the external environment in this *differentiation subphase* (about 5-10 months). The *practicing subphase* (about 10-15 months) follows and is marked by the child's increased locomotor abilities allowing greater exploration and a growing ability to tolerate maternal absence. The third subphase, *rapprochement* (between 15-22 months), denotes the child's growing awareness of his or her own separate psychological existence. During this time, the child appears conflicted between the desire for separateness and the wish to recreate symbiotic fusion. The result of this tension culminates in the rapprochement crisis, resolved only gradually through the building of a stable internal image of the primary caretaker. The fourth subphase, *consolidation of individuality and beginnings of emotional object constancy*, is open-ended, denoting the child's internalization of a stable and secure caretaker representation, coupled with an appreciation of the external caretaker as a physically separate person.

While Mahler's scheme has not been without criticism (e.g., Harter, 1983; Stern, 1985), it has served as the theoretical basis for various adaptations describing adolescent intrapsychic reorganization. Blos (1967) was the first writer to recognize the potential applicability of Mahler's observations to the adolescent passage. In his discussion of the second individuation process, he noted that while the psychological work of infancy is to separate from the caretaker of reality by internalizing the image, it is disengagement from this very internalized object that remains the intrapsychic work of adolescence. Blos did not continue, however, to detail any specific subphases in the adolescent separation-individuation process comparable to those suggested by Mahler nor did he elaborate upon different defensive modes used by some adolescents to maintain internalized object ties.

Later theorists have proposed some modifications to or elaborations of Blos's account. Brandt (1977) has identified specific parallels between infant and adolescent subphases of separation-individuation. The second separation-individuation process, Brandt believes, spans from puberty to late adolescence. He argues that adolescent differentiation begins at puberty as one starts to modify the existing body image and that libidinal object constancy can be observed in late adolescence when youths adopt social roles and become capable of relating to parents in a new way. In Josselson's (1980) view, the second individuation process spans the time of latency and adolescence; parallels to infant symbiosis, differentiation, and practicing are to be found in the latency phrase alone. Symbiosis is reflected in the child's emotional dependence on parents. Practicing is demonstrated by the child's increasing locomotor and interpersonal abilities. Esman (1980) has depicted early adolescence as a time of "massive hatching," with parallels to the infant differentiation subphase. Mid-adolescence is seen as a time of practicing, and late adolescence as a time of integration and consolidation parallel to Mahler's final separation-individuation subphase. I have suggested that the second individuation process is a phenomenon generally addressed in late (rather than early or mid) adolescence, based on longitudinal research exploring intrapsychic structural features of the identity statuses (Kroger, 1989).

Normative adolescent separation-individuation has been investigated empirically through identity and intimacy status research and research on egocentrism. Currie (1983), Josselson (1987), Kroger (1985), Kroger and Haslett (1988), Kroger (1990), and Papini, Micka, and Barnett (1989) have all examined separation-individuation issues in relation to the identity statuses; furthermore, all of these studies found foreclosure subjects to evidence a structural organization still governed by the parental introjects. Additionally, all studies found identity achievements to be more differentiated from the parental introjects than foreclosures. Moratoriums of these identity status investigations generally evidenced more mixed patterns on separation-individuation measures, possibly reflecting different intrapsychic subphases that may underlie this transitional identity status. Bellew-Smith and Korn (1986), Levitz-Jones and Orlofsky (1985), and Millis (1983) have all examined the second separation-individuation process in relation to Orlofsky's intimacy statuses (Levitz-Jones & Orlofsky, 1985). All three studies found more disorders of separation-individuation in low (stereotypic, pseudointimate, and isolate) and merger intimacy statuses than in high (pre-intimate and intimate) intimacy groups. Using Levine, Green, and Millon's (1986) Separation-Individuation Test of Adolescence in cross-sectional research, Lapsley, Fitzgerald, Rice, and Jackson (1989) have indicated that the imaginary audience and personal fable may serve different functions during the second separation-individuation process; the imaginary audience may be an expression of anxiety associated with the loss of internalized objects, while the personal fable may serve as a defense against such loss.

Investigating the Adolescent Second
Separation-Individuation Process:
Conceptual and Methodological Issues

Further theoretical refinements in the application of Mahler's separation-individuation construct to adolescence should aim to examine, more precisely, the process and timing by which the internalized representation of the primary caretaking figure is relinquished. Both infants and adolescents are faced with the need to modify existing body images; however, application of the separation-individuation model to describe alterations in adolescent self-image due to changes in body structure (i. e., Brandt, 1977) does not address the underlying intrapsychic dynamics of differentiating from the parental introject. Josselson's (1980) descriptions also present some problems in interpretation. For example, latency is described not only as a time of practicing but also as one of symbiosis in relation to the internalized parent; early adolescence is later described in what may be seen as a return to the differentiation subphase (Feldberg, 1986). Lack of precision in drawing parallels to Mahler's subphases continues in Josselson's silence regarding both differentiation as well as the final separation-individuation subphase of libidinal object constancy. Additionally, there has often been lack of clear distinction between internalized and external objects in theoretical discussions of adolescent separation-individuation, as well as great diversity in descriptions of timing for the second individuation process. Future research should aim to more precisely delineate specific changes in both internalized and external relationships throughout the adolescent years in order to reconcile present conflicting descriptions of both content and timing of the second individuation process. Peers and other significant adults may be serving as transitional objects in a movement that is far lengthier than our present accounts indicate; there may be even more than one cycle of separation-individuation as adolescents come to relinquish the parental introject and then transitional objects in restructuring the intrapsychic foundations of identity.

Additional conceptual problems have occurred in accounts of the second separation-individuation process. At times, "separation-individuation" has been equated with "separation" by some adolescent theorists and researchers, depicted as movement away from relatedness or as movement from dependence to independence. This bipolar conceptualization does not reflect the meaning of the separation-individuation process described by Mahler. Through the separation-individuation subphases of infancy, Mahler describes a series of qualitatively different levels in the ways by which a child comes to attain a newfound sense of autonomy as well as a new kind of relationship to the primary caregiver of reality. Indeed, the healthy outcome of libidinal object constancy is this very ability to integrate both dependence and independence needs (Mahler et al., 1975). Josselson (1987, 1988) makes an important plea for the integration of autonomy and relationship in our theories of adolescent and adult development. However, she, too, at times appears to conceptualize separation-individuation in bipolar terms as movement away from relationship: "To study separation-individuation in women is a disorienting task because women tend to grow within rather than out of relationships" (Josselson, 1987, p. 189). Movement out of relationship is not at issue in any second separation-individuation process of adolescence; rather, change in the quality of how one is both related and autonomous as a result of differentiation from internalized object ties are its hallmarks for both sexes.

Levine (1987) has articulated a similar point of concern in his discussion of measurement instruments designed to assess any adolescent separation-individuation process. Levine argues, for example, that the Psychological Separation Inventory developed by Hoffman (1984) purports to extend Mahler's concept of the separation-individuation process to adolescence but, in fact, assesses only aspects of independence. By conceptualizing separation-individuation as movement from dependence to independence, Hoffman assumes that the phenomenon can be measured on some interval scale; separation-individuation is thus an entity that one "has," to greater or lesser degree. This approach clearly does not address any sequence of qualitatively distinct integrations implied through Mahler's model of separation-individuation subphases. Efforts that evaluate various qualitative dimensions of adolescent separation-individuation, such as the Separation-Individuation Theme Scale (Coonerty, 1989) and Levine, Green, and Millon's (1986) Separation-Individuation Test of Adolescence, may prove more useful tools in examining this movement process. Future instruments attempting to assess separation-individuation in adolescence must be conceptually clear about the phenomena they purport to measure. The "quality" rather than "quantity" of differentiation and relatedness must be addressed in any measures of the second separation-individuation process.

In general, empirical investigations of adolescent separation-individuation reviewed earlier have pointed to structural change from an organization governed by the parental introjects to one that has restructured these object ties. However, from some of these same investigations there is also evidence that different defensive operations may be used within both foreclosed and achieved identity status groupings. Foreclosed subjects have shown both high separation anxiety as well as high detachment scores on a measure of separation anxiety (Kroger 1985; Kroger

& Haslett, 1988); furthermore, Levitz-Jones and Orlofsky (1985) note that merger and low intimacy groups may be dealing with threats of internalized object loss through the desire either for fusion or for detachment. The work of Lapsley et al. (1989) also notes the possibility of different defensive strategies used to maintain object ties. A surprisingly high percentage of identity achieved subjects have shown patterns of excessive self-sufficiency or detachment in addition to the most common secure attachment profile (Kroger & Haslett, 1988, unpublished raw data). Further attention to the nature of defenses maintaining intrapsychic structural arrangements are in order.

Contributions from Constructive-Developmental Theory and Research: Kegan and Noam

Robert Kegan (1982) has offered a life-span model of ego developmental change. The ego, in Kegan's view, is an internal unitary structure or balance between that which is taken to be self and that which is regarded as other. Ego development over the course of the life span is a dynamic process, "a creative motion" of finding, relinquishing, and creating new balances between self and other. Developmental stands, such as Piagetian stages of logic and Kohlberg's stages of moral reasoning, arise from a "bigger context" according to Kegan; this "bigger context" is an intrapsychic organization, a self-other balance, which subtends both cognition and affect and gives rise to all meaning-making activity.

Basic to Kegan's model are a sequence of hierarchically organized self-other stages that reflect increasing levels of differentiation and integration. Self (or subject) refers to that which one *is*—to that in which one is embedded and is unable to gain distance from or take a perspective on. Thus, the young child *is* its impulses and perceptions and is unable to take a perspective on them. Other (or object) refers to that which one is able to take a perspective upon and relate to. Thus, this child (originally a self embedded in impulses and perceptions) gradually develops a self that is able to coordinate its impulses and perceptions (now object). It is only when a self has emerged capable of coordinating its own impulses and perceptions (other) that this child no longer believes it is the external world which goes dark upon closing the eyes (Kegan, 1982).

Kegan's life-span developmental model traces changing boundaries between that which is taken as self and that regarded as other through five stages (incorporative [0], impulsive [1], imperial [2], interpersonal [3], institutional [4], and interindividual [5]). The infant enters the world without self-other boundary; during this incorporative stage (0), his or her world lacks any distinction between internal and external—the infant *is* its reflexes and sensations. Gradually, object permanence and separation anxiety come into existence. Kegan suggests that these abilities may be cognitive and affective expressions of a single underlying phenomenon—a self now separating from an embeddedness in its reflexes and beginning to organize them as elements of a more complicated system. By holding in memory the image of an object or person (requirements for both object permanence and separation anxiety), the self of the infant now is a large system capable of organizing its reflexes and sensations; to hold in memory one's own experiencing (to have it rather than be it) requires a more differentiated system than that present during the incorporative stage. Thus, the impulsive self (stage 1) of the preschool years gradually emerges. Now able to take as object its own reflexes and sensations, the child becomes embedded in a new system—that of impulses and perceptions. Here, the self *is* its impulses and perceptions, unable to differentiate from, organize, or act upon them. "Though the child has become differentiated enough to recognize that the whole world is not an extension of herself, she remains embedded in her impulses and perceptions and confuses real others with these" (Kegan, Noam, & Rogers, 1982). It is from this balance that the child views people in the distance to *be* the size of ants—not to *appear like* the size of ants (Kegan, 1982). Transformation from this balance involves yet another loss, as that which was subject (impulses and perceptions) becomes object to still another more complicated system—a self now embedded in its own needs and wishes. This imperial (stage 2) self of the primary school-aged child is capable of organizing or taking as object its impulses and perceptions. Here, one can no longer be fooled by how things look—a dessert pastry cut in half still has the same amount, even though it has been cut in two pieces. However, this same imperial self is unable internally to hold more than one point of view; in this organization, "there is only one guy home inside" and what makes sense is how the world can best meet *his* needs.

What, then, are the self-other balances normatively observed during adolescence? With time, that childhood imperial self embedded in his or her own needs evolves into an adolescent interpersonal self (stage 3) now internally able to coordinate these needs and wishes with those of other people: "*She* becomes something more as the interpersonal and intrapsychic coordinator between needs perspectives" (Kegan, Noam, & Rogers, 1982, p. 113, italics added). At the same time, however, the individual within the interpersonal balance is intrapsychically embedded in a context of mutuality that sets new limits to the self's way of creating sense. Now one *is* one's relationships; no subject exists apart from the interpersonal matrix to be able to organize or take a perspective upon its relationships. What or how the self feels is a direct result of another person's evaluation, for there is not yet a more differentiated internal structure itself capable of evaluating this other's response. The result of the interpersonal (stage 3) to institutional (stage 4) shift is self-authorship, generally not seen until late adolescence or adulthood. The self of the institutional stage (4) now is able to speak from an internal authority, differentiated from its former embeddedness in shared realities and capable of taking as object these contents of its experience. "The strength of stage 4 is its psychological self-employment, its capacity to own oneself, rather than having all the pieces of oneself owned by various shared contexts" (Kegan, Noam, & Rogers, 1982, p. 115). It is only now that one can *have* (rather than be) his or her relationships, for a self now exists that is no longer subject to mutuality. Yet within the institutional balance, there is a new form of self-embeddedness, which, in turn, sets new limits to ways of making sense. Now, the self is subject to its own ideologies, with no larger context from which to organize these belief systems and take a perspective upon them. Kegan cites Erikson here in noting that the stage 4 self is inevitably ideological, requiring recognition and support by a group upholding those principles in which the self has now become embedded. Thus, for those late adolescents in the institutional balance, there is a self that has chosen its own commitments and affiliations but is not yet able to organize or reflect upon these valuing systems. It is only from the stage 5 interpersonal balance that this capacity is present. Here, the interpersonal self is no longer embedded in or identified with *what* it authors, but can now take a perspective on *how* it generates its own valuing systems. Kegan has found this stage 5 structure of meaning-making only rarely in his studies of adult subjects.

Assessment of subject-object balance is done through an extensive semistructured interview developed by Kegan and his colleagues (Lahey et al., 1987). This interview, lasting approximately 1-1/2 hours, asks the interviewee to select from among a series of key emotions (e.g., anger, success, anxiety) one that brings to mind a particular situation; the interviewer then carefully probes the subject's construction of his or her experience. The focus is not on the *content* of the issue (*why* one is angry), but rather on *structure*—on *how* the self must be constructed in order to experience the particular emotion in this way. The interview rating system also identifies four transition points along the continuum between all adjacent subject-object balances. The interview and assessment training manual reports four studies of interrater reliability, one of test-retest reliability, and one of inter-item consistency (Lahey et al., 1987). When interrater agreement of subject-object balance is defined as falling within one discrimination (1/5 stage), agreement percentages between two raters were 82%, 100%, 100%, and 100% across the four studies. The one study of test-retest reliability conducted to date reports a Pearson $r = .834$ ($p<.0001$) when agreement is defined as falling within one discrimination (1/5 stage). From the one study addressing the issue of inter-item consistency, correlation of scores between two forms of the interview was .96.

Research utilizing the constructive-developmental approach to explore questions of subject-object balance during late adolescence have been limited, in part as a result of the model's own infancy. Noam and his associates have been developing a subject-object interview to explore consistency across different domains of concern in adolescence (Noam, 1989). In a small pilot study, I have explored possible links between Kegan's constructive-developmental stages of meaning-making with other "deep" measures of ego development in adolescence (Kroger, 1989), and a more extensive longitudinal investigation is currently in progress. Research might usefully ask what intrapsychic predictors (if any) appear for those adolescents likely to remain arrested within the imperial or interpersonal balances during their late adolescent and adult years.

Constructive Developmental Theory:
Conceptual and Methodological Issues

Criticism of Kegan's constructive-developmental scheme has come from several directions. Questions have been raised regarding structural unity, the relationship between development and psychopathology, and the very nature of the balances serving as the basis of the evolutionary scheme itself (Damon & Hart, 1988; Noam, 1988). Noam has questioned the underlying logical structure of Kegan's scheme in asking what the impulses defining stage 1, the needs of stage 2, the relationships of stage 3, the institutions of stage 4, and the interdependence of stage 5 have in common that make them part of one developmental sequence. I would argue here that briefly presenting such issues in a way that emphasizes contents has caused the underlying nature of structural systems to be lost. When subject-object balances are viewed in terms of an underlying organizational system disembedding from increasingly more comprehensive systems of order or authority—for example, one's own need's and wishes (stage 2), the needs and wishes of other people (stage 3), and then one's own values and ideologies (stage 4)—the logic to this ordering system becomes more apparent.

In an attempt to present a more comprehensive model of development, Noam has introduced the notions of encapsulation and core theme. He suggests that encapsulations, or pockets of old meaning systems that are governed by the logic at the time of origin, sometimes remain unaccommodated when structural transformation occurs. In this way, structural change may take place in late adolescence, yet various encapsulations of earlier life experience remain unchanged, coexisting with a higher level of subject-object balance and producing ways of making sense that may seem to fluctuate considerably between less mature and more mature organizations. Certain core themes, based on previous life experiences, may actually arrest structural development (for example, being abandoned by an important other in childhood may make transition to the interpersonal stage difficult in adolescence). Noam suggests that some larger, more comprehensive system of individual biography may, in fact, "hold" subject-object balances.

Kegan and Rogers (1989), on the other hand, argue that such accounts still interpret present functioning in terms of early trauma or developmental failure and do not address the specifically adolescent or adult forms that psychopathology may take. Rather than conceptualizing psychopathology as lack of *integration* between structure and encapsulations as does Noam, Kegan and Rogers seek to understand psychopathology as dispositional qualities within existing structural organizations—in other words, Kegan and Rogers address questions of both *what* is taken as subject and object as well as *how* the object is taken within one's present structural framework. Research addressing *how* an object is held could serve to clarify the nature of the relationship between current subject-object balance and biography, particularly in studies of late adolescence when psychopathology often first appears.

As an assessment technique, Kegan's subject-object interview requires great skill as well as time to administer and rate; however, an alternative format would risk misrepresentation of underlying structure by not allowing a subject to demonstrate the limits of his or her own meaning-making system. Not only do subject-object interviews aim to identify a subject's meaning-making balance but they also must demonstrate that no alternative organization could be an accurate descriptor of the interviewee's meaning-making structure. Such thoroughness in assessment is commendable. Attention to specific phases of organization in the transition process is also a valuable contribution made by the subject-object interviewing procedure to our understanding of developmental processes.

THE QUESTION OF A UNITARY SELF

Within each of the three developmental models reviewed, critics have questioned a conceptualization of the ego as a *unitary* structural organization that undergoes developmental change. From Marcia's elaboration of Erikson's fifth developmental stage, Waterman (1985) and others have questioned the meaning of a global identity assessment when ratings across domains are so frequently discrepant. Within object relations theory, Stern (1985) has critiqued Mahler's unitary model of infant ego development, arguing that four different senses of self emerge from birth and remain fully functioning and coexisting throughout the life cycle. Noam (1988) and Damon and Hart (1988) have questioned Kegan's (1982) assumption of a unitary structure, subtending both cognition and affect. Arguments from all of these critics draw upon issues of inconsistency in patterns of development that have been demonstrated across domains of self. It would seem important, therefore, to address the meaning of the term *consistency* before generating any conclusions about the nature of structural unity.

In relation to the question of structural unity, consistency can be understood in several ways (Lahey, 1986). Consistency can refer to a single organizing tendency that implies people will demonstrate a common rating across issues when participating in interviews designed to tap any deep structure of ego organization. Consistency can also be understood in terms of the use of different though closely related structural organizations. In terms of Kegan's model, Lahey (1986) has noted that consistency can also be expressed when one uses two (but no more than two) different subject-object structures. When a structural organization is in transition, there will not be uniformity of ratings across domains, but rather a mix of ratings from adjacent developmental positions.

Continuing from Lahey's comments, most identity status research has been conducted with late adolescents and young adults in university settings, an age span and social context in which structural transition is anticipated. To test for consistency during such a time and make claims against the case of structural unity is inappropriate, given such sample bias. However, we may learn much through such sample populations about the course of structural transition. Studying identity status ratings across domains in samples of young adult employees, for example, would seem a better test of consistency and structural unity within the identity status model. Lahey's (1986) constructive-developmental investigation of consistency among young adult subjects was made with this issue in mind. Additionally, the identity status interview may be tapping issues that are simply not salient for assessing an individual's underlying identity structure, thereby producing results with varying congruences across domains. An identity status interview that allows the individual choice in the domains for assessment may provide both a more accurate index of identity structure and a better test of the consistency hypothesis. Such a procedure is presently employed in assessment of subject-object balances by Kegan and his associates (Lahey et al., 1987). At this point, there have been too few investigations probing structural dimensions of identity within any given model to present answers to questions regarding unity of organization. However, when consistency is viewed in terms of the meanings described previously, limited evidence supports the notion of a unitary structure underlying the various domains of identity (Berzonsky, 1988; Carroll, 1986; Kroger, 1986, 1988; Lahey, 1986; Rogow, Marcia, & Slugoski, 1983). When further investigations are undertaken, it is important to consider both the meanings consistency holds as well as the salience of domains used to assess structural organization.

SUMMARY AND DIRECTIONS FOR FUTURE RESEARCH

This chapter has reviewed three theoretical models addressing intrapsychic reorganization during late adolescence; each is based upon a structural rather than functional conceptualization of the ego. Though speaking through different languages, Erikson ego psychoanalytic psychology, adaptations of Mahler's object relations approach, and constructive-developmental theory have all described intrapsychic restructuring during late adolescence as a process in which internalized points of view (or identifications), which have previously determined the self's organization, now instead become mediated by it. Within ego psychoanalytic psychology, cautions have been raised regarding the meaning of Marcia's identity statuses when applied to age spans other than late adolescence; questions have also been raised about the value of various identity status assessment techniques for identifying underlying structural organization. Theoretical discussions of the second separation-individuation process point to the need for greater conceptual clarity and precision in examining the relationship between internalized self and object representations as the parental introject is relinquished. Constructive-developmental accounts of normative development in late adolescence have provided some of the most comprehensive descriptions of mechanisms underlying structural change, though research is still in its infancy. Questions have also been raised regarding the concept of a unitary self; this chapter has stressed the need to consider various meanings of consistency as well as methods of assessment when empirically testing its existence. Theoretical refinement and future research should aim for greater precision in addressing qualitatively different integrations of internalized self and object representations during the process of ego restructuring during late adolescence.

REFERENCES

Adams, G. R., & Fitch, S. A. (1981). Ego stage and identity status development: A cross-lag analysis. *Journal of Adolescence, 4*, 163-171.

Adams, G. R., & Shea, J. A. (1979). The relationship between identity status, locus of control, and ego development. *Journal of Youth and Adolescence, 8*, 81-89.

Archer, S. L. (1982). The lower age boundaries of identity development. *Child Development, 53*, 1551-1556.

Bellew-Smith, M., & Korn, J. H. (1986). Merger intimacy status in adult women. *Journal of Personality and Social Psychology, 50*, 1186-1191.

Berzonsky, M. D. (1988, March). *The structure of identity.* Paper presented at the biennial meeting of the Society for Research on Adolescence, Alexandria, VA.

Blos, P. (1967). The second individuation process of adolescence. *Psychoanalytic Study of the Child, 22*, 162-186.

Bourne, E. (1978). The state of research on ego identity: A review and appraisal. Part II. *Journal of Youth and Adolescence, 8*, 371-392.

Brandt, D. E. (1977). Separation and identity in adolescence: Mahler and Erikson—some similarities. *Contemporary Psychology, 13*, 507-518.

Carroll, B. (1986). *Subject and object: Changes in structure between the ages of five and seven.* Unpublished doctoral dissertation, Harvard University.

Coonerty, S. (1989, April). An exploration of change in separation-individuation themes in the borderline disorder. In W. H. Berman (Chair), *Separation-Individuation and attachment: Contributions of empirical research to psychoanalytic theory.* Symposium conducted at the annual meeting of Division of Psychoanalysis, American Psychological Association, Boston.

Currie, P. S. (1983). Current attachment patterns, attachment history, and religiosity as predictors of ego-identity status in fundamentalist Christian adolescents. *Dissertation Abstracts International, 44*B, 1955B (University Microfilms No. DA83223811).

Damon, W., & Hart, D. (1988). *Self-understanding in childhood and adolescence.* Cambridge: Cambridge University Press.

Donovan, J. M. (1975a). Identity status and interpersonal style. *Journal of Youth and Adolescence, 4*, 37-55.

Donovan, J. M. (1975b). Identity status: Its relationship to Rorschach performance and to daily life pattern. *Adolescence, 10*, 29-44.

Erikson, E. H. (1968). *Identity: Youth and crisis.* New York: Norton.

Esman, A. H. (1980). *Adolescent Psychiatry, 8*, 320-331.

Feldberg, A. (1986). Adolescent separation, individuation, and identity (re)formation: Theoretical extension and modifications. *Dissertation Abstracts International, 46*B, 2834B (University Microfilms No. DA8523268).

Ginsburg, S. D., & Orlofsky, J. L. (1981). Ego identity status, ego development, and locus of control in college women. *Journal of Youth and Adolescence, 10,* 297-307.

Grotevant, H. D. (1983). The contribution of the family to the facilitation of identity formation in early adolescence. *Journal of Early Adolescence, 3,* 225-237.

Harter, S. (1983). Developmental perspectives on the self-system. In P. H. Mussen (Ed.), *Handbook of child psychology* (Vol. 4). New York: John Wiley.

Hoffman, J. A. (1984). Psychological separation of late adolescents from their parents. *Journal of Counseling Psychology, 31,* 170-178.

Hopkins, L. B. (1982). Assessment of identity status in college women using outer space and inner space interviews. *Sex Roles, 8,* 557-566.

Josselson, R. L. (1973). Psychodynamic aspects of identity formation in college women. *Journal of Youth and Adolescence, 2,* 3-52.

Josselson, R. (1980). Ego development in adolescence. In J. Adelson (Ed.), *Handbook of adolescent psychology.* New York: John Wiley.

Josselson, R. (1982). Personality structure and identity status in women viewed through early memories. *Journal of Youth and Adolescence, 11,* 293-299.

Josselson, R. (1987). *Finding herself: Pathways to identity development in women.* San Francisco: Jossey-Bass.

Josselson, R. (1988). The embedded self: I and thou revisited. In D. K. Lapsley & F. C. Power (Eds.), *Self, ego, and identity: Integrative approaches* (pp. 91-108). New York: Springer-Verlag.

Kegan, R. (1982). *The evolving self: Problem and process in human development.* Cambridge, MA: Harvard University Press.

Kegan, R., Noam, G., & Rogers, L. (1982). The psychologic of emotion: A neo-Piagetian view. In D. Chichetti & P. Hesse (Eds.) *New directions for child development: No. 16. Emotional development.* San Francisco: Jossey-Bass.

Kegan, R., & Rogers, L. (1989, May). *"Mental growth" and "mental health" as distinct concepts in the study of developmental psychopathology: Theory, research, and clinical implications.* Paper presented at the First Harvard Conference on Development and Psychopathology, Cambridge, MA.

Kirshner, L. A. (1988). Implications of Loevinger's theory of ego development for time-limited psychotherapy. *Psychotherapy, 25,* 220-226.

Kroger, J. (1985). Separation-individuation and ego identity status in New Zealand university students. *Journal of Youth and Adolescence, 14,* 133-147.

Kroger, J. (1986). The relative importance of identity status interview components: Replication and extension. *Journal of Adolescence, 9,* 337-354.

Kroger, J. (1988). A longitudinal study of ego identity status interview domains. *Journal of Adolescence, 11,* 49-64.

Kroger, J. (1989). *Identity in adolescence: The balance between self and other.* London: Routledge.

Kroger, J. (1990). Ego structuralization in late adolescence as seen through early memories and ego identity status. *Journal of Adolescence, 13,* 65-77.

Kroger, J., & Haslett, S. J. (1987). A retrospective study of ego identity status change by mid-life adults. *Social and Behavioral Sciences Documents, 17* (Ms. No. 2797).

Kroger, J., & Haslett, S. J. (1988). Separation-individuation and ego identity status in late adolescence: A two-year longitudinal study. *Journal of Youth and Adolescence, 17,* 59-79.

Lahey, L. (1986). *Males' and females' construction of conflict in work and love.* Unpublished doctoral dissertation, Harvard University.

Lahey, L., Souvaine, E., Kegan, R., Goodman, R., & Felix, S. (1987). *A guide to the subject-object interview: Its administration and interpretation.* Unpublished manuscript, Harvard University Graduate School of Education.

Lapsley, D. K., Fitzgerald, D. P., Rice, K. G., & Jackson, S. (1989). Separation-individuation and the "new look" at the imaginary audience and personal fable: A test of an integrative model. *Journal of Adolescent Research, 4,* 483-505.

Levine, J. B. (1987). A comprehensive analysis of the discriminant and external validity, normative properties, and theoretical contributions of the separation-individuation test of adolescence. *Dissertation Abstracts International, 48B,* 1155B (University Microfilms No. DA8716165).

Levine, J. B., Green, C. J., & Millon, T. (1986). Separation-individuation test of adolescence. *Journal of Personality Assessment, 50,* 123-137.

Levitz-Jones, E. M., & Orlofsky, J. L. (1985). Separation-individuation and intimacy capacity in college women. *Journal of Personality and Social Psychology, 49,* 156-169.

Loevinger, J. (1976). *Ego development: Conceptions and theories.* San Francisco: Jossey-Bass.

Mahler, M., Pine, F., & Bergman, A. (1975). *The psychological birth of the human infant.* New York: Basic Books.

Marcia, J. E. (1966). Development and validation of ego identity status. *Journal of Personality and Social Psychology, 3,* 551-558.

Marcia, J. E. (1980). Identity in adolescence. In J. Adelson (Ed.), *Handbook of adolescent psychology* (pp. 159-187). New York: John Wiley.

Marcia, J. E. (1989, July). Implications of methodologies for identity theory: The identity status interview. In H. E. Bosma & J. E. Marcia (Chairs), *Different approaches in identity research in adolescence: An unnecessary or an essential proliferation.* Symposium conducted at the biennial meeting of the International Society for the Study of Behavioral Development, Jyvaskyla, Finland.

Mills, S. R. (1984). Separation-individuation and intimacy status in young adulthood. *Dissertation Abstracts International, 45B,* 2695B. (University Microfilms No. DA8425396).

Noam, G. (1988). A constructivist approach to developmental psychopathology. In E. D. Nannis & P. A. Cowan (Eds.), *New directions for child development: No. 39. Developmental psychopathology and its treatment.* San Francisco: Jossey-Bass.

Noam, G. (1989). *Interpersonal self and biography interview.* Unpublished manuscript, McLean Hospital, Harvard Medical School.

Orlofsky, J., & Frank, M. (1986). Personality structure as viewed through early memories and identity status in college men and women. *Journal of Personality and Social Psychology, 50,* 580-586.

Papini, D. R., Micka, J. C., & Barnett, J. K. (1989). Perceptions of intrapsychic and extrapsychic functioning as bases of adolescent ego identity statuses. *Journal of Adolescent Research, 4,* 462-482.

Rogow, A. M., Marcia, J. E., & Slugoski, B. R. The relative importance of identity status interview components. *Journal of Youth and Adolescence,* 1983, *12,* 387-400.

Schmid-Kitsikis, E. (1972). Exploratory studies in cognitive development. In F. J. Monks, W. W. Hartup, & J. de Wit (Eds.), *Determinants of behavioral development.* New York: Academic Press.

Snarey, J., Kohlberg, L., & Noam, G. (1983). Ego development in perspective: Structural stage, functional phase, and cultural age-period models. *Developmental Review, 3,* 303-338.

Stern, D. N. (1985). *The interpersonal world of the infant.* New York: Basic Books.

Waterman, A. S. (1985). Identity in the context of adolescent psychology. In A. S. Waterman (Ed.), *New Directions for child development: No. 30. Identity in adolescence: Processes and contents.* San Francisco: Jossey-Bass.

8. Ethnic Identity in Adolescence: Process, Context, and Outcome

Jean S. Phinney
California State University, Los Angeles

Doreen A. Rosenthal
The University of Melbourne

INTRODUCTION

The achievement of a positive, coherent identity is a fundamental goal for adolescents (Erikson, 1968). Their critical task is to select and integrate childhood identifications, together with personal inclinations and the opportunities afforded by society, in order to construct a sense of who they are and what they will become. An understanding of this process requires an appreciation of the psychological, social, and cultural web in which the individual grows and changes.

For adolescents from ethnic minority groups, the process of identity formation has an added dimension due to their exposure to alternative sources of identification, their own ethnic group and the mainstream or dominant culture. Growing up in a society where the mainstream culture may differ significantly in values and beliefs from their culture of origin, these youth face the task of achieving a satisfactory and satisfying integration of ethnic identity into a self-identity. The ease, or difficulty, with which this task is accomplished depends on a number of factors, which are the focus of this chapter. In particular, minority adolescents may have to confront issues of prejudice and discrimination, structural barriers which limit their aspirations and hinder their achievements, and other features of the mainstream society that differentiate them from the majority. If minority youth are to construct a strong, positive, and stable self-identity, then they must be able to incorporate into that sense of self a positively valued ethnic identity.

145

Ethnic identity has been studied almost exclusively as a phenomenon of relevance to minority groups. Although the concept of ethnic identity can be extended to majority group adolescents, ethnicity is generally not salient for them (Deschamps, 1982; McGuire, McGuire, Child, & Fujioka, 1978), and thus it has little or no importance as an identity issue (Driedger, 1976; Phinney & Alipuria, 1990; Phinney & Tarver, 1988). There is little research on this topic, and this chapter does not address it.

Our purpose is to examine the process of ethnic identity formation in youth from a variety of ethnic minorities, focusing particularly on the interaction between contextual and developmental factors as this process unfolds. Of course, the experiences of minority youth vary widely. In the United States, the focus of research has been on African-Americans, Hispanics, Asian-Americans, and Native Americans, in large part because of the problems these groups have faced, for both historical and social reasons. Other ethnic minorities, primarily those from European backgrounds, have been subject to fewer negative messages from the mainstream society. For these adolescents the path to acceptance of and pride in their ethnicity may be less problematic.

There is little research that examines the distinction between Caucasian minority groups and minority groups of color; that is, between racial identity and ethnic identity within a racial group. Researchers comparing ethnic identity across groups have generally made comparisons within racial categories (Driedger, 1976; Rosenthal & Hrynevich, 1985) or compared racially different groups with the Caucasian majority (Phinney & Alipuria, 1990). However, there are several obvious differences between ethnic identity based only on culture or country of origin and that based on race. First, racially similar minority groups can eventually assimilate into a dominant society (although this may be difficult for recent immigrants). The option of complete assimilation is not present for racially distinct groups. Therefore, for minorities of color there is less latitude in the ways of establishing an ethnic identity. Second, although prejudice and discrimination have existed against some racially similar groups, such as European immigrants in the United States and Australia, negative attitudes and behaviors have been far less widespread and less virulent than against racially distinct minorities. Phinney, Lochner, and Murphy (1990) suggest that dealing with prejudice and discrimination is a central aspect of ethnic identity formation, especially for minorities of color.

In addition, there are crucial distinctions among various ethnic groups. Each ethnic group has both its own culture and traditions and its own history within a particular society. Ogbu (1987) points out that ethnic groups have become part of another culture for widely differing reasons, including conquest, slavery, political asylum, and economic opportunity. They have brought their own values, attitudes, and practices to the interface with another culture. They have been faced with varying degrees of acceptance and rejection by the dominant group.

It is with differences such as these in mind that we turn to an analysis of the development of ethnic identity in minority youth. We examine the ways in which ethnic identity is conceptualized and the contexts in which ethnic identity formation takes place— the family, the community, and the wider society. The last section reviews evidence regarding the relationships of ethnic identity to self-esteem. The chapter concludes with an integration of these various strands and implications for future research.

THE CONCEPTUALIZATION OF ETHNIC IDENTITY IN ADOLESCENCE

Ethnic identity refers to "one's sense of belonging to an ethnic group and the part of one's thinking, perception, feelings, and behavior that is due to ethnic group membership" (Rotheram & Phinney, 1987, p. 13). Most writers agree that the construct includes some or all of the following components: self-identification as member of a group, feelings of belonging and commitment to a group, positive (or negative) attitudes toward the group, a sense of shared attitudes and values, and specific ethnic traditions and practices, such as language, behavior, and customs. Each of these components highlights a different dimension of the construct. Self-identification, or the ethnic label used to describe oneself, is important since it locates the individual within a particular cultural framework. However, an individual may self-identify without feeling strongly committed to the group, so an expressed sense of attachment is also important. The extent to which individuals adopt the ways of their culture is indicated by their participation in activities such as language, friendship networks, religious affiliation, food preference, exogamy, and traditional customs. Finally, since identification with an ethnic group is not necessarily accompanied by positive feelings about that group, the evaluative meaning given to group membership is a critical component.

In studying ethnic identity, researchers have generally selected certain of these components and developed their own measures for application to a particular ethnic group (e.g., Driedger, 1976; Giles, Taylor, Lambert, & Albert, 1976; Rosenthal & Hrynevich, 1985; Taft, 1985; Ting-Toomey, 1981). While this research has yielded rich findings about particular groups, the use of widely differing definitions and measures limits the ability to make comparisons and generalizations across studies (see Phinney, 1990, for a recent review).

A general measure of ethnic identity that can be used with adolescents and young adults from various groups has recently been proposed (Phinney, 1992). The measure focuses on aspects that are common across all groups, assessing attitudes toward the group and feelings of belonging, as well as the process of ethnic identity formation: the extent of exploration of, and commitment to, one's ethnicity. In ethnically diverse high school and college samples, all the components were found to load on a single factor, suggesting a unified construct. This measure, however, does not include other aspects of identification with one's ethnic group, such as language usage or specific cultural knowledge and practices, which many writers have considered to be central to ethnic identity. There is a growing body of research that demonstrates the importance of conceptualizing ethnic identity as a multifaceted, dynamic construct (Garcia, 1982; Giles et al., 1976; Giles, Llado, McKirnan, & Taylor, 1979; Rosenthal & Hrynevich, 1985), with complex and subtle interactions between different elements of ethnic identity and external forces (Rosenthal & Feldman, in press a, in press b).

Nevertheless, most researchers have typically taken a "snapshot" approach to studying ethnic identity, with little attention given to the ways in which it develops. Much research stemming from a social psychological perspective, and in particular social identity theory as elaborated by Tajfel and his colleagues (1978, 1981), focuses on ethnic identity at a given point in the adolescent's history and attempts, for example, to map those elements that are salient for a particular group, or to explore correlates of ethnic identity.

In contrast, a smaller body of work has taken a developmental perspective and has looked at the process of ethnic identity formation. Much of this work has dealt with African-Americans, although other minority groups have been considered from this perspective (Arce, 1981; Atkinson, Morten, & Sue, 1983; Cross, 1978; Parham & Helms, 1981). Ethnic or racial identity is seen in this work as developing from a state of low ethnic awareness, and often preference for the majority culture, to an appreciation for and acceptance of one's ethnicity. In an extension of this process approach, Phinney and her associates (Phinney, 1989, 1990; Phinney & Alipuria, 1990) have drawn on the ego identity literature (Erikson, 1968; Marcia, 1980) as their conceptual framework, placing ethnic identity within the context of ego identity development.

Before turning to work linking ego identity and ethnic identity, it is important to note differences between the two concepts: (a) Ethnic identity is a social identity; its meaning is embedded in the culture to which one belongs. Although ego identity research has given increasing recognition to the impact of the family on identity formation, there has been little attention to the role of the wider context. (b) Ethnic identity deals with a given, one's heritage; it cannot be chosen in the way one can choose a profession or political identity, although the extent or manner of expressing ethnic identity can vary. The ego identity literature has emphasized those aspects of the self where youth can make choices among clear alternatives. (c) The importance and salience of ethnic identity vary among ethnic groups, and between majority and minority group members. The process of ego identity formation is assumed to be comparable for all adolescents, although research has focused on Caucasian youth from Western cultures. (d) Finally, ego identity has been studied primarily by psychologists focusing on adolescence, and by clinical psychologists and psychoanalysts, while ethnic identity has been studied from a wide range of theoretical perspectives, by social and developmental psychologists, sociologists, and anthropologists.

In spite of these differences, the ego identity framework provides important parallels to the study of ethnic identity. It is useful to think of ethnic identity as an additional domain of identity development for minority youth, and, in fact, ethnic identity achievement has been found to be significantly related to high scores on an independent measure of ego identity (Phinney, 1989). The three-stage model of ethnic identity formation proposed by Phinney (1989, 1990) integrates the process models of Arce (1981), Atkinson, Morten, and Sue (1983), Cross (1978), and Parham and Helms (1981), among others, and relates them to the model of ego identity formation proposed by Marcia (1980). Ethnic identity is seen as developing through a series of stages in a manner similar to that described by Waterman (1982) for ego identity.

The first stage is an unexamined ethnic identity. Early adolescents, as a result of negative ethnic images and stereotypes, may express an out-group preference. Alternatively, because of socialization in the family or community, they may have a positive sense of attachment to their ethnic group. In either case, attitudes at this stage have not been arrived at independently, but are derived from others, for example, their parents, community, or the larger society. By analogy with ego identity, ethnic identity at this stage may be thought of as foreclosed. In contrast, some adolescents, perhaps because of the absence of conflicts or salient experiences related to ethnicity, may have given little thought to or have been unconcerned about issues related to ethnicity and can be said to have a diffuse ethnic identity.

At some point, typically during adolescence, an experience that makes ethnicity salient is seen as triggering an exploration of what it means to be a member of a specific minority group in society. It is not clear what initiates the exploration (termed "encounter" by Cross, 1978); it may be a specific instance of prejudice, involvement in a structured ethnic awareness program, identity exploration in other domains, or experiences related to the gradual widening of the adolescent's world through school or work. This period is equivalent to the identity crisis or moratorium described by Erikson (1968) and studied by Marcia (1980) and others. Some of the issues that must be examined at this time are cultural differences between their group and the dominant group, the images and stereotypes of their group held by society, and the experiences of prejudice and discrimination (Phinney, et al., 1990).

The exploration stage is, ideally, followed by a resolution of the conflicts and contradictions posed by minority status in society. At this point, individuals make a commitment to a particular way of being a member of their group; they have an achieved ethnic identity, characterized by a secure sense of themselves as ethnic group members. Cross (1978) has termed this "internalization."

A recent longitudinal study (Phinney & Chavira, in press) showed a significant movement from lower to higher stages of ethnic identity between the ages of 16 and 19. In addition, interview studies of minority youth (Phinney, 1989; Phinney & Tarver, 1988) showed that more African-American 10th graders than 8th graders had explored their ethnicity. College undergraduates scored significantly higher than high school 11th and 12th graders on a questionnaire measure of ethnic identity achievement (Phinney, 1992). It appears that with increasing age, minority youth are more likely to have explored and resolved questions about the meaning of ethnicity as a component of their identity, that is, to have an achieved ethnic identity. However, as with ego identity (Marcia & Kowaz, 1988; Waterman, 1982), there may be regressions and reexaminations at various stages in the process. Even after achieving an ethnic identity, the issues may be reexamined subsequently as new conflicts or contradictions come to the fore (Parham, 1989).

In summary, while ethnic identity has been conceptualized as dynamic and multidimensional, studies have generally addressed only selected aspects of the construct, and relatively few have considered it developmentally. An adequate understanding requires an appreciation of the way developmental and contextual factors interact in the formation of ethnic identity in adolescence.

ETHNIC IDENTITY FORMATION: THE INTERACTION OF DEVELOPMENT AND CONTEXT

To understand the task faced by adolescents, we must consider both the early environment in which children first acquire a sense of themselves as ethnic group members and the contextual factors that influence their adolescent years. The family provides the earliest context for a developing sense of ethnicity and is a continuing influence throughout adolescence. Furthermore, the family's effectiveness in socializing a child as an ethnic group member will depend on the supports provided by the ethnic community. But even when the parents present a positive ethnic image and the ethnic community reinforces that image, the developing child is susceptible to society's images of the group, which may differ radically from their own. Young adolescents, then, facing the major task of ego identity achievement, must make sense of the variety of often contradictory knowledge, experience, attitudes, and images relative to their ethnicity that derive from their social context.

Family Influences on Ethnic Identity

There is considerable evidence that family environment shapes the development of minority adolescents in areas as diverse as socio-emotional development and school outcomes (see Spencer & Dornbusch, 1990, for a review). It is reasonable to expect that family influences on the formation and maintenance of ethnic identity in childhood are powerful and pervasive. The family is the source of children's first experiences related to ethnicity, and it is generally with the parents and other family members that children make their first identifications as part of a group. Family and significant others are the principal sources of information and influence providing a cultural context, a lens through which the child views the world. Families that participate with pleasure in their cultural traditions and express positive feelings about their group are likely to lay a basis for a positive ethnic identity.

Research with African-American families suggests that many African-American parents socialize their children to be proud of their race, with the goal of ensuring that the child develops positive feelings and self-confidence as an African-American individual (e.g., Harrison, 1985; Jaynes & Williams, 1989; Nobles, 1973; Peters, 1985; Thornton, Chatters, Taylor, & Allen, 1990). None of these studies actually takes the next step of evaluating whether this parental goal is realized, that is, whether racial socialization does have a significant impact on children's ethnic identity, although Spencer (1983) has shown that Eurocentric (out-group) attitudes are less common among young African-American children whose parents discuss racial discrimination and teach their children about African-American history.

What is clear is that the child brings to adolescence a view of his or her ethnic heritage that has been largely shaped by family influences. But to what extent does this influence extend to adolescence, and how do parental attitudes impact on adolescents' ethnic identity? There is a surprising dearth of research directed at exploring the ways in which parents and family shape an adolescent's sense of belonging to an ethnic group. At a very general level, it appears that parents' involvement in the ethnic community is related to their adolescent's sense of ethnic identity (Rosenthal & Cichello, 1986). However, the same study found that, with Italian adolescents, parental maintenance of traditional customs and norms of behavior was unrelated to adolescents' ethnic identity. A culturally traditional family may even create an environment in which adolescents have difficulty reconciling their ethnicity with their involvement in the mainstream culture (Rosenthal, 1987). Szapozcnik and Kurtines (1980) describe the conflicts that can result when rapidly acculturating adolescents clash with their more traditional parents over values and behaviors. Statements by Asian-American and Mexican-American high school students (Phinney & Chavira, in preparation) illustrate the kinds of family conflicts experienced by some minority youth:

> My parents are sort of old-fashioned, so they tell me that I have to do things. . . . Like, I am a girl so I am always sent to the kitchen to cook. . . . I am more Americanized and I don't believe in that girl thing. We end up in an argument and it does not get solved.

> Mexican culture is more inclined to hold you back as an adolescent. [Parents] try to hold you back and try to protect you more. . . . I try to talk it over with them; they still try to protect me.

Phinney and her colleagues (Phinney & Nakayama, 1991) have demonstrated that parental sensitivity to cultural diversity has positive outcomes for adolescent ethnic identity. Asian-American, African-American, and Mexican-American adolescents who scored high on a measure of ethnic identity (including ethnic practices, attitudes, and commitment) had parents who were significantly more likely than parents of low scorers to state that they had personally tried to prepare their son or daughter for living in a culturally diverse society.

In addition to modeling or discussing ethnic issues specifically, parents may influence adolescents in indirect ways. In a recent study with first- and second-generation Chinese adolescents in two Western cultures, Rosenthal and Feldman (in press a) showed that warm, regulating, autonomy-promoting parenting behaviors, which have been shown to lead to positive, well-socialized outcomes in children and adolescents (Maccoby & Martin, 1983; Steinberg, 1990), were predictive of ethnic pride, but not ethnic behaviors or knowledge. They suggest that adolescents whose parents act as positive role models are likely to take on other aspects of parental behaviors and values, specifically the value given by parents to their ethnic heritage.

In other studies of family context, the focus has been on structural factors, such as ethnic intermarriage and transracial adoption, both of which are assumed to result in a weakening of ethnic ties. The sparse evidence available suggests that children of interethnic marriages retain a positive identification with their ethnic origins (Alba & Chamin, 1983; Salgado de Snyder, Lopez, & Padilla, 1982; Yogev & Jamsky, 1983). Two studies of transracial adoption demonstrated a strong relationship between parents' attitudes and adolescents' self-definition. African-American adolescents who had been raised by Caucasian parents who deemphasized their adoptive children's racial or ethnic origins claimed a mixed (African-American/Caucasian) identity rather than considering themselves African-American (McRoy, Zurcher, Lauderdale, & Anderson, 1984). Similarly, Hispanic adolescents raised by non-Hispanic parents defined themselves as American rather than Mexican-American (Andujo, 1988). It seems that adoptive parents who realistically perceive their child's racial or ethnic identity as different from their own and are accepting of that difference will provide a family environment that is conducive to the development of a positive group identification.

While parents are the primary socializers of their children, they are not the only influence. At adolescence the impact of external forces is likely to be considerably more potent than earlier in the life span. If we are to explain the apparent shifts in various aspects of ethnic identity, we must take account of features of the ethnic community and larger society.

The Ethnic Community

The cultural context provided by the family is reinforced when the ethnic community provides a subculture that allows for many of the activities central to an individual's life (e.g., school, religion, recreation) to be carried out within the group, that is, the group has a high level of institutional completeness (Breton, 1964). The importance for ethnic identity of being part of a group that is cohesive and structured, and whose institutions are central to one's life, is demonstrated in several studies. In Australia, the Greek immigrant community is more cohesive and structured than is the Italian. Rosenthal and Hrynevich (1985) found, not surprisingly, that Greek-Australian adolescents valued their Greek identity, while their Italian peers placed less emphasis on maintaining their cultural heritage and favored assimilation into the host culture. Driedger (1976) found in Canada that status within the society interacted with institutional completeness so that groups high on both status and completeness (French and Jews) had the strongest sense of ethnic identity. Lowest levels of ethnic identity were found among Germans, Ukrainians, and Poles, whose groups have low status and only low to moderate levels of institutional completeness.

When the community lacks cohesiveness and a sense of kinship (Stack, 1974) and also cannot provide role models for ways of being a successful member of a group, adolescents may have little to identify with. Two interview studies of African-American young (Taylor, 1989) contrast the strong parental models, which have influenced college students, with the lack of models for inner-city youth. Among college youth, parental models played a more decisive role than peers. In contrast, many inner-city African-American youth viewed their fathers, if available at all, as unattractive role models and turned more to their peers. Many of these youth lack models whom they regard as resources for knowledge, skills, and social support (Hunt & Hunt, 1977; Silverstein & Krate, 1975). Lack of identification with parents or other adults in the community may leave poor African-American youth at particular risk in the attempt to develop a positive sense of their blackness.

Another characteristic that affects attachment to the ethnic group is whether the ethnic community is present in substantial numbers in a neighborhood or is a small minority (Garcia & Lega, 1979). There are conflicting findings, with low ethnic density related to loss of ethnic identity of Caucasian minorities in one study (Alba & Chamlin, 1983), and to retention of ethnic ties among

Mexican-Americans in another (Padilla, 1980). Social identity theory enables us to reconcile these findings in terms of group distinctiveness (McGuire et al., 1978). Members of the Caucasian minorities have more readily available to them the option of blending or "passing" into the mainstream group than do the visibly different Mexican-Americans. This distinctiveness, so social identity theorists argue, results in heightened salience of ethnic identity. However, adolescents who are part of a large minority (Chinese in San Francisco) were found to be similar in terms of levels and nature of ethnic identity to those in a small, dispersed minority, namely Chinese in Melbourne, Australia (Rosenthal & Feldman, in press b).

Furthermore, for immigrant groups, the ethnic community changes over time, as successive generations become more acculturated. While several studies have shown a weakening of ethnic identity among later generations of immigrants, other studies have suggested that ethnic identity remains stable after the second generation or that a resurgence occurs, with stronger identification occurring in third and subsequent generations. Some researchers (e.g., Keefe & Padilla, 1987; Triandis, Kashima, Shimada, & Villareal, 1986) have suggested that elements of the culture that are central (e.g., values) may be more resistant to change than those that are peripheral (e.g., behaviors). Keefe and Padilla (1987), in a study of Mexican-American adults, found that cultural awareness (defined as familiarity with Mexican culture) declined across generations; however, ethnic loyalty, involving an individual's attitudes and feeling about the Mexican culture and people and about discrimination, remained almost constant from the second to the fourth generation. Similarly, in their study of first- and second-generation Chinese-Australian and Chinese-American high school students, Rosenthal and Feldman (in press b) found that ethnic knowledge and behavior decreased over time, but there was no change in the importance accorded to ethnic identity or the positive evaluation of that identity.

Clearly, many characteristics of the ethnic community, including its structure, cohesiveness, density, and the recency of immigration of its members, influence the ethnic identity of its adolescents. Yet the community functions within a broader societal context that strongly affects the developing adolescent.

The Ethnic Group in the Larger Society

The impact on ethnic identity of the position of the minority group in society and the relationship between minority and majority group, at both the individual and group levels, have been the focus of considerably more conceptual and empirical attention than have the family and the community. Social identity theory (Tajfel, 1978, 1981) stresses the dynamic nature of the relationship between the individual and society, explicitly dealing with group belongingness or social identity as a product of individuals' representations of their social world and their place in that world. The outcome of this interaction will be determined by the need individuals have to achieve a positive sense of self-identity via membership in various groups. Tajfel (1978) points out that members of disparaged minority groups face the problem of having to live with negative images of their group. Individuals who accept the negative images of society toward their group face the risk of self-image problems and may show a preference for or identification with another group. Alternatively, individuals may try to leave the group, by assimilation or passing, or they may seek to change the situation, by attempting to re-evaluate and enhance the image of the group.

The tendency to identify with or prefer the majority culture is seen in much research with minority children. Although virtually all minority children can correctly identify their own ethnic group membership by age 8 or 9 (Aboud, 1987; Bernal, Knight, Garza, Ocampo, & Cota, 1990), many continue to show a preference for the majority culture (out-group preference) throughout and beyond childhood (Bernal et al., 1990; Davey, 1983; George & Hoppe, 1979; Semaj, 1980; Spencer, 1982). Thus, there is strong evidence that at least some minority children approach adolescence without a clear preference for their own group. There are fewer studies of preference beyond childhood. Ullah (1985) reports that 9% of second-generation Irish 14- to 18-year-olds in England "sometimes" or "often" hide the fact that they are of Irish descent. Evidence from interviews shows a persistence of out-group preference among some adolescents (Phinney, 1989), although more frequently mentioned are feelings of having wished at a younger age to be a member of the dominant group (Phinney & Chavira, in preparation):

Before, there was an internal type of conflict. I remember I would not say I was Hispanic. My friends . . . were White and Oriental and I tried so hard to fit in with them.

I am proud of who I am and I tell people when they ask me; I admit I used to try to hide it.

A preference for mainstream culture, or the wish to be a member of the dominant group, would seem to be incompatible with a secure ethnic identity. As adolescents explore identity options, other strategies suggested by Tajfel may come into play, such as trying to "pass," a strategy used by adolescent Indian boys in Britain (Hogg, Abrams, & Patel, 1987).

Alternatively, minority youth may attempt to change the group's image by stressing positive aspects of their own culture. In contrast to earlier studies showing identification with the Caucasian majority, Milner (1984) found that young British-born West Indians have turned to alternative and positive cultural identities with the emergence of a black British youth culture stressing the positive and unique features of black identity. As with Milner's West Indian adolescents, Ullah (1985, 1987) found that Irish youth in Britain, an ethnic minority that is the target of prejudice and discrimination, are redefining group membership by enhancing their own group characteristics compared with the out-group, in this case the dominant English majority. A similar strategy is evident among Greek-Australian high school students (Giles, Rosenthal, & Young, 1985), who held exaggerated views of their group's economic and business influence. Movements stressing ethnic pride have likewise developed among African-American and Mexican-American groups in the United States.

The notion of duality, double consciousness, or biculturality is a persistent theme in much research on ethnic minorities (see, for example, Jaynes & Williams, 1989). The description of African-Americans as having "two warring idols in one dark body" (DuBois, 1963, p. 17) is a good example of the commonly expressed view that individuals must choose between two conflicting or competing identities. Yet most studies suggest that ethnic identity is not a bipolar dimension, with ties to the ethnic minority at one end and to the host culture at the other. Rather than considering maintenance of an ethnic identity to be incompatible with identification with the dominant culture, Berry (1980) argues that the two are independent; it is possible to maintain or enhance one's ties with both groups, to varying degrees. Studies of Indians living in Britain (Hutnik, 1986), Armenian-Americans (Der-Karabetian, 1980), Jewish-Americans (Zak, 1973), Chinese-Americans (Ting-Toomey, 1981), and Greek- and Italian-Australians (Rosenthal & Hrynevich, 1985) have all shown two coexisting identities without evidence of conflict between the two.

Nevertheless, other studies report a more complex picture. Elias and Blanton (1987) explored affective, behavioral, and cognitive dimensions of ethnic identity in Israeli-Jewish families living in the United States and found that the relationship between Israeli, Jewish, and American identities differed, depending on the dimension. Other studies using ethnographic methods have shown that the ways in which minority youth relate to the dominant culture involve not just more or less identification with each group but rather qualitatively different ways of relating. Vigil (1979) and Matute-Bianchi (1986) provide descriptions of high school students of Mexican descent, who choose among various ethnic identities: Mexican-oriented, Anglo-oriented, Mexican-American, Chicano, or Cholo. These identities are characterized by varying attitudes toward Mexican culture and toward the mainstream culture of the high school, as well as differing personal styles, academic performance, and proficiency in Spanish. Likewise, Ogbu (1985) reviews studies that identify various types of adaptation to inner-city life among African-American adolescents; the Square or Ivy Leaguer (mainstream oriented), the Regular or the Cool Cat (street-wise), the Jester (prankster), and the Antagonist (fighter). A case study of a West Indian adolescent in Britain (Weinreich, 1979) illustrates the process by which youth examine identity options.

Focusing specifically on African-American youth, several writers discuss extreme choices made by some youth, of either an "oppositional" identity, that is, defining themselves in contrast to the Caucasian culture (Ogbu, 1987), or becoming "raceless," that is, rejecting their blackness (Fordham, 1988; Fordham & Ogbu, 1986). African-American youth who try to achieve success by Caucasian standards face opposition from other African-Americans; "their behaviors tend to be interpreted not only as 'acting White' but also as a betrayal of Black people" (Ogbu, 1987, p. 166). Thus,

African-American students have to choose between "acting Black" and "acting White." Those who develop an oppositional identity limit their opportunities in the mainstream culture; those who opt for success in school and in the mainstream do so by "minimizing their relationship to the Black community and to the stigma attached to 'Blackness' " (Fordham, 1988, p. 57).

Yet some minority youth appear to have developed strategies for handling such conflicts (Phinney & Chavira, in preparation). As one Mexican-American male high school student puts it:

> [Some Hispanic friends] say that I am never going to make it. They try and hold me down . . . I get angry but that anger makes me strive for more . . . I don't fight against them, I just leave them alone and try to strive more for myself.

Others feel that they are able to negotiate the demands made on them in differing cultural contexts:

> Being invited to someone's house, I have to change my ways of how I act at home, because of culture differences. I would have to follow what they do . . . I am used to it now, switching off between the two. It is not difficult.

> When I am around my people, I feel more Hispanic. Like at school, it is all English and at my job it is all English . . . I can really be both. I know what to do and what to expect. No problem.

In summary, society presents a range of conflicting messages to minority youth, who adapt to these pressures in many different ways. Ultimately, how they deal with their ethnicity is likely to have important implications for their self-concept.

ETHNIC IDENTITY AND SELF-CONCEPT

In earlier sections of this chapter, we have assumed that achieving a positive sense of ethnic identity is a healthy outcome for minority youth. We can explore this assumption further by investigating the link between ethnic identity and feelings of self-worth in adolescents. There is a good precedent for this strategy since there is evidence from studies of adolescent identity that an achieved ego identity is associated with high self-esteem (e.g., Waterman, 1984). Adolescence is a time of intense preoccupation with self and self-presentation. How they appear to others is a matter of great consequence to adolescents (Elkind, 1967). Imagining the reactions of others to one's self is likely to have a profound effect on one's self-esteem, especially for adolescents who are not part of the mainstream, who are "different" from their peers.

In early research on the self-esteem of ethnic minority children and youth, the underlying expectation was that poor self-esteem would result from factors such as low status, poverty, and perceptions of prejudice and discrimination. In an extended discussion of this question, Tajfel (1978) states that "People who are members of minorities . . . share one difficult psychological problem, which can be described . . . as a conflict between a satisfactory self-realization and the restrictions imposed upon it by the realities of membership in a minority group" (p. 9). However, most recent studies have shown no relationship between ethnicity and self-esteem. A difficulty with much research on this topic has been the lack of a clear distinction between ethnicity and ethnic identity; that is, while purporting to measure ethnic identity, researchers simply use ethnic group membership as the variable of interest, without assessing the adolescent's sense of belonging to the group (self-identification), evaluation of his or her group membership (ethnic pride), or any other aspect of ethnic identity.

In several studies which have examined more closely the effect of levels of ethnic identity on self-esteem, ethnic group membership coupled with a sense of ethnic pride has shown a positive relationship to adolescents' sense of self-worth. Grossman, Wirt, and Davids (1985) found that ethnic esteem mediated between ethnic group and self-esteem in a sample of Chicano adolescents, and racial acceptance was positively correlated with self-esteem in African-Americans (Paul & Fisher, 1980).

Two recent studies of Italian-Australian and Anglo-Australian young women (Grieve, Rosenthal, & Cavallo, 1988; Rosenthal & Grieve, 1990) provide insights into the complexity of the relationship between ethnic identity and self-esteem. In a study of high school students, levels of self-esteem were similar in the two groups, but the correlates of self-esteem differed. Unlike the Anglo-Australians, whose self-esteem was associated also with masculine characteristics, the self-esteem of the Italian-Australian girls was associated with stereotypic feminine attributes and preoccupations. In an older sample of college students, those young women who were more highly identified with their Italian culture were both more traditional in their attitudes to the role of women in society (and especially motherhood) and more satisfied with being female than were their more assimilated peers. At the same time, these young women held firmly to a belief in the importance of a career. Rosenthal and Grieve concluded that these contradictory sets of attitudes, especially for those who strongly identified with their ethnic group, may be a source of difficulty should these young women attempt to combine a career with motherhood.

This line of research suggests that the consequences of minority group membership for an individual's sense of self-worth are not due to minority status per se but are mediated by other factors, such as the gender role prescriptions in a society. Research in Australia suggests that minority girls are more likely to be at risk when they come from cultures where sex roles are sharply differentiated and males are accorded greater prestige (Rosenthal, Moore, & Taylor, 1983). Other societal features that have been implicated as mediating the self-esteem of minority adolescents are the presence or absence of a strong and structured ethnic community whose members are involved and committed, and the extent to which adolescents perceive prejudice and discrimination toward the group (Rosenthal & Cichello, 1986; Rosenthal et al., 1983).

Another mediating factor is the process by which adolescents consciously deal with the realities of their ethnic group membership. Some of these strategies have been discussed earlier, in examining the research on social identity. Research that focuses on the issue developmentally provides another perspective. Just as other research indicates that positive psychological outcomes are associated with an achieved identity (Marcia, 1980), Phinney and her colleagues (Phinney, 1989; Phinney & Alipuria, 1990) propose that an achieved ethnic identity (that is, exploration of the issues raised by one's ethnicity, resulting in a resolution of these issues and a commitment to an ethnic identity) contributes positively to self-esteem. They suggest that commitment to an ethnic identity is a critical feature of the self-concept of minority youth and one that mediates the impact of minority status on adjustment (Phinney, Lochner, & Murphy, 1990). This prediction has been supported in a series of studies. Phinney (1989) found that African-American, Asian-American, and Mexican-American adolescents who showed greater resolution of their ethnic identity had significantly higher scores on four measures of psychological adjustment, including self-esteem. This relationship was confirmed in further studies of high school students and college students (Phinney, 1992; Phinney & Alipuria, 1990). Of interest in these studies was the finding that there was generally little relationship between ethnic identity and self-esteem for the Caucasian college students, supporting the conclusions that an achieved ethnic identity is more closely tied to self-esteem for minority youth than majority youth.

The study by Phinney and Alipuria (1990) highlights the complex nature of the interaction between ethnic identity and self-esteem. The results showed consistently higher correlations with self-esteem for ethnic commitment than ethnic search, and fluctuations in these correlations as a function of ethnic group and of gender. Asian-Americans (and females in particular) were more like their Western peers, with only modest correlations between ethnic identity and self-esteem. More substantial correlations were found for African-American and Mexican-American youth. A possible explanation is that the Asian-Americans enjoy special status and prestige as models and high-achieving students, a position not shared by their African-American and Mexican-American peers.

A study of Mexican-American and Japanese American high-school students (Matute-Bianchi, 1986) supports this view. For the students of Japanese descent, the issue of their identity as a distinct ethnic group was not relevant to their identity as students, and they tended not to engage in ethnically linked activities; rather, they were active in the mainstream clubs of the school. In contrast, the students of Mexican descent used ethnic identity as a response to their subordinate status in the school community and were more invested in their ethnicity.

The actual process by which minority youth wrestle with and resolve issues associated with cultural conflict, stereotypes, or discrimination, in order to maintain a positive self-concept, is further elucidated in interviews with Asian-American, African-

American, and Hispanic high school students (Phinney & Chavira, in preparation). Interviews were conducted with two groups of students, those scoring relatively high or relatively low on ethnic identity. The issues and conflicts about their ethnicity faced by these youth are similar in both groups; for example:

> I am not ashamed of being Hispanic but . . . I am disappointed because I compare the Hispanic race to other races. . . . We have not done much.
>
> I am very proud of my ethnicity, I am very proud of some of the good things my culture has done, and then again, there are certain things like in every culture, there are always some people who have to ruin it for everybody.

Most of the students had experience with both stereotypes and discrimination, and both high and low ethnic identity students felt that it was appropriate at times to ignore ethnic slurs and prejudice. However, significantly more high ethnic identity youth, when asked how they dealt with such incidents, stated that they would respond actively, by pointing out why stereotypes were inaccurate or why discrimination was wrong; for example:

> I'm going to let them know, just because you see that on TV, that's not reality.

> You talk about it and you try to change things. You try to make people see you not as White, Black, Asian, just see for who you are and what you can do.

> The people I can help, the people I can reach, I try to talk to them.

Furthermore, a high ethnic identity was associated with an understanding that the prejudice was not personally directed at oneself:

> A lot of times we have been put down. Before, it used to hurt me a lot emotionally, because I did kind of feel that I was not as good as [the Caucasian students] were. . . . I think I matured. . . . What I saw is how ignorant people could be to think that another person who is of a different color or of a different ethnic group is not as smart.

Adolescents who have achieved a secure, comfortable ethnic identity have dealt with their ambivalence, rejected negative stereotypes, and resolved for themselves conflicts associated with their ethnicity. They feel good about themselves:

> I am what I am, and I don't know if that is Asian or if that is American . . . I usually think of myself as totally Americanized, [but] I know I don't want to American [i.e., Caucasian], like brown hair and blue eyes. I am proud to be Japanese American.

> I am proud of my heritage and I am also proud that I know how to speak English and that I was born and raised here. I am happy the way I am.

In summary, it is clear that the links between self-esteem, ethnicity, and ethnic identity are not straightforward. The relationship between ethnic identity and psychological well-being varies depending on the particular ethnic group, including the cohesiveness of the group and its status in society; environmental factors, such as family, school, and peers; as well as the adolescent's way of dealing with his or her ethnicity within a particular social context. This complexity highlights the need to go beyond simple correlations between ethnic identity and self-esteem, if we are to "unpackage" the true contributions of ethnic identity to well-being.

SUMMARY AND CONCLUSIONS

The material presented in this chapter establishes that ethnic identity is a critical developmental issue for ethnic minority adolescents. In spite of differences among groups, it is clear that the family, community, and societal contexts in which adolescents develop pose a number of conflicts that minority youth must resolve in establishing an ethnic identity. These issues and conflicts do not necessarily result in psychological problems for minority youth, who are no more likely than other adolescents to suffer from low self-esteem. Rather, minority youth, like all adolescents, face a specific range of identity questions, depending on their own particular life experiences and the resources they bring to deal with these questions. As with many issues faced by adolescents, questions about ethnicity are likely to involve competing, often ambivalent feelings. They are not a matter of a simple choice, for example, between close family ties and relationships with members of other groups, or between preference for one's own group and admiration for the mainstream culture. In each instance, elements of contrasting views are likely to coexist to varying degrees. One's ethnicity can provide supportive roots and also limiting stereotypes; it can be a source of pride but also discomfort. The identity task is to integrate these contrasting elements, together with one's own inclinations and options, to achieve a unified sense of self as an ethnic group member.

The research to date has provided only a sketchy, fragmented picture of this process, both because of limitations in the theoretical frameworks used for studying ethnic identity and because of methodological problems in the research itself. Much of the work has been atheoretical, and studies of the same issues have drawn on widely differing theoretical frameworks. The central empirical problem to be dealt with is the multifaceted nature of ethnic identity and the complex and subtle relationships among its components, some of which are specific to particular groups while others apply across all groups. Reliable measures are needed for both specific components, such as particular ethnic practices and attitudes, and general aspects, such as a sense of belonging and commitment (Phinney, 1990). Furthermore, we need to ensure that the study of ethnic identity includes not only members of disparaged minorities (such as African-Americans, Hispanics, and indigenous minorities) but also minority groups that are admired, at least in some respects, by members of the mainstream culture (such as Asians).

A critical task in furthering our understanding is to provide a solid theoretical base by integrating developmental and social psychological perspectives, together with a consideration of contextual factors, as a foundation for future research. Erikson's theory provides a broad developmental view within which ethnic identity can be located. One point of interest is the relationship of ethnic identity to other aspects of ego identity, such as gender, political, and religious identities. Do these develop in synchrony? To what extent are they subject to common influences? What processes enable the minority adolescent to integrate ethnic identity with other identities into a "meta-identity"?

While adolescence is seen as the focal period for ethnic identity formation, a life-span developmental perspective is essential, in order to elucidate the precursors of adolescent ethnic identity and to trace its impact beyond adolescence. We need, for example, to ask what are the antecedents in childhood of a positive ethnic identity at adolescence. What happens to ethnic identity in early and later adulthood, when the relatively sheltered environments of home and school are replaced by work and greater contact with the mainstream society? Questions such as these imply an urgent need for well-planned cross-lagged research designs, by means of which we can obtain information over time and over several cohorts.

The social psychological perspective, especially social identity theory, also has an important contribution to make to our understanding of the ways in which ethnic youth deal with minority status. For example, research is needed to explore why some youth can be comfortable living in, and moving between, two cultures, while others either separate themselves from the mainstream or attempt to assimilate completely. The impact of social class is an important area that has largely been ignored in ethnic identity research. Other broad contextual factors, such as the extent to which the society embraces pluralism, are likely to be critical. What are the consequences for minority youth of living in a mainstream culture that has a "melting pot," assimilationist ethos, versus a multicultural, pluralistic society? How does ethnic identity manifest itself in xenophobic societies where "outsiders" are never truly accepted?

Bronfenbrenner's (1979) ecological model of development provides a valuable framework for addressing contextual influences on ethnic identity development. His work and the research outlined in this chapter emphasize the need to consider these factors not in isolation but in interaction with each other. It is clear from research cited here that contextual factors, such as parenting practices or community supports, do not exert an influence individually but interact in ways that demand multivariate research designs if we are to do justice to the complexity of family and social influences. We can extend Lerner's goodness-of-fit notion (Lerner, Lerner, & Tubman, 1989) to the important issue of the match between what the environment demands of minority youth, *qua* minority youth, and the special competencies, needs, and attitudes of these youth. When the expectations of the environment and youth match, we can expect positive outcomes for ethnic identity development.

Finally, we need also to consider the conditions under which ethnic identity becomes a salient issue for majority youth. In times of changing demographics and economic uncertainty, when majority group numbers are shrinking relative to those in ethnic minorities, when there is considerable movement between societies, and when there appears to be a resurgence of ethnic pride among many minorities, then majority youth may also be forced to confront the meaning and value that their ethnic group membership has for them.

REFERENCES

Aboud, F. (1987). The development of ethnic self-identification and attitudes. In J. Phinney & M. Rotheram (Eds.), *Children's ethnic socialization: Pluralism and development*. Newbury Park, CA: Sage.

Alba, R., & Chamin, M. D. (1983). A preliminary examination of ethnic identification among whites. *American Sociological Review, 48*, 240-242.

Andujo, E. (1988). Ethnic identity of transethnically adopted Hispanic adolescents. *Social Work, 33*, 531-535.

Arce, C. (1981). A reconsideration of Chicano culture and identity. *Daedalus, 110* (2), 177-192.

Atkinson, D., Morten, G., & Sue, D. (1983). *Counseling American minorities*. Dubuque, IA: Wm. C. Brown.

Bernal, M., Knight, G., Garza, C., Ocampo, K., & Cota, M. (1990). The development of ethnic identity in Mexican American children. *Hispanic Journal of Behavioral Sciences, 12*, 3-24.

Berry, J. (1980). Acculturation as varieties of adaption. In A. Padilla (Ed.), *Acculturation: Theory, models, and some new findings*. Boulder, CO: Westview.

Breton, R. (1964). Institutional completeness of ethnic communities and the personal relations of immigrants. *American Journal of Sociology, 70*, 193-205.

Bronfenbrenner, U. (1979). *The ecology of human development*. Cambridge, MA: Harvard University Press.

Cross, W. (1978). The Thomas and Cross models of psychological nigrescence: A literature review. *Journal of Black Psychology, 4*, 13-31.

Davey, A. (1983). *Learning to be prejudiced: Growing up in multi-ethnic Britain*. London: Edward Arnold.

Der-Karabetian, A. (1980). Relation of two cultural identities of Armenian-Americans. *Psychological Reports, 47*, 123-128.

Deschamps, J. C. (1982). Social identity and relations of power between groups. In H. Tajfel (Ed.), *Social identity and intergroup relations*. Cambridge: Cambridge University Press.

Driedger, L. (1976). Ethnic self-identity: A comparison of ingroup evaluations. *Sociometry, 39*, 131-141.

DuBois, W.E.B. (1963). *An ABC of color.* Berlin: Seven Seas Books.

Elias, N., & Blanton, J. (1987). Dimensions of ethnic identity in Israeli Jewish families living in the United States. *Psychological Reports, 60*, 367-375.

Elkind, D. (1967). Egocentrism in adolescence. *Child Development, 38*, 1025-1034.

Erikson, E. H. (1968). *Identity: Youth and crisis.* New York: Norton.

Fordham, S. (1988). Racelessness as a factor in black students' school success: Pragmatic strategy or Pyrrhic victory? *Harvard Educational Review, 58*, 54-84.

Fordham, S., & Ogbu, J. (1986). Black students' school success: Coping with the burden of "acting white." *The Urban Review, 18*, 176-206.

Garcia, J. (1982). Ethnicity and Chicanos: Measurement of ethnic identification, identity, and consciousness. *Hispanic Journal of Behavioral Sciences, 4*, 295-314.

Garcia, M., & Lega, L. (1979). Development of Cuban ethnic identity questionnaire. *Hispanic Journal of Behavioral Sciences, 1*, 247-261.

George, R., & Hoppe, R. (1979). Racial identification, preference, and self-concept. *Journal of Cross-Cultural Psychology, 10*, 85-100.

Giles, H., Llado, N., McKirnan, D. H., & Taylor, D. M. (1979). Social identity in Puerto Rico. *International Journal of Psychology, 14*, 185-201.

Giles, H., Rosenthal, D. A., & Young, L. (1985). Perceived ethnolinguistic vitality: The Anglo- and Greek-Australian setting. *Journal of Multilingual and Multicultural Development, 6*, 253-269.

Giles, H., Taylor, D. M., Lambert, W. E., & Albert, G. (1976). Dimensions of ethnic identity: An example from Northern Maine. *Journal of Social Psychology, 100*, 11-19.

Grieve, N. R., Rosenthal, D. A., & Cavallo, A. (1988). Self-esteem and sex-role attitudes: A comparison of Italian- and Anglo-Australian adolescent girls. *Psychology of Women Quarterly, 12*, 175-189.

Grossman, B., Wirt, R., & Davids, A. (1985). Self-esteem, ethnic identity, and behavioral adjustment among Anglo and Chicano adolescents in West Texas. *Journal of Adolescence, 8*, 57-68.

Harrison, A. O. (1985). The black family's socializing environment: Self-esteem and ethnic attitude among black children. In H. P. McAdoo & J. L. McAdoo (Eds.), *Black children* (pp. 174-193). Newbury Park, CA: Sage.

Hogg, A., Abrams, D., & Patel, Y. (1987). Ethnic identity, self esteem and occupational aspirations of Indian and Anglo-Saxon British adolescents. *Genetic, Social and General Psychology Monographs, 113*, 487-508.

Hunt, J., & Hunt, L. (1977). Racial inequality and self-image: Identity maintenance as identity diffusion. *Sociology and Social Research, 61*, 539-559.

Hutnik, N. (1986). Patterns of ethnic minority identification and modes of social adaption. *Ethnic and Racial Studies, 9*, 150-167.

Jaynes, G., & Williams, R. (1989). *A common destiny: Blacks and American society* (Chapter 4). Washington, DC: National Academy Press.

Keefe, S., & Padilla, A. (1987). *Chicano ethnicity.* Albuquerque: University of New Mexico Press.

Lerner, R., Lerner, J., & Tubman, J. (1989). Organismic and contextual biases of development in adolescence: A developmental contextual view. In G. Adams, R. Montemayor, & T. Gullotta (Eds.), *Biology of adolescent behavior and development.* Newbury Park, CA: Sage.

Maccoby, E. E., & Martin, J. (1983). Socialization in the context of the family: Parent-child interaction. In M. E. Hetherington (Ed.), *Handbook of child psychology: Vol. 4. Socialization, personality, and social development* (pp. 1-102). New York: John Wiley.

Marcia, J. (1980). Identity in adolescence. In J. Adelson (Ed.), *Handbook of adolescent psychology* (pp. 159-187). New York: John Wiley.

Marcia, J., & Kowaz, A. (1988, April). *Current research directions in psychological development theory.* Paper presented at the Western Psychological Association meeting, Burlingame, CA.

Matute-Bianchi, M. (1986). Ethnic identities and pattern of school success and failure among Mexican-descent and Japanese-American students in a California high school: An ethnographic analysis. *American Journal of Education, 95,* 233-255.

McGuire, W., McGuire, C., Child, P., & Fujioka, T. (1978). Salience of ethnicity in the spontaneous self-concept as a function of one's ethnic distinctiveness in the social environment. *Journal of Personality and Social Psychology, 36,* 511-520.

McRoy, R., Zurcher, L., Lauderdale, M., & Anderson, R. (1984). The identity of transracial adoptees. *Social Casework, 65,* 34-39.

Milner, D. (1984). The development of ethnic attitudes. In H. Tajfel (Ed.), *The social dimension: European developments in social psychology* (Vol. 1). Cambridge: Cambridge University Press.

Nobles, W. W. (1973). Psychological research and the black self-concept: A critical review. *Journal of Social Issues, 29,* 11-31.

Ogbu, J. (1985). A cultural ecology of competence among inner-city blacks. In M. Spencer, G. Brooks, & W. Allen (Eds.), *Beginnings: The social and affective development of black children.* Hillsdale, NJ: Lawrence Erlbaum.

Ogbu, J. (1987). Opportunity structure, cultural boundaries and literacy. In J. Langer (Ed.), *Language, literacy, and culture: Issues of society and schooling.* Norwood, NJ: Ablex.

Padilla, A. M. (1980). The role of cultural awareness and ethnic loyalty in acculturation. In A. M. Padilla (Ed.), *Acculturation: Theory, models and some new findings,* Boulder, CO: Westview.

Parham, T. (1989). Cycles of psychological nigrescence. *The Counseling Psychologist, 17,* 187-226.

Parham, T., & Helms, J. (1981). Influence of a black student's racial identity attitudes on preference for counselor race. *Journal of Counseling Psychology, 28,* 250-257.

Paul, M., & Fischer, J. (1980). Correlates of self-concept among black early adolescents. *Journal of Youth and Adolescence, 9,* 163-173.

Peters, M. F. (1985). Racial socialization of young black children. In H. P. McAdoo & J. L. McAdoo (Eds.), *Black children* (pp. 159-173). Newbury Park, CA: Sage.

Phinney, J. (1989). Stages of ethnic identity development in minority group adolescents. *Journal of Early Adolescence, 9,* 34-49.

Phinney, J. (1990). Ethnic identity in adolescents and adults: A review of research. *Psychological Bulletin, 180,* 499-514.

Phinney, J. (1992). The multigroup ethnic identity measure: A new scale for use with adolescents and young adults from diverse groups. *Journal of Adolescent Research, 2.*

Phinney, J., & Chavira, V. (in press). Ethnic identity and self-esteem: An exploratory longitudinal study. *Journal of Adolescence.*

Phinney, J., & Chavira, V. (in preparation). Parental ethnic socialization and adolescents' ethnic attitudes.

Phinney, J., & Alipuria, L. (1990). Ethnic identity in college students from four ethnic groups. *Journal of Adolescence, 13,* 171-183.

Phinney, J., Lochner, B. T., & Murphy, R. (1990). Ethnic identity development and psychological adjustment in adolescence. In A. Stiffman & L. Davis (Eds.), *Ethnic issues in adolescent mental health.* Newbury Park, CA: Sage.

Phinney, J., & Nakayama, S. (1991, April). Parental influence on ethnic identity formation in minority adolescents. Paper presented at the biennial meeting of the Society for Research on Child Development, Seattle, WA.

Phinney, J., & Tarver, S. (1988). Ethnic identity search and commitment in black and white eighth graders. *Journal of Early Adolescences, 8,* 265-277.

Rosenthal, D. A. (1987). Ethnic identity development in adolescents. In J. S. Phinney & M. J. Rotheram (Eds.), *Children's ethnic socialization: Pluralism and development.* Newbury Park, CA: Sage.

Rosenthal, D. A., & Cichello, A. (1986). The meeting of two cultures: Ethnic identity and psychological adjustment of Italian-Australian adolescents. *International Journal of Psychology, 21,* 487-501.

Rosenthal, D. A., & Feldman, S. S. (in press a). The nature and stability of ethnic identity in Chinese youth: Effects of length of residence in two cultural contexts. *Journal of Cross-Cultural Psychology.*

Rosenthal, D. A., & Feldman, S. S. (in press b). The relationship between parenting behavior and ethnic identity in Chinese-American and Chinese-Australian adolescents. *International Journal of Psychology.*

Rosenthal, D. A., & Grieve, N. R. (1990). Attitudes to the gender culture: A comparison of Italian-Australian and Anglo-Australian female tertiary students. *Australian Psychologist, 25,* 282-292.

Rosenthal, D. A., & Hrynevich, C. (1985). Ethnicity and ethnic identity: A comparative study of Greek-, Italian-, and Anglo-Australian adolescents. *International Journal of Psychology, 20,* 723-742.

Rosenthal, D. A., Moore, S. M., & Taylor, M. J. (1983). Ethnicity and adjustment: A study of the self-image of Anglo-, Greek-, and Italian-Australian working-class adolescents. *Journal of Youth and Adolescence, 12,* 117-135.

Rotheram, M., & Phinney, J. (1987). Definitions and perspectives in the study of children's ethnic socialization. In J. Phinney & M. Rotheram (Eds.), *Children's ethnic socialization: Pluralism and development.* Newbury Park, CA: Sage.

Salgado de Snyder, N., Lopez, C. M., & Padilla, A. M. (1982). Ethnic identity and cultural awareness among the offspring of Mexican interethnic marriages. *Journal of Early Adolescence, 2,* 277-282.

Semaj, L. (1980). The development of racial evaluation and preference: A cognitive approach. *The Journal of Black Psychology, 6,* 59-79.

Silverstein, B., & Krate, R. (1975). *Children of the dark ghetto.* New York: Praeger.

Spencer, M. (1982). Personal and group identity of black children: An alternative synthesis. *Genetic Psychology Monographs, 106,* 59-84.

Spencer, M. (1983). Children's cultural values and parental child rearing strategies. *Developmental Review, 4,* 351-370.

Spencer, M., & Dornbusch, S. M. (1990). Minority youth in America. In S. S. Feldman & G. R. Elliott (Eds.), *At the threshold: The developing adolescent* (pp. 123-146). Cambridge, MA: Harvard University Press.

Stack, C. B. (1974). *All our kin.* New York: Harper & Row.

Steinberg, L. D. (1990). Interdependency in the family: Autonomy, conflict and harmony in the parent-adolescent relationship. In S. S. Feldman & G. R. Elliott (Eds.), *At the threshold: The developing adolescent* (pp. 255-276). Cambridge, MA: Harvard University Press.

Szapocznik, J., & Kurtines, W. (1980). Acculturation, biculturalism, and adjustment among Cuban Americans. In A. M. Padilla (Ed.), *Acculturation: Theory, models, and some new findings*. Boulder, CO: Westview.

Taft, R. (1985). The psychological study of the adjustment and adaptation of immigrants in Australia. In N. T. Feather (Ed.), *Australian psychology: Review of research*. Sydney: Allen & Unwin.

Tajfel, H. (1978). *The social psychology of minorities*. New York: Minority Rights Group.

Tajfel, H. (1981). *Human groups and social categories: Studies in social psychology*. New York: Cambridge University Press.

Taylor, R. (1989). Black youth, role models, and the social construction of identity. In R. Jones (Ed.), *Black adolescents*. Berkeley, CA: Cobb & Henry.

Thornton, M. C., Chatters, L. M., Taylor, R. J., & Allen, W. R. (1990). Sociodemographic and environmental correlates of racial socialization by black parents. *Child Development, 61*, 401-409.

Ting-Toomey, S. (1981). Ethnic identity and close friendship in Chinese-American college students. *International Journal of Intercultural Relations, 5*, 383-406.

Triandis, H. C., Kashima, Y., Shimada, E., & Villareal, M. (1986). Acculturation indices as a means of confirming cultural differences. *International Journal of Psychology, 21* 43-70.

Ullah, P. (1985). Second generation Irish youth: Identity and ethnicity. *New Community, 12*, 310-320.

Ullah, P. (1987). Self-definition and psychological group formation in an ethnic minority. *British Journal of Social Psychology, 26*, 17-23.

Vigil, D. (1979). Adaptation strategies and cultural life styles of Mexican-American adolescents. *Hispanic Journal of Behavioral Sciences, 1*, 375-392.

Waterman, A. (1982). Identity development from adolescence to adulthood: An extension of theory and a review of research. *Developmental Psychology, 18*, 341-358.

Waterman, A. (1984). *The psychology of individualism*. New York: Praeger.

Weinreich, P. (1979). Cross-ethnic identification and self-rejection in a black adolescent. In G. Verma & C. Bagley (Eds.), *Race, education, and identity*. New York: St. Martin's Press.

Yogev, A., & Jamsky, H. (1983). Children of ethnic intermarriage in Israeli schools: Are they marginal? *Journal of Marriage and the Family, 45*, 965-973.

Zak, I. (1973). Dimensions of Jewish-American identity. *Psychological Reports, 33*, 891-900.

9. A Consideration of Intervening Factors in Adolescent Identity Formation

Carol Markstrom-Adams
University of Guelph

INTRODUCTION

The major psychosocial task of adolescence is the construction of a healthy identity (Erikson, 1968). There are several distinguishable characteristics of a healthy identity, such as: (a) an understanding of the sameness and continuity of the self over space and time; (b) having direction and purpose for one's life as shown through identifiable values and goals; (c) a self that is integrated and characterized by a sense of wholeness; and (d) the self that is defined is valued by significant others.

Identity, like other constructs of development, is thought to occur through the course of normal maturational processes within appropriate, supportive social contexts. According to Eriksonian theory (1963, 1968), one of the primary factor operating in identity resolution is the individual's negotiation of earlier psychosocial stages. While this component of Erikson's theory is difficult to falsify through empirical research, it remains a central tenet of the theory. It is apparent in reading the research literature that social scientists are interested in identifying additional factors that interact with identity formation. Perhaps an unstated assumption of many of these research attempts is that through understanding intervening factors in identity formation, intervention efforts might be targeted toward adolescents who are exhibiting less mature forms of identity.

The purpose of this chapter is to identify and discuss intervening factors in the formation of identity that have been targeted in a broad body of theoretical and empirical literature. Much of this literature is embedded in Marcia's (1966) identity status model; thus, in this chapter, linkages are made between intervening factors in identity formation and the four identity statuses. For discussion purposes, this chapter is organized in three sections: (a) social contextual factors of the family, ethnicity and race, and religion; (b) cognitive factors of formal operations, assimilation and accommodation, perspective-taking and egocentrism, cognitive complexity, and the failure to conceptualize the continuity of the self; and (c) factors related to certain adolescent psychopathological conditions.

SOCIAL CONTEXTUAL
FACTORS IN IDENTITY FORMATION

Contextual factors pertinent to identity formation encompass issues that close social relationships and the sociocultural milieu present to the adolescent. Identity formation is not wholly an individualistic process; rather, the social environment exerts its forms of power and influence. Three social contextual factors identified in relation to identity include family relationships, ethnic and racial group membership, and religiosity.

Family Relationships

There is a great deal of research that has been conducted on the relation between identity formation and parental socialization styles. Adams, Dyk, and Bennion (1987) summarize findings from Adams (1985), Adams and Jones (1983), and Campbell, Adams, and Dobson (1984) on family correlates of identity formation. Diffusion is related to adolescent perceptions of maternal and paternal rejection and poor affectionate relationship with mother, paternal perceptions of rejection-control and withdrawn behavior, and maternal perceptions of low affection. Foreclosure is related to adolescent perceptions of affectionate relationship with mother, maternal perceptions of companionship and high affection, and paternal perceptions of withdrawn behavior. Moratorium and achievement are associated with adolescent perceptions of low maternal control/regulation, maternal encouragement of independence, father's fairness in discipline with moderation in praise, high companionship, physical affection, support of parents, and both maternal and paternal perceptions of independence. Further, moratorium is characterized by maternal perception of low affection; while achievement is characterized by maternal perception of high affection.

Consistent with the Adams et al. (1987) report, Donovan (1975) and Jordan (1971, as cited in Baumeister, 1986) found that foreclosure is associated with close relationships with parents. Not surprisingly, diffusion is associated with strained and distant relationships between adolescents and their parents (Donovan, 1975), and with sons' perceptions of their parents being disapproving and rejecting (Jordan, 1971). Jordan also reported that sons who currently were in crisis or had been in crisis reported inconsistent and ambivalent relationships with their parents. Baumeister (1986) goes on to conclude, from the clinical and psychoanalytic literature, that ambivalence is conducive to the identity crisis, explaining that: "Negative feelings toward the parents help set off the repudiation of parental values, and the positive influence of parents produces the inner resources needed in the struggle to achieve a new identity" (p. 204).

Cooper, Grotevant, and Condon (1983) and Grotevant and Cooper (1985) suggest that the promotion of both individuality and connectedness in the family system provides bases for adolescent exploration in identity, as opposed to either too little or too much cohesion and affection. While their findings are correlational in nature, they found that four factors of individuation (self-assertion, separateness, permeability, and mutuality) were related to adolescent exploration in identity formation. Based on their findings, Cooper et al. (1983) conclude that:

[T]he leaving process is facilitated by individual family relationships, characterized by separateness, which gives the adolescent permission to develop his or her own point of view, in the context of connectedness, which provides a secure base from which the adolescent can explore worlds outside the family. (p. 56)

In summary, several investigators have identified certain familial intervening factors in identity formation. It is important to note that the research on this topic is correlational in nature; thus it cannot be unequivocally stated that a particular socialization style creates a certain effect on adolescent identity formation. Nonetheless, the findings are compelling and warrant further investigation.

Ethnic and Racial Group Membership

For adolescents who are members of ethnic and racial minority groups, the task of identity formation becomes especially complex due to several intervening factors. For example, Spencer and Markstrom-Adams (1990) attribute such complexity to issues of color, behavioral distinctions, language differences, physical features, and social stereotypes. A problem recognized by many professionals interested in minority mental health is the fact that ethnic and racial minorities are confronted with two sets of cultural values—those of their own minority group and those of the mainstream culture (LaFromboise & Low, 1989; Mendelberg, 1986; Sue, 1981). In the process of identity formation, the values of the larger culture and minority culture conflict. Sorting through the two sets of values and selecting those to incorporate into one's identity may, for some minority individuals, yield a no-win scenario. That is, adopting an identity consistent with values of the dominant culture may result in ostracism from one's minority group. The contrary also may occur, that is, the result of rejecting the dominant culture's values and accepting the values of one's own group may result in limited options for interaction in the larger society. Some individuals, who are unable to make a coherent blend of the two sets of cultural values, may exhibit confusion in their identities by swinging back and forth between an Anglo identity and an identity consistent with the values of their ethnic group (Katz, 1981). Identity diffusion may then be the result.

Other problematic intervening factors in identity formation have been identified by Berlin (1986) in respect to Native Americans. These factors include: (a) insufficient number of adults who can role model healthy outcomes to the task of identity formation; (b) limited opportunities for identity exploration; and (c) earlier developmental failures. These barriers may be applicable to other ethnic minority groups as well. Ethnic and racial discrimination may limit opportunities for employment and social interaction, thereby inhibiting identity exploration among minority individuals. Discrimination also may impede progress in psychosocial stages prior to adolescence.

Consistent with the above remarks, there is evidence to suggest that minority adolescents engage in less exploration than their

Anglo counterparts. Streitmatter (1988) found Anglo adolescents significantly less foreclosed in both interpersonal and ideological identities than minority (i.e., African-American, Native American, Asian, Hispanic, and "other") adolescents. Similarly, Abraham (1986) found Mexican-American adolescents more foreclosed in ideological identity than Anglo adolescents, and Markstrom (1987) reported that Native American adolescents (and, to a lesser degree, Mexican-Americans and African-Americans) scored higher on foreclosure than did their Anglo peers. Hauser (1972a, 1972b) also found African-American adolescents to be characterized by greater foreclosure in identity. Since foreclosure is an identity status characterized by an absence of exploration, these studies are consistent with Berlin's (1986) remarks that minority individuals may have fewer options for exploration available to them. Further, the effects of racial prejudice and discrimination may contribute to a disinclination among some minority youths to explore outside of their own groups, resulting then in identity foreclosure.

In summary, a salient feature in identity formation among ethnic and racial minorities includes the necessity of sifting through two sets of cultural values and identity options. Further, ethnic and racial prejudice and discrimination may result in limited opportunities for exploration in the identity process.

Religiosity

In respect to religious identity formation, certain factors may contribute to premature foreclosure into a religious identity that is based in either a formal religious organization or a religious cult. For example, tempo and process may be intervening factors in religious identity formation. Parker (1985) found that those individuals who engaged in gradual conversion processes had higher rates of identity achievement than those who did not. Further, he identified a group of individuals who resembled achievement in their religious convictions, but reported hasty and dramatic conversion experiences. It may be that such individuals prematurely foreclose in identity in order to reduce anxiety that is associated with the identity search process. Parker states that these individuals, while reporting a crisis, do not have religious identity crises. Rather, the crisis is centered on a decision of whether or not to submit to a higher authority figure. Consistent with Parker's ideas, Masterson (1988) has recognized a group of teenagers who resist the tasks of emancipation and identity formation by blindly following religious authority leaders. Foreclosing to such authority figures does not require these adolescents to take responsibility for themselves—which is precisely what they are trying to avoid.

Formal religious organizations, while being in positions to assist adolescents in the identity search process, often abdicate such a role (Davis, 1986). Arnold (1983) notes that "moral and spiritual confusion is decreased by anticipating with youth what the normal feelings, questions, issues, and decisions will be and helping them test these in advance" (p. 117). While some religious organizations may be equipped to aid adolescents in their identity quests, some adolescents may be uncomfortable utilizing formal religion as a source of support and guidance in identity formation. Such reluctance may then be disadvantageous for some adolescents, as Feinstein (1980) notes: "An inability to make use of the transitional structures of society (school, dating, working, and other psychosocial moratoria) creates anxiety and diffusion of identity" (p. 12). The risk is that if the adolescent's search process is not facilitated within organized religion, the adolescent will turn to other agencies, for example, cults (Dean, 1982; Feinstein, 1980). For those adolescents who are overwhelmed with the anxieties of moratoria, cults provide absolute answers and an imposed structure.

In summary, some adolescents may be prone to foreclosure in identity, particularly religious identity, when the ambiguity of moratorium is not acceptable. It is this group of adolescents who have been identified in the literature as being particularly susceptible to the influence of cults. In some instances, organized religion may be at fault in failing to provide the necessary support and structure to young people who are attempting to successfully negotiate the task of identity formation. In other cases of premature foreclosure, the adolescent does not have coping mechanisms at his or her disposal to control the normal anxiety of moratoria and thereby forecloses in identity by surrendering his or her will to an authority figure.

COGNITIVE BARRIERS IN IDENTITY FORMATION

The second major section of this chapter deals with cognitive intervening factors of formal operational reasoning, cognitive assimilation and accommodation, perspective-taking and egocentrism, cognitive complexity, and the failure to conceptualize continuity of the self. As opposed to the previous section in which the social environment of the adolescent was taken into account, the factors discussed in this section may be categorized as individual developmental factors.

Formal Operations

In close reading of the works of Erikson and Piaget, the suggestion that formal operations is a prerequisite to identity formation can be found. Erikson (1968) identifies the formal operational ability of thinking about the possible as enhancing adolescent tasks of development, stating:

> Such cognitive orientation forms not a contrast but a complement to the need of the young person to develop a sense of identity, for, from among all possible and imaginable relations, he must make a series of ever-narrowing selections of personal, occupational, sexual, and ideological commitments. (p. 245)

In a similar vein, Inhelder and Piaget (1958) have written that the changes that occur in the personality and in the social arena at adolescence are a result of the development of formal structures. Piaget's view is very similar to Erikson's since it is thought that the ability to reason hypothetically allows the adolescent's interest to expand beyond what one has immediately experienced to the consideration of many social possibilities (Piaget, 1972; Piaget & Inhelder, 1969). More specifically in terms of the cognitive-developmental framework, Kohlberg and Gilligan (1971) have placed the resolution of the identity crisis as "dependent upon attainment of formal logical thought and of questioning of conventional morality" (p. 1078).

There have been several studies on the relation between ego identity and formal operations, with discrepant findings reported. No relations between ego identity and formal thought were found among undergraduates in studies by Cauble (1976) and Berzonsky, Weiner, and Raphael (1975). Mixed results were reported by Wagner (1987), who reported that both formal operations and ego identity were found to increase with age for males and females 10 to 18 years of age. Positive relations between ego identity and formal operations have been reported by Rowe and Marcia (1980) in a study carried out among college men and women. Significant positive relations between ego identity and formal operations also were reported by Protinsky and Wilkerson (1986), among subjects ranging from ages 13 to 24, and among high school boys in a study by Leadbetter and Dionne (1981).

Taken together, it is difficult to interpret the results of these studies due to a variety of methodological inconsistencies among studies. The problems associated with the contradictory findings among studies assessing the relation between formal operations and identity development have been elucidated by Hill and Palmquist (1978). They assert that many researchers have failed to provide a rationale for using certain cognitive tasks in these studies, adding, "Not only is a rationale for the particular measures not provided but a conceptual analysis of why some aspect of formal reasoning should be related to some aspect of identity formation is lacking as well" (p. 25). Similar observations have been made by Leadbetter and Dionne (1981), who have noted Piaget's (1972) remarks that due to adolescents' interests and aptitudes, they may be likely to engage in formal operations in some areas but not in others. Thus, adolescents who exhibit formal operational reasoning in the traditional Piagetian sense may not be inclined to apply such reasoning to identity issues. Indeed, Leadbetter and Dionne observed that in most studies on the topic, the measures of formal operations have been unrelated to issues of identity.

An inability to examine several possible identity alternatives does not allow the individual to progress through moratorium. Thus, the individual is confined to ego identity statuses of foreclosure or diffusion. Using occupational identity as an example, the individual who cannot imagine the self performing various occupational roles may foreclose to an occupation based on parental suggestions. Diffusion is another probable outcome resulting in occupational instability or job dissatisfaction due to making a random or impulsive occupational choice.

Assimilation and Accommodation

The suggestion that assimilation and accommodation are operative in identity formation has been advanced by various writers (Gordon, 1988; Parker, 1985; Whitbourne, 1986). For example, Parker notes that the tension between assimilation and accommodation propels the individual to resolve inconsistencies and conflicts that arise in development. In an attempt to link deficits in formal operations and adolescent psychopathology, Gordon argues that assimilation and accommodation "underlie structural formal operational deficits, since it is these mechanisms that both create and modify cognitive structures" (p. 53). Gordon goes on to say that functional disturbances in assimilation and accommodation may result from:

1. lack of opportunity for assimilation and accommodation either globally or within a specific domain;
2. functional imbalance, or a strong and nonadaptive predominance of either assimilation or accommodation; and
3. difficulty intercoordinating reasoning across different domains of knowledge. (p. 63)

The second point has the most pertinence to the present discussion, particularly in light of Whitbourne's model of adult identity development. As a fundamental assumption, the individual, in his or her identity, strives to feel good about the self which, when achieved, results in feelings of happiness. To the contrary, when doubts are experienced in identity, associated feelings are anxiety and depression. According to Whitbourne, "Identity assimilation refers to the process through which the adult tries to interpret experiences in a manner that is consistent with an identity as a loving, competent, and good person" (p. 18). Accommodation occurs "when the experiences one has are so discordant with an identity as a worthwhile person" (p. 18). Equilibrium occurs when both assimilation and accommodation are used to interpret and integrate experiences into one's identity. Disequilibrium can occur when the individual has an overreliance on either assimilation or accommodation. In the case of assimilation, the individual exhibits resistance to change and has limited self-awareness. In an overreliance on accommodation, the individual is characterized by an underdefined identity and an admission of external factors, as opposed to individual factors, that dictate decision-making.

In summary, it is possible to examine how an overreliance on either assimilation or accommodation may interact with the identity statuses. With disequilibrium, in the form of heightened assimilation in the absence of accommodation, the outcome may be identity foreclosure. Through what Whitbourne identifies as defensive rigidity and lack of insight, the individual is not engaging in exploration. Further, the individual engages in self-justification and identity projection to psychologically defend the fragile sense of self he or she has defined. The individual may engage in such defensive behavior until the discrepancies between self-perception and environmental feedback become so enormous that they can no longer be ignored. If the person continues to resist accommodation in identity, professional intervention may be required to prompt the individual to examine alternatives.

While ongoing accommodation in identity is desirable, an overreliance on the use of accommodation in the absence of assimilation also may be detrimental to the individual's psychosocial development. If the individual is continually engaging in critical analysis of his or her identity and does not begin to defend some sense of self, the result may be identity diffusion or an elongated moratoria, in which the person is continually doubting identity choices and incessantly asking the question, "Who am I?" In the case of overaccommodation, as well, therapeutic intervention may be required to aid the individual in bringing some sense of closure to the identity process.

Perspective-Taking and Egocentrism

While Enright and Deist (1979) support Erikson's (1968) notion that formal operations is prerequisite to identity formation, they identify social cognitive skills as a more appropriate underlying construct of identity formation. Specifically, Enright and Deist suggest that advanced social perspective-taking abilities, as delineated in Selman's (1980) model, are prerequisite to identity formation. In empirical investigations on this topic, Enright, Ganiere, Buss, Lapsley, and Olson (1983) and Enright, Olson, Ganiere, Lapsley, and Buss (1984) report that social perspective-taking training was found to enhance ego identity formation of high school students and college students. While findings by Markstrom-Adams, Ascione, Braegger, and Adams (under review) were mixed, they found Enright's social perspective-taking training and their own form of ideological perspective-taking training to enhance ideological achievement.

Enright and Deist (1979) and Buss and Enright (1987) provide information on the mechanisms of social perspective-taking that they believe produce change in ego identity formation. They assert that in order to understand the self or to form an identity, one must first start by understanding others. Then the individual must determine how he or she is both similar to and different from others. Social perspective-taking establishes such a process by allowing the individual to reflect upon the self from the perspectives of other individuals, other groups, and society as a whole. It is the ability to take broad, global perspectives (Level 4 of social perspective-taking), especially, that facilitates identity formation, since multiple perspectives may be taken.

Two essential aspects of identity, which arise from engaging in social perspective-taking, are an understanding of both what one has in common with others and how the self is unique and different from others (Enright & Deist, 1979). An overemphasis on the perspectives of others is said to lead to rigidity, while too much emphasis on the self's perspective may lead to adolescent egocentrism. This is quite similar to Gordon's (1988) discussion of assimilation and accommodation in interpersonal experiences. Limited opportunities to encounter the perspectives of others may prevent both assimilation and accommodation.

The negative counterpart of social perspective-taking and a potential barrier to identity formation is egocentrism. Egocentrism is defined as a lack of differentiation between one's own point of view and the point of view of others (Inhelder & Piaget, 1958). Piaget's conceptualization of the constructivist epistemology has bearing on this discussion; that is, children (and adults) construct their notions of reality out of their own experiences with the environment (Elkind, 1979). Reality is not perceived accurately; rather, reality is the construction of one's perceptions of reality. As the child grows older, his/her perceptions of reality become more accurate, and egocentric thought is replaced by more socially oriented thinking (Elkind, 1979).

According to Looft (1971, 1972), social interaction contributes to the child's ability to decenter and become less egocentric over time. A decline in egocentrism is marked by the ability to account for the feelings of others, which involves perspective-taking (Looft, 1971). Thus, cognitive decentering is accompanied by an awareness of the points of view of others (Muuss, 1982). Inhelder and Piaget (1958) note that it is through social interaction in the peer group, especially, where the adolescent's egocentric theories about reality are tested and changed. So, as social perspective-taking skills expand, childhood egocentrism diminishes.

In support of the notion that egocentrism may be counterproductive to identity formation, Adams, Abraham, and Markstrom (1987) found that those in less mature identity statuses scored higher on egocentrism (as measured by self-consciousness and self-focusing behavior) than those in identity achievement.

In summary, the failure to attain identity achievement may be due to a barrier in identity formation among adolescents who have difficulties in replacing normative early adolescent egocentrism with greater sociocentric thinking and perspective-taking skills. Ongoing engagement in self-focusing and self-consciousness inhibits the usage of perspective-taking ability, which has been suggested as a prerequisite to identity formation. Such adolescents may be in need of intervention in which the teaching of perspective-taking skills is specifically targeted.

Cognitive Complexity

Several investigators have investigated the role of cognitive complexity in identity formation and have suggested that individuals characterized by greater cognitive complexity are more mature in identity. For example, Waterman (1984) hypothesized in regard to various individualistic qualities (e.g., identity) that "Those persons most characterized by individualistic qualities will be more likely than others to provide evidence of the use of more sophisticated and efficient modes of cognitive functioning" (p. 63).

Two characteristics of cognitive complexity, differentiation and integration, have been identified as playing facilitative roles in ego identity formation. However, research on identity and cognitive complexity (differentiation and integration) has been mixed.

Berzonsky and Neimeyer (1988) found those in diffusion and moratorium as highly differentiated, and did not find a relation between ego identity and integration. Similarly, Cote and Reker (1979) found diffusions characterized by high differentiation. When cognitive complexity alone (not distinguishing between differentiation and integration) has been studied in relation to ego identity, a curvilinear relation emerges (Kirby, 1977; Tzuriel & Klein, 1977). That is, those low and high in identity scored more complex than those moderate in ego identity. As a less direct measure of cognitive complexity, Adams and Fitch (1981, 1982) and Adams and Shea (1979) found a positive relation between ego development, as conceptualized by Loevinger (1976), and identity.

Due to the findings of these reports and others, Slugoski, Marcia, and Koopman (1984) offered a proposal that it is the integrative component of cognitive complexity which is especially salient in identity development. Indeed, Slugoski et al. (1984) found that subjects in identity achievement and moratorium scored higher on their integrative capacities, while those in less mature ego identity statuses scored lower on integrative capacities.

While the research on the role of cognitive complexity in identity formation is inconclusive, conceptually an argument can be made as to how the inability to engage in cognitive differentiation and integration could hinder identity formation. In differentiation, the adolescent is required to examine various complexities of the personality and distinguish between the various components of the psyche. Baumeister (1986) argues that differentiation in both broad (e.g., gender) and narrow (e.g., one's name) facets of identity are important. Thus, the adolescent can examine likes and dislikes, interests, values, motives, and so on. The inability to introspect to this degree may be reflected in a tendency to prematurely foreclose to an identity or to opt out of the identity search process, as in the case of diffusion.

Some individuals may be able to engage in differentiation, but are unable to integrate. In such cases, individuals are caught in ongoing states of moratoria. That is, they are perpetually engaging in experimentation without committing to lasting or meaningful identities. Commitments in adulthood are short-term and may be quite anxiety-provoking to these individuals.

Failure to Conceptualize the Continuity of the Self

One important component to identity resolution is the ability to conceptualize the self as having an existence over time (Akhtar, 1984; Baumeister, 1986; Erikson, 1968). In conceptualizing the self's existence over time, there is an understanding of the continuities between the self in prior life experiences, at the present, and who one will be in the future. Ball and Chandler (1989) suggest that the inability to conceptualize one's identity over time is a critical factor in suicidal tendencies of adolescents, stating:

> Such individuals, lacking any personally computable means of making meaningful connections between their own past, present, and likely futures, could be expected to also lack the usual care and concern that others normally express about their future well-being and so would be hypothesized to be at special risk to behaving in ways that are potentially self-destructive. (p. 263)

Empirical evidence reported by Ball and Chandler (1989) and Bar-Joseph and Tzuriel (1990) supports this assertion. It is possible to further speculate on other disorders that are likely to be seen in adolescents who have difficulty in conceptualizing the self over time, for example, delinquency and substance abuse.

In essence, if the adolescent is not working toward positive future goals, the future becomes irrelevant. For depressed adolescents the result may be suicide attempts. For other adolescents, their behavior is likely to exemplify a quest for present gratification without regard to future consequences. It is reasonable to state that many of these adolescents are diffused in identity.

In summary, the failure to conceptualize the continuity of the self over time may render a severe handicap to identity formation. Failing to recognize the pertinence of one's past to one's present identity, and failing to integrate that past into one's current understanding of the self, may result in feelings of aimlessness and meaninglessness. Certainly, the adolescent is likely to be characterized as being diffused in identity and may exhibit disturbing behavioral symptoms. Other adolescents may become foreclosed in identity as they make commitments based on the suggestions of others. In short, they have greater confidence in the assessments of others concerning the self than they do about their own.

They make identity commitments without considering the future implications of such decisions.

ADOLESCENT PSYCHOPATHOLOGY

Adolescent theorists from the earlier part of this century suggested that psychopathological symptoms were normative during adolescence. For example, Hall (1904) depicted adolescence as a time of "storm and stress"; while Anna Freud (1971) called the period of adolescence a "developmental disturbance." More recent writers have challenged such assertions (e.g., Masterson, 1988; Offer & Offer, 1975). As a psychiatrist, Masterson (1988) has observed that severe symptoms of pathology are not normative for adolescence. The many healthy adolescents have at their disposal the autonomy and skills to successfully negotiate the tasks of adolescence. However, some adolescents do exhibit psychopathological symptoms to the degree to which professional intervention is required. It is this group that will be targeted for discussion purposes in this section.

Many psychopathological disturbances observed among some adolescents are accompanied by disturbances in identity. For example, identity disturbances are evident in identity disorders and borderline personalities (American Psychiatric Association, 1987). While not explicitly writing of the identity crisis, Masterson's (1988) ideas on borderline adolescents are quite salient to identity disturbances found in this form of psychopathology. For example, Masterson has noted the fear of independence and self-expression commonly found in borderline adolescents. He attributes these fears to what he calls the "abandonment depression." The abandonment depression arises from the failure of the real self's emergence. The efforts made by the real self to assert itself are thwarted in early childhood, often by mothers (and sometimes fathers) who fail to provide the child with the support and encouragement necessary for the emergence of autonomy. Oftentimes the parents of these adolescents are characterized as having impaired senses of selves, as are their adolescents.

Masterson notes that the abandonment depression reemerges when adolescents and adults confront separation experiences. The individual continues to tell the self a message that has been internalized from early childhood, that is, it is not all right to be an autonomous, unique individual. According to Masterson, manifestation of the abandonment depression can be observed in four different ways. Some adolescents become borderline and are at risk for a breakdown due to the stresses of emancipation and mastering the sex drive. A second group of adolescents simply drops out of society for a time through avoiding commitment and responsibility. Some adolescents may join cults or religious groups, where a powerful authority figure will provide a system of structure and rules for them. By joining cults, these adolescents also avoid taking responsibility for the self. A fourth group of adolescents, while appearing to be functioning better than those in the other groups, often seek therapy for other pathologies, such as phobias, psychosomatic symptoms, and anorexia.

In addition to borderline disorders, some writers have observed an association between the narcissistic personality disorder and identity disturbances. While a degree of self-focusing behavior is typical of adolescence (Elkind, 1968, 1979), Blatt (1983) observes that some adolescents do engage in narcissism to a degree that it is dysfunctional. Unhealthy narcissism is observed in the individual who engages in highly defensive gestures in order to prevent a confrontation with underlying feelings of being unloved, loneliness, inauthenticity, and emptiness (Blatt, 1983). Attachments to others are minimized to protect the frail sense of self from exposure. These observations are quite similar to Masterson's (1988) discussion of the real self and the false self.

Burch (1985) has written of a form of identity foreclosure observed in narcissistic adolescents. These adolescents, as children, were given too much independence and decision-making power by their parents. Further, their parents were quite willing to meet their children's narcissistic demands. Rather than working through the normal moratoria of adolescence, these individuals prematurely foreclose to their identities and expect to be treated as peers by adults.

In summary, the presence of psychopathology in adolescence, particularly borderline and narcissistic disorders, is strongly implicated in identity formation. Borderline disturbances bear strong resemblance to identity diffusion in that some borderline adolescents simply drop out of the identity search and commitment process. Other borderline adolescents may be susceptible to making foreclosed commitments at the urging of strong authority figures. Narcissic disorders also pose problems in identity formation of adolescents. It has been suggested that this group of adolescents is at risk for identity foreclosure. Self-exploration is too threatening to the narcissistic individual who rigidly defends the fragile sense of self.

SUMMARY

In this chapter, an attempt was made to highlight intervening factors in adolescent identity formation. Research on this topic is only suggestive due to its largely correlational nature. Thus, the conclusions drawn in this chapter should be regarded as speculative, but nonetheless are compelling in terms of topics for future research. Clinicians and adolescent practitioners, as well, may pay heed to the intervening factors of identity formation.

From the diverse topics covered in this chapter, it becomes apparent that there are many factors that interact with the formation of identity. While Erikson suggests that the earlier psychosocial stages are foundational to successful resolution of the identity conflict, in this chapter social contextual factors, cognitive factors, and factors within adolescent psychopathology were targeted as playing roles in the task of identity establishment. Some conditions may complicate the task of identity formation (e.g., ethnic and racial group membership and psychopathological disorders); while in other cases, the absence of certain capabilities may serve as barriers to identity formation (e.g., formal operations and cognitive complexity).

REFERENCES

Abraham, K. G. (1986). Ego-identity differences among Anglo-American and Mexican-American adolescents. *Journal of Adolescence, 9*, 151-166.

Adams, G. R. (1985). Family correlates of female adolescents' ego identity development. *Journal of Adolescence, 8*, 69-82.

Adams, G. R., Abraham, K. G., & Markstrom, C. A. (1987). The relationship between identity development, self-consciousness, and self-focusing during middle and late adolescence. *Developmental Psychology, 23*, 292-297.

Adams, G. R., Dyk, P., & Bennion, L. D. (1987). Parent-adolescent relationships and identity formation. *Family Perspective, 21,* 249-260.

Adams, G. R., & Fitch, S. A. (1981). Ego stage and identity status development: A cross-lag analysis. *Journal of Adolescence, 4,* 163-171.

Adams, G. R., & Fitch, S. A. (1982). Ego stage and identity status development: A cross-sequential analysis. *Journal of Personality and Social Psychology, 43,* 574-583.

Adams, G. R., & Jones, R. M. (1983). Female adolescents' identity development: Age comparisons and perceived childrearing experiences. *Developmental Psychology, 19,* 249-256.

Adams, G. R., & Shea, J. A. (1979). The relationship between identity status, locus of control, and ego development. *Journal of Youth and Adolescence, 8,* 81-89.

Akhtar, S. (1984). The syndrome of identity diffusion. *American Journal of Psychiatry, 141,* 1381-1385.

American Psychiatric Association (1987). *Diagnostic and statistical manual of mental disorders* (3rd ed. revised). Washington, DC: American Psychiatric Association.

Arnold, L. E. (1983). *Preventing adolescent alienation.* Lexington, MA: Lexington Books.

Ball, L., & Chandler, M. (1989). Identity formation in suicidal and nonsuicidal youth: The role of self-continuity. *Development and Psychopathology, 1,* 257-275.

Bar-Joseph, H., & Tzuriel, D. (1990). Suicidal tendencies and ego identity in adolescence. *Adolescence, 25,* 215-223.

Baumeister, R. F. (1986). *Identity: Cultural change and the struggle for self.* New York: Oxford University Press.

Berlin, I. N. (1986). Psychopathology and its antecedents among American Indian adolescents. In B. B. Lahey & A. E. Kazdin (Eds.), *Advances in clinical child psychology* (Vol. 9.) (pp. 125-152). New York: Plenum.

Berzonsky, M. D., & Neimeyer, G. J. (1988). Identity status and personal construct systems. *Journal of Adolescence, 11,* 195-204.

Berzonsky, M. D., Weiner, A. S., & Raphael, D. (1975). Interdependence of formal reasoning. *Developmental Psychology, 11,* 258.

Blatt, S. J. (1983). Narcissism and egocentrism as concepts in individual and cultural development. *Psychoanalysis and Contemporary Thought, 6,* 291-303.

Burch, C. A. (1985). Identity foreclosure in early adolescence: A problem of narcissistic equilibrium. *Adolescent Psychiatry, 12,* 145-161.

Buss, R. R., & Enright, R. D. (1987). Helping adolescents improve their ego identity. In J. C. Coleman (Ed.), *Working with troubled adolescents* (pp. 153-166). London: Academic Press.

Campbell, E., Adams, G. R., & Dobson, W. R. (1984). Familial correlates of identity formation in late adolescence. *Journal of Youth and Adolescence, 13,* 509-525.

Cauble, M. A. (1976). Formal operations, ego identity and principled morality: Are they related? *Developmental Psychology, 12,* 363-364.

Cooper, C. R., Grotevant, H. D., & Condon, S. M. (1983). Individuality and connectedness in the family as a context for adolescent identity formation and role-taking skill. In H. D. Grotevant & C. R. Cooper (Eds.), *New directions for child development: Vol. 22. Adolescent development in the family* (pp. 43-59). San Francisco: Jossey-Bass.

Cote, J. E., & Reker, G. T. (1979). Cognitive complexity and ego identity formation: A synthesis of cognitive and ego psychology. *Social Behavior and Personality, 7,* 107-112.

Davis, G. L. (1986). Spiritual direction: A model for adolescent catechesis. *Religious Education, 81,* 267-278.

Dean, R. A. (1982). Youth: Moonies' target population. *Adolescence, 17,* 567-574.

Donovan, J. M. (1975). Identity status and interpersonal style. *Journal of Youth and Adolescence, 4*, 37-55.

Elkind, D. (1968). Cognitive structure and adolescent experience. *Adolescence, 2*, 427-434.

Elkind, D. (1979). *The child and society: Essays in applied child development*. New York: Oxford University Press.

Enright, R. D., & Deist, S. H. (1979). Social perspective taking as a component of identity formation. *Adolescence, 14*, 517-522.

Enright, R. D., Ganiere, D. M., Buss, R. R., Lapsley, D. K., & Olson, L. M. (1983). Promoting identity development in adolescents. *Journal of Early Adolescence, 3*, 247-255.

Enright, R. D., Olson, L. M., Ganiere, D., Lapsley, D. K., & Buss, R. R. (1984). A clinical model for enhancing adolescent ego identity. *Journal of Adolescence, 7*, 119-130.

Erikson, E. H. (1963). *Childhood and society* (2nd ed.). New York: Norton.

Erikson, E. H. (1968). *Identity: Youth and crisis*. New York: Norton.

Feinstein, S. C. (1980). The cult phenomenon: Transition, repression, and regression. *Adolescent Psychiatry*, 113-122.

Freud, A. (1971). *The writings of Anna Freud: Problems of psychoanalytic training, diagnosis and techniques of therapy* (Vol. 7). New York: International Universities Press.

Gordon, D. E. (1988). Formal operations and interpersonal and affective disturbances in adolescents. In E. D. Nannis & P. A. Cowan (Eds.), *New directions for child development: Vol. 39. Developmental Psychopathology and its Treatment* (pp. 51-73). San Francisco: Jossey-Bass.

Grotevant, H. D., & Cooper, C. R. (1985). Patterns of interaction in family relationships and the development of identity exploration in adolescence. *Child Development, 56*, 415-428.

Hall, G. S. (1904). *Adolescence* (Vols. 1 & 2). Englewood Cliffs, NJ: Prentice-Hall.

Hauser, S. T. (1972a). Black and white identity development: Aspects and perspectives. *Journal of Youth and Adolescence, 1*, 113-130.

Hauser, S. T. (1972b). Adolescent self-image development. *Archives of General Psychiatry, 27*, 537-541.

Hill, J. P., & Palmquist, W. J. (1978). Social cognition and social relations in early adolescence. *International Journal of Behavioral Development, 1*, 1-36.

Inhelder, B., & Piaget, J. (1958). *The growth of logical thinking from childhood to adolescence*. New York: Basic Books.

Jordon, D. (1971). Parental antecedents and personality characteristics of ego identity statuses. Unpublished doctoral dissertation, State University of New York at Buffalo.

Katz, P. (1981). Psychotherapy with Native adolescents. *Canadian Journal of Psychiatry, 26*, 455-459.

Kirby, C. S. (1977). *Complexity-simplicity as a dimension of identity formation*. Unpublished doctoral dissertation, Michigan State University.

Kohlberg, L., & Gilligan, C. (1971). The adolescent as a philosopher: The discovery of the self in a post-conventional world. *Daedalus, 100*, 1051-1086.

LaFromboise, T. D., & Low, K. G. (1989). American Indian children and adolescents. In J. T. Gibbs & L. N. Huang (Eds.), *Children of color* (pp. 114-147). San Francisco: Jossey-Bass.

Leadbetter, B. J., & Dionne, J. (1981). The adolescent's use of formal operational thinking in solving problems related to identity resolution. *Adolescence, 16*, 111-121.

Loevinger, J. (1976). *Ego development*. San Francisco: Jossey-Bass.

Looft, W. R. (1971). Egocentrism and social interaction in adolescence. *Adolescence, 6*, 485-494.

Looft, W. R. (1972). Egocentrism and social interaction across the life span. *Psychological Bulletin, 78*, 73-92.

Marcia, J. E. (1966). Development and validation of ego identity status. *Journal of Personality and Social Psychology, 3*, 551-558.

Markstrom, C. A. (1987, April). *A comparison of psychosocial maturity between four ethnic groups during middle adolescence.* Paper presented at the biennial meetings of the Society of Research on Child Development, Baltimore, MD.

Markstrom-Adams, C., Ascione, F. R., Braegger, D., & Adams, G. (under review). The effects of two forms of perspective-taking training on ego identity formation in late adolescence.

Masterson, J. F. (1988). *The search for the real self: Unmasking the personality disorders of our age.* New York: Free Press.

Mendelberg, H. E. (1986). Identity conflict in Mexican-American adolescents. *Adolescence, 21*, 215-222.

Muuss, R. E. (1982). *Theories of adolescence* (4th ed.). New York: Random House.

Offer, E., & Offer, J. (1975). *From teenage to young manhood.* New York: Basic Books.

Parker, M. S. (1985). Identity and the development of religious thinking. In A. S. Waterman (Ed.), *New directions for child development: Vol. 30. Identity in adolescence: Processes and contents* (pp. 43-60). San Francisco: Jossey-Bass.

Piaget, J. (1972). Intellectual evolution from adolescence to adulthood. *Human Development, 15*, 1-12.

Piaget, J., & Inhelder, B. (1969). *The psychology of the child.* New York: Basic Books.

Protinsky, H., & Wilkerson, J. (1986). Ego identity, egocentrism, and formal operations. *Adolescence, 21*, 461-466.

Rowe, L., & Marcia, J. E. (1980). Ego identity status, formal operations, and moral development. *Journal of Youth and Adolescence, 9*, 87-99.

Selman, R. L. (1980). *The growth of interpersonal understanding: Development and clinical analysis.* New York: Academic Press.

Slugoski, B. R., Marcia, M. E., & Koopman, R. F. (1984). Cognitive and social interactional characteristics of ego identity statuses in college males. *Journal of Personality and Social Psychology, 47*, 646-661.

Spencer, M. B., & Markstrom-Adams, C. (1990). Identity processes among American cultural minority group children. *Child Development, 61*, 290-310.

Streitmatter, J. L. (1988). Ethnicity as a mediating variable of early adolescent identity development. *Journal of Adolescence, 11*, 335-346.

Sue, D. W. (1981). *Counseling the culturally different: Theory and practice.* New York: John Wiley.

Tzuriel, D., & Klein, M. M. (1977). Ego identity: Effect of ethnocentrism, ethnic identification, and cognitive complexity in Israeli, Oriental, and Western ethnic groups. *Psychological Reports, 40*, 1099-1110.

Wagner, J. A. (1987). Formal operations and ego identity in adolescence. *Adolescence, 22*, 23-35.

Waterman, A. S. (1984). *The psychology of individualism.* New York: Praeger.

Whitbourne, S. K. (1986). *The me I know: A study of adult identity.* New York: Springer-Verlag.

10. A Process Perspective on Identity and Stress Management

Michael D. Berzonsky
State University of New York at Cortland

INTRODUCTION

According to Erikson's (1968) life-span theory of personality development, adolescents are confronted with the task of constructing a clear sense of self-identity. Identity emerges as prior identifications and residuals from childhood conflicts are integrated and structured. This self-structure provides a subjective sense of inner unity and a feeling of integrative continuity over time. Although Erikson does not discuss it this way, identity can be conceptualized as a self-constructed theory of the self (Berzonsky, 1989a; Epstein, 1973). This self-structure serves as the conceptual framework within which life experiences are interpreted and it provides the basis for attempts to cope with stressors and personal problems.

To operationally define identity most researchers have relied on Marcia's (1966) identity status paradigm. Even though the paradigm has its critics (e.g., Blasi, 1988; Cote & Levine, 1988, but compare Waterman, 1988), over the past two decades it has dominated the field of identity research (see Berzonsky, 1988; Bourne, 1978; Marcia, 1980; Waterman, 1982, for reviews). Within Marcia's scheme, the presence or absence of self-reported self-exploration crisis and commitment serve to designate four identity classifications: *Foreclosure* (commitment without current or past self-exploration crises); *Diffusion* (neither commitment nor self-exploration present); *Moratorium* (ongoing self-exploration in the absence of commitment); and *Achiever* (commitment present and past self-exploration indicated).

Within the status model identity is typically construed as an outcome variable: a relatively stable personality *structure* that is conserved over time and situations (compare, however, Grotevant,

1987; Marcia, 1988). In this chapter I elaborate a model of identity development that highlights individual differences in the *process* by which self-relevant experience is encoded, represented, and utilized. It is argued that individuals within Marcia's (1966) identity statuses differ in the social-cognitive processes they use to make decisions, cope with problems, and negotiate identity issues (see Berzonsky, 1990). More specifically, three processing orientations are proposed to underlie the four statuses (Berzonsky, 1988, 1989a). Self-exploring moratoriums and achievers are hypothesized to be (or to have been) *information-oriented*; they effortfully seek out, elaborate, and evaluate relevant information before attempting to deal with problems and make decisions. Individuals in the diffusion category tend to be *avoidant oriented*; they characteristically procrastinate and try to avoid dealing with problems and decisions as long as possible. Finally, the model proposes that identity foreclosures tend to employ a *normative orientation*; they conform to the normative expectations and prescriptions held by significant others, such as parental figures.

I begin with an overview of the model. (A more detailed description appears in Berzonsky, 1988, 1990). Next, evidence supporting the relationship between identity status and the three processing orientations is reviewed. My major purpose in this chapter is to extend the model to individual differences in the way in which adolescents cope with personal problems and manage stress.

A PROCESS MODEL OF IDENTITY

The present model derives from the premise that individuals are capable of actively processing information and that, at least in the long run, information-based decisions will maximize adaptation. Following theorists such as Fritz Heider (1958), George Kelly (1955), Jean Piaget (1950), and others, I use a person-as-scientist metaphor to characterize identity development over the life-span (Berzonsky, 1990). As individuals live and adapt within environmental and social contexts, self-relevant experiences occur and problems are encountered. To adapt effectively, individuals function as *intuitive* "scientists," attempting to construct "theories" and make causal inferences about themselves, the contexts within which they live, and Self by Context interactions (Berzonsky, 1989a).

Person-as-Intuitive-Scientist

The person-as-scientist metaphor does not imply that individuals deliberately theorize about themselves in a formal manner nor does it suggest that individuals are able or willing to construct a valid theory about their "true" nature (see Berzonsky, 1986a, 1986b; but compare Waterman, 1986). The self-constructions that are comprised in one's identity may be unwittingly generated and only vaguely understood. In terms of George Kelly's (1955) *construction corollary*, people are able to cope effectively in their lives because over time they notice, abstract, and interpret the recurrent themes and regularities in their experience. These interpretations or self-constructions, not the objective events-in-themselves, influence what individuals do.

Epstein (1973) suggested that the self-concept or identity structure is actually a self-theory—a conceptual structure about oneself that is *unconsciously* constructed. This self-structure serves the same functions as any theory in that it is the framework within which self-relevant information is interpreted, and it contains the cognitive schemata and scripted behavioral strategies (Neisser, 1976; Schank & Abelson, 1977) that govern problem-solving. Successful adaptation involves a dialectical interchange between assimilative and accommodative processes (Berzonsky, 1990). In the course of daily living, the identity structure or self-theory directs initial efforts to resolve problems and obstacles as they arise, and it provides a basis for assimilating and construing experiences. Such assimilative processing requires minimal attentional effort; it is considered to be relatively "mindless" and automatic (e.g., Langer, Blank, & Chanowitz, 1978; Shiffrin & Schneider, 1977). While such processing is very efficient (see Hansen, 1985), it can also lead to structure-driven distortions of reality. For resourceful coping, therefore, there needs to be continual monitoring and evaluating of feedback about the effectiveness of a particular approach. When assimilative efforts fail, a state of dissonance exists and accommodative efforts to revise the schema or strategy are necessitated. In the long run, optimal adaptation would result from a flexible and balanced deployment of assimilative and accommodative processes (see Berzonsky, 1990; Block, 1982; Showers & Cantor, 1985).

Status Differences in Self-Construction

It is proposed that the four statuses in Marcia's paradigm reflect three different styles of personal problem solving and decision making. By definition, individuals classified as moratoriums and achievers in Marcia's scheme are, or at least have been, engaged in an *information-oriented* process of self-exploration; they deliberately seek out (or have sought out) self-relevant information before making identity-relevant decisions and committing themselves. They differ on the commitment identity dimension; achievers have made firm decisions, moratoriums have not. Foreclosures have used a *normative-oriented* approach to making identity commitments; they have dealt with problems by internalizing the norms and expectations held for them by parents and significant others. Diffusions, like moratoriums, lack firm identity commitments. Instead of actively attending to and processing relevant information, however, they tend to be *avoidant-oriented*; they delay and procrastinate until the hedonic cues in the immediate situation dictate a course of action.

These orientations comprise the processing components used to encode, integrate, evaluate, and revise self-relevant information in various life domains. It is assumed that these processes operate on at least three different planes (Berzonsky, 1990). The most basic level consists of *actual* behavioral and cognitive responses that individuals use to solve problems and cope in the course of day-to-day living. *Social-cognitive strategies* are systematic collections of the more basic acts and cognitive representations. For example, depending on the nature of a problem, an information-oriented strategy might take the form of reading, talking to knowledgeable others, or trial-and-error personal experimenting. In each instance, the goal is to obtain and evaluate relevant information before (if?) it is utilized. *Identity style* refers to the strategy that an individual characteristically uses or, reportedly, would prefer to deploy. By late adolescence, virtually all normal individuals would be capable of utilizing all three social-cognitive strategies. Consequently, motivational factors may tend to account for individual differences in identity style (see Berzonsky, 1990). Also, strategy utilization may be affected by situational factors, such as environmental demands and problems. Individuals who ordinarily would operate in a normative- or avoidant/diffuse-oriented fashion may engage in effortful analyses of problem-relevant information under specific conditions, such as volitional freedom (Wicklund & Brehm, 1976), accountability (Tetlock, Skitka, & Boettger, 1989), and personal relevance (Petty, Cacioppo, & Goldman, 1981). Finally, processing orientation may be influenced by the extent to which existing information and beliefs are integrated and crystallized: Structure and process are reciprocally related. Well-organized self-constructs and firm identity commitments may "drive" assimilation and processing in an efficient but biased manner (see, for example, Berzonsky, 1989b; Hansen, 1985; Markus, 1977).

In the following section, research suggesting a parallel between these social-cognitive orientations and identity status is reviewed. First, investigations of status differences on social cognitive variables are considered, followed by a review of research on identity style.

IDENTITY STATUS AND SOCIAL COGNITION

Normative-Oriented Foreclosures

Status comparisons on measures of authoritarianism suggest that foreclosures possess rigid belief systems, are intolerant of ambiguity, and are closed to potentially dissonant information (Berzonsky & Neimeyer, 1988; Marcia, 1966, 1967; Schenkel & Marcia, 1972). On measures of interpersonal style and attentional focus, Read, Adams, and Dobson (1984) found that foreclosures had the greatest difficulty evaluating and integrating information from multiple perspectives, and that both foreclosures and diffusions were closed to relevant information because of a restricted attentional focus. Likewise, findings by Slugoski, Marcia, and Koopman (1984) reveal that foreclosures and diffusions had problems assuming a self-determined perspective within which conflicting sources of information could be integrated and evaluated. In a self-presentation experiment, Berzonsky, Schlenker, and McKillop (1987) found that foreclosures displayed a significant tendency to *resist* internalizing a positive public self-presentation (i.e., playing the role of a very sociable applicant in a simulated job interview). Finally, correlational findings indicate that identity foreclosure is positively associated with a socially defined identity, public self-consciousness, other-directed self-monitoring, and other-oriented problem-solving strategies (Berzonsky, Trudeau, & Brennan, 1988; Grotevant & Adams, 1984). The picture that emerges is one of individuals with inflexible belief and value systems who tend to be overly reliant on the normative expectations of others.

Information-Oriented Self-Explorers

Slugoski et al. (1984) found that cognitive integrative complexity was characteristic of self-reflective moratoriums and achievers. In the aforementioned Read et al. (1984) investigation, moratoriums and achievers, in contrast to foreclosures and diffusions, made fewer mistakes as information load increased, processed greater amounts of information, and were more self-certain about their own judgments. However, the data suggest that social-cognitive processing among self-explorers may be qualified by an individual's level of identity commitment.

For instance, studies of personal-construct-system differentiation indicated that *ongoing* (a moratorium state) but *not past* (achiever) self-exploration is associated with increased cognitive complexity (Berzonsky & Neimeyer, 1988; Berzonsky, Rice, & Neimeyer, 1990). Differences in social-cognitive correlates of the two self-exploration statuses have also been reported. Berzonsky et al. (1988) found that achievement was positively associated with personally defined identity content (see Cheek & Briggs, 1982), but moratorium scores were not. Likewise, other-directed self-monitoring (Snyder, 1974) was negatively correlated with achievement, but positively associated with moratorium scores. One explanation is that during the process of self-exploration, one may look to others for information and alternatives to consider and evaluate. Once commitments have been made, one is less apt to do this in at least a nondiscriminating fashion. Indeed, Adams, Ryan, Hoffman, Dobson, and Nielsen (1985, Study 3) found that although identity achieved subjects were not susceptible to the vagaries of peer-conformity pressures, they did indicate that they conform for instrumental purposes, such as achieving a goal. (The possible influence that structural commitments exert on processing orientation is considered below.)

Avoidant-Oriented Diffusions

Grotevant and Adams (1984) found that diffusions reported a tendency to avoid confronting personal problems. Berzonsky et al. (1988) found that identity diffuseness was negatively correlated with a personally defined identity and private self-consciousness, but positively associated with other-directed self-monitoring and a tendency to act in a manner consistent with current situational demands. Finally, in the Berzonsky et al. (1987) self-presentation experiment mentioned above, the subjects were randomly assigned to three role-playing contexts: a face-to-face encounter with a confederate, a written interview, and an anonymous presentation condition. Diffuseness was significantly correlated with internalizing the self-presentation in the actual face-to-face encounter but not the other two conditions. These findings are consistent with the notion that diffusions tend to operate in a situation-specific fashion since minimal immediate consequences would occur in the written and anonymous conditions (see Berzonsky, 1988).

PROCESSING ORIENTATION: IDENTITY STYLE

In order to investigate these processing orientations more directly, I have constructed a self-report measure of identity style (Berzonsky, 1989b, 1990). It should be noted that these orientations are assumed to operate on at least three planes (see above). Identity style is the most *general* level and refers to the orientation that *reportedly* an individual typically uses or would prefer to employ.

An Identity Style Inventory (ISI) was developed by uncoupling the commitment and self-exploration components that would be confounded in statements about identity status. For example, "I've more or less always operated according to the values I was brought up with" (normative); "It doesn't pay to worry about values in advance: I decide things as they happen" (avoidant/diffuse); and "I've spent a lot of time and talked to a lot of people, trying to develop a set of values that makes sense to me" (information). Six items were written for each scale. In addition, a 10-item commitment scale was developed: "I'm not sure which values I really hold." Subjects rate on a Likert scale the extent to which they consider the statements to be self-descriptive. The inventory yields three style scores—diffuse/avoidant orientation (diff); information orientation (info); and normative orientation (norm)—and a commitment (comm) index. Internal reliability coefficients (alpha) ranged from .52 (norm) to .77 (comm), and test-retest correlations over a 5-week interval varied from .78 (diff) to .84 (comm) (Berzonsky, 1989b). A revised version of the ISI (Berzonsky, in press) contains a 10-item diff scale (coefficient alpha = .73), 10-item info scale (coefficient alpha = .62), 9-item norm scale (coefficient alpha = .66) in addition to the 10-item comm scale. Revised Scale × Original Scale correlations (N = 171) were: .70 (diff), .72 (norm), and .75 (info). (Additional information about the ISI is provided in Berzonsky, 1989b, 1990, in press.)

Social-Cognitive Correlates of Identity Style

Research indicates that reported use of an information-oriented identity style is associated with facilitative anxiety reactions and an internal locus of control (Berzonsky, 1989b) and a number of social-cognitive dimensions, including a need for cognition, openness to ideas, a personal identity emphasis, and introspectiveness (Berzonsky, 1990). Reported use of an avoidant/diffuse style has been found to be correlated positively with external-control expectancies, other-directed self-monitoring, and debilitative anxiety reactions (Berzonsky, 1989b), and inversely associated with introspectiveness and an openness to personal feelings (Berzonsky, 1990). Finally, individuals who use a normative style appear to close off "core" areas of the self, such as value and belief systems: Negative correlations have been obtained between a normative orientation and openness to ideas, values, and actions (Berzonsky, 1990).

Identity Status and Identity Style

According to the process model being developed, the three processing orientations or styles can be mapped onto Marcia's (1966) four identity statuses (see Berzonsky, 1988, 1989a). Berzonsky (1989b, Study 2) used the Grotevant and Adams (1984) measure to assess identity status. As predicted, the Normative × Foreclosure and Diffuse/Avoidant × Diffusion correlations were significant. These relationships were replicated in a follow-up investigation in which Melgosa's (1985) index of occupational identity status was used (Berzonsky, 1990).

The relationship between an information-oriented style and identity status appears to be complicated. For instance, Berzonsky (1989b, Study 2), found a significant Information × Achiever zero-order correlation ($r = .25$, $p<.05$). However, when achiever scores were regressed on the ISI variables, a *normative* orientation was the only style variable that accounted for a significant portion of the variation in achiever scores beyond that attributed to commitment. In addition, Berzonsky (1989b, Study 2) found that the zero-order Moratorium Status × Information Style relationship was not significant ($r= .06$). However, a significant partial Information × Moratorium correlation ($r = .34$, $p<.01$) was obtained when the effect of commitment was statistically controlled. This finding has been replicated with Melgosa's (1985) measure of occupational identity status (Berzonsky, 1990): A significant Information × Moratorium correlation was not obtained until the effect of commitment was statistically removed ($r = .10$; partial $r = .27$, $p<.01$). Thus commitment may serve to suppress the extent to which an information orientation is utilized: It may be inefficient to continually reconsider issues and problems after decisions have been made.

These correlational analyses ignore qualitative distinctions among the status categories. We just completed an investigation of the hypothesized Status × Style relationships within a large-scale sample of "pure" status types (Berzonsky & Neimeyer, 1990). The 148 subjects included in these analyses were culled from a sample of 560 undergraduate late adolescents who had been administered the Extended Objective Measure of Ego Identity Development (Adams, Shea, & Fitch, 1979). There were 55 achievers, 28 moratoriums, 28 foreclosures, and 37 diffusions. A

Table 10.1 Mean Style Scores on Identity Status Indices

Identity Status Style Orientations	Achievers (N = 55)	Moratoriums (N = 28)	Foreclosures (N = 28)	Diffusions (N = 37)	F Ratio	p
Information	39.35$_{ab}$	36.59$_a$	36.36$_b$	33.41$_{ab}$	10.78	<.01
Normative	29.45$_{acd}$	25.67$_{ac}$	32.43$_{ab}$	25.89$_{bd}$	12.26	<.01
Avoidant/ Diffuse	21.67$_a$	23.89$_b$	23.92$_c$	27.24$_{abc}$	6.25	<.01
Commitment	43.39$_{ab}$	33.07$_a$	39.82$_{ab}$	35.00$_b$	34.52	<.01

NOTE: Within rows, means with a common single-letter subscript differ by at least $p<.05$. For all univariate F-tests, df= 3, 144.

multiple analysis of variance (MANOVA) indicated a significant effect of status (Pillais), $F = 9.86$, $p<.01$. All univariate F-tests were significant (see Table 10.1).

As expected, foreclosures had the highest normative scores, and diffusions were highest on the avoidant/diffuse dimension. Consistent with the previous correlational data, the pattern of findings for the self-exploring statuses was complex. First, the normative scores of achievers were significantly higher than those of both moratoriums and diffusions. Second, the information-orientation scores of moratoriums were significantly lower than those of achievers, and not significantly higher than those of foreclosures (see Table 10.1). The statuses differed as predicted along the commitment dimension: achievers > foreclosures > diffusions = moratoriums.

Regression analyses indicated that commitment accounted for a significant proportion of the variance in each of the three style variables. A 4 (Status) × 3 (Style) MANCOVA with the ISI commitment index as a covariate was significant (Pillais), $F = 3.99$ $p<.01$. The univariate analyses and adjusted style means appear in Table 10.2.

The covariance analysis appears to shed some light on the hypothesized Information Orientation × Self-Explorer Statuses relationships. With the effect of commitment statistically controlled, self-exploring moratoriums were found to have the highest information orientation, significantly higher than foreclosures and diffusions. Also, when the effect of commitment was removed, the normative scores of achievers did not differ from those of moratoriums and diffusions.

Table 10.2 Adjusted Style Scores on Identity Status Indices

Style Orientations	Achievers (N = 55)	Moratoriums (N = 28)	Foreclosures (N = 28)	Diffusions (N = 37)	F Ratio	p
Information	37.24_c	38.39_{ab}	35.59_a	34.47_{bc}	4.73	<.01
Normative	27.34_a	27.46_b	31.67_{abc}	26.94_c	6.60	<.01
Avoidant/ Diffuse	23.61_b	22.23_a	24.63_c	24.26_{ab}	2.37	<.10

NOTE: Style scores adjusted for the effect of commitment. Within rows, means with a common single-letter subscript differ by at least $p<.05$. For all univariate F-tests, df = 3, 143.

These findings suggest that processing orientation cannot be considered independent from structural aspects of identity. That is to say, an information-oriented self-explorer (a.k.a. moratorium) seeks out, processes, and evaluates self-relevant information when dealing with problems, stressors, and decisions. Information that proves to be useful and effective will over time become schematized and crystallized. Such well-integrated and organized self-constructs may then tend to "drive" subsequent processing and problem-solving in a more biased "normative" fashion (see Hansen 1985; Kihlstrom & Cantor, 1984). Processing orientation or preferences may be influenced by the extent to which an individual's global self-identity (or specific relevant aspects of it) is structurally integrated and consolidated. Once personal decisions and commitments have been "achieved," there may be a tendency for problem solving and information processing to become more focused and restricted.

Longitudinal data on changes in processing orientation and structural integration over time would be one way of investigating this hypothesis (see Berzonsky et al., 1990). An alternative approach was employed by Neimeyer, Prichard, Berzonsky, and Metzler (1990). Subjects within the four identity statuses were randomly assigned to one of three occupational relevance conditions: high personal relevance, moderate personal relevance, and low personal relevance. (The subjects had previously rated the self-relevance of 12 occupations.) The subjects read a description of the assigned occupation and then completed a hypothesis-generation task designed to have them assess their *suitability* or *unsuitability* for that occupation; they were instructed to generate any thoughts and ideas that they considered to be relevant to making a decision about this occupation (see Blustein & Strohmer, 1987). Overall, information-oriented subjects (achievers and moratoriums) generated significantly more total hypotheses than foreclosures and diffusions. This main effect, however, was qualified by a marginal Identity Processing Orientation × Occupational Relevance × Hypothesis Type Interaction. Specifically, when generating hypotheses about highly relevant or irrelevant occupations, *all* participants demonstrated a pronounced *confirmation* bias. Regardless of identity orientation, occupations about which the subjects already held firm, well-organized views resulted in biased, schema-driven hypothesis-testing. In the moderate-relevant condition, however, self-explorers generated significantly more self-unsuited hypotheses than did the nonself-explorers. Thus, the self-exploring statuses employed a balanced, information-oriented approach, but only in the condition where they did not already hold firm views. Interestingly, this effect was not qualified by the subjects' level of global identity commitments; both moratoriums and achievers displayed the balanced strategy in the moderate-relevant condition. In the other two conditions, committed foreclosures (and achievers) and uncommitted moratoriums (and diffusions) were equally one-sided in their hypothesis production. These results are consistent with the view that structural consolidation and specific content may influence, even override, processing orientation (see Berzonsky, 1990; Neimeyer et al., 1990).

We now turn to the major concern of this chapter: What role does identity processing orientation play in coping with stressors? Stress management is considered in terms of Lazarus and Folkman's (1984) model of cognitive appraisal and coping style.

COPING WITH STRESSORS

Stress has been conceptualized as a relational concept involving a Person × Environmental Event (stressor) interaction (Folkman, 1984). Stress results when a person encounters a pressure to change in an undesired way. Since the time of G. Stanley Hall, adolescence has been described as a period of extraordinary stress. While there are opposing views and explanations of this description (compare, e.g., Bandura, 1964; Blos, 1962; and Coleman, 1978), one conclusion seems inescapable: At least some adolescents experience considerable stress and anxiety (Berzonsky, 1982; Coleman, 1978).

Normal adolescence is marked by a multiplicity of transitions and potential stressors, including puberty, peer pressures, changing academic and social demands, dating experiences, and expectations for developing independence. Yet not all adolescents experience a "turbulent decade" (see Bandura, 1964; Douvan & Adelson, 1966; Offer, 1969). A relevant question to ask is, "Why do some adolescents seem to be more vulnerable to or at risk for these potential stressors?" Or, to state it more positively, "What accounts for inter-individual differences in how effectively adolescents cope with stressors and personal problems?"

Coping has been defined in terms of the deliberate, controlled efforts that are made in reaction to a potential stressor. Lazarus (1966) and his colleagues (e.g., Folkman & Lazarus, 1980, 1985) have distinguished two types of strategies. *Problem-focused* coping is aimed at altering the event or situation that is producing the strain: for example, seeking relevant information and options, generating alternative solutions, making decisions, and acting to alter the stress-inducing situation. *Emotion-focused* coping is aimed at alleviating or regulating the emotional distress being experienced by utilizing defensive tactics, such as denial, wishful thinking, distancing, attempting to reduce the tension being experience, or seeking emotional solace from others—avoiding the cause of the stress (Folkman & Lazarus, 1980, 1985).

These strategies as conceptualized by Folkman and Lazarus (1985) are *not* considered to be stable individual dispositions. According to their model, the use of problem-focused or emotion-focused coping depends on a two-step process of cognitive appraisals. The primary appraisal involves an assessment of the personal implications of the stressor: Is the stressor seen as being threatening or challenging? Is it a question of possible harm (bodily or psychological injury) and loss (self-esteem) or development and improvement? The secondary appraisal considers the availability of personal, social, and physical resources: What can I do? (Folkman, 1984). Generally, emotion-focused coping strategies are employed whenever individuals decide they cannot solve the problem or do something constructive. Positive or optimistic appraisals about personal resourcefulness are associated with problem-focused coping (Folkman & Lazarus, 1980). Research has demonstrated the existence of these two coping strategies in populations of early adolescents (Compas, 1987), late adolescents, and adults (Folkman & Lazarus, 1980, 1985).

The process model of identity development presented above suggests that there may be dispositional differences in the way in which individuals appraise and attempt to manage stressors. Information-oriented individuals should generally construe stressors as being manageable and, therefore, resort to problem-focused coping efforts. The avoidant/diffuse style is assumed to be characterized by procrastination and problem avoidance; attempts to escape from the emotional distress with little regard for adaptive, long-term *problem* solutions should occur. A normative style involves reliance on social authorities, referent groups, and significant others.

Identity Status and Stress Management

According to Erikson's (1968) theory, a coherent sense of ego identity furnishes the basis for adapting effectively with the vicissitudes of life. However, research on identity and stress management is scant. Marcia (1966) did find that identity achievers performed more effectively than the other statuses (especially diffusions) on a concept attainment task administered under externally imposed stress. Other studies (see Berzonsky et al., 1988; Grotevant & Adams, 1984) reveal the following: Self-exploration (achievement) is characterized by reported tendencies to confront stressors with self-directed strategies and an absence of other-directed, self-monitoring; foreclosure is associated with public self-consciousness, and other-directed, self-monitoring and proble solving; diffusions reportedly avoid coping with problems and are other-oriented. (See Jorgensen & Dusek, in press; Lobel & Gilat, 1987; and Reischl & Hirsch, 1989, for recent attempts to investigate identity and coping outside of the identity status framework.)

Identity Style and Stress Management

I have recently completed several studies relevant to the hypothesized relationship between identity orientation and coping with stress. For instance, debilitative test anxiety reactions and external control expectancies were found to be positively associated with an avoidant/diffuse identity style, but inversely correlated with an information orientation. In addition, facilitative test anxiety was characteristic of individuals who were information-oriented (Berzonsky, 1989b, Study 1).

In an initial attempt to examine directly the relationship between coping with stress and identity style, 98 late-adolescent undergraduates were administered the Identity Style Inventory and Folkman and Lazarus's (1985) Ways-of-Coping checklist (see Berzonsky, 1990). The participants were asked to respond to the Ways-of-Coping checklist in terms of a *specific academic* situation (e.g., test or paper assignment) that had actually created stress for them. The results indicated that *problem-focused* coping efforts were positively associated with an information-oriented identity style, and negatively correlated with an avoidant/diffuse style. Emotion-focused coping strategies, such as wishful thinking, tension reduction, and detachment, were positively associated with the avoidant/diffuse orientation. A normative identity style was positively correlated with social-support seeking and tendencies to engage in wishful thinking and detachment. These findings have been replicated and extended in a recent unpublished investigation (Berzonsky, in press).

The ISI, Ways-of-Coping checklist, and the Alpert and Haber (1960) measure of facilitative and debilitative test anxiety were administered to 171 (102 females, 69 males) late adolescents. Participants were asked to think about an actual stressful academic event when they completed the coping checklist. The correlation matrix by sex appears in Table 10.3.

The general pattern of Style × Coping correlates is consistent for males and females and tends to be comparable to those reported above (cf. Berzonsky, 1990). For both males and females emotion-focused coping is positively correlated with both an avoidant/diffuse and normative orientation. With females the normative style is also associated with social-support seeking. An information orientation in both sexes was related to both problem-focused and

Table 10.3 Intercorrelations Between Identity and Stress-Management Variables

Variable	A	B	C	D	E	F	G	H	I	J	K
Identity Variables											
A. Information	—	-.04	-.24**	.39**	.46**	.25**	-.23**	-.26**	.01	.27**	-.22**
B. Normative	.07	—	.15	.38**	-.03	.17*	.26**	.28**	.12	-.14	.13
C. Avoidant/Diffuse	-.22*	.12	—	-.39**	-.24**	.06	.43**	.53**	.24**	.00	.10
D. Commitment	.39**	.38**	-.24**	—	.22**	.18*	-.15	-.26**	-.10	-.04	-.05
Coping Variables											
E. Problem-Focused	.47**	.07	-.03	.20*	—	.40**	-.21*	-.23**	.11	.27**	-.08
F. Social Seeking	.25**	.00	-.15	.02	.34**	—	.21*	-.02	.30**	.04	.10
G. Wishful Thinking	-.09	.33**	.38**	.02	.01	.29**	—	.52**	.42**	-.17*	.37**
H. Detachment	-.07	.42**	.34**	-.08	-.13	.01	.46**	—	.37**	-.03	.18*
I. Tension Reduction	.04	.08	.14	.19	.22*	.24*	.37**	.18	—	.02	.23**
Test Anxiety Variables											
J. Facilitative	.01	-.16	.02	.05	.12	-.07	-.32**	-.33**	-.12	—	-.57**
K. Debilitative	-.01	.28**	.13	.11	-.02	.21*	.43**	.43**	.11	-.47**	—

NOTE: Correlations for Females (N = 102) are listed above the diagonal; males (N = 69) are listed below. *p<.05, **p<.01

Table 10.4 Stepwise Regression Analyses of Stress-Management Component Scores on ISI Variables

Analysis	R	R^2	Adjusted R^2	R^2 Change	Beta
DV: Emotion-Focused Coping					
Step 1: Avoidant/Diffuse					
Orientation	.50	.25	.25		.41**
Step 2: Normative					
Orientation	.55	.30	.29	.05**	.29**
Step 3: Commitment	.56	.32	.31	.02**	−.16*
DV: Problem-Focused Coping					
Step 1: Information					
Orientation	.42	.18	.18		.42**
DV: Negative Test Anxiety					
Step 1: No variables					
were entered					

NOTE: *p<.05 , ** p<.01

social-support-seeking coping efforts. Investigators have pointed out (see Carver, Scheier, & Weintraub, 1989; Folkman & Lazarus, 1985) that the seeking of social support may occur for different reasons, that is, instrumental or emotional support motives. Thus, information-oriented individuals may look to others in order to obtain relevant information and options before they make a personal decision, whereas normative-oriented individuals may look to others for emotional support or "the solution." (The latter "expressive" concern may be associated with a feminine sex role.)

In order to clarify further the interrelationships between identity orientation and stress-management style, I did some additional analyses on these data. First, to identify general coping styles, the five ways-of-coping and two test-anxiety variables were submitted to a principal components analysis. Three components were extracted and rotated to the varimax criterion. Component I was marked by detachment (.81), wishful thinking (.77), and tension reduction (.70) and was labelled Emotion-Focused Coping. The significant loadings of debilitative (.82) and facilitative (−.89) test anxiety served to identify Component II as Negative Test Anxiety. The third component, Problem-Focused Coping, was defined by the problem-focused (.82) and social-support seeking (.80) indices. Component scores were then computed for each subject and entered as dependent variables in a series of stepwise multiple regression analyses.

As predicted, an avoidant/diffuse orientation accounted for the largest portion of the variance in emotion-focused coping, $R = .50$, $R^2 = .25$ (see Table 10.4). In addition, a normative orientation and commitment independently accounted for a significant portion of the variation in emotion-focused coping. The beta weights indicate that the two style variables were positively associated with an emotional focus, while commitment was inversely related to the reported utilization of this method of stress management. An information-oriented style accounted for a significant portion of the variance in problem-focused coping ($R = .42$, $R^2 = .18$). Neither any of the style variables nor commitment were correlated with negative-test-anxiety reactions.

These findings support the process view of identity explicated above. Individuals who characteristically use an information-oriented approach to decision making and problem solving reportedly dealt with stressors by focusing on problem-relevant information and considerations. An avoidant/diffuse style was accompanied by concerns about managing the emotional distress itself rather than the underlying causal factors. Interestingly, a normative orientation was also linked to emotion-focused coping and problem avoidance. One possibility is that emotion-focused avoidance is a means by which foreclosed commitments can be maintained. Consistent with this view is evidence indicating that a normative orientation is associated with a tendency to be closed and inflexible in "hard core" aspects of the self, such as values (Berzonsky, 1990). Such defensive tactics may serve to insulate individuals from information that might threaten or invalidate critical self-views. It should be emphasized that commitment was entered into the regression model *after* the influence of a normative orientation was statistically controlled. At step 1, before the normative variable was entered, the Commitment × Emotion-Focused Coping correlation was nonsignificant, $r = -.02$, ns. Thus emotion-focused avoidance appears to be enhanced by norm-oriented commitments, but depressed by commitments not associated with a normative style.

CONCLUDING THOUGHTS

This chapter has focused on a process interpretation of identity development. Specifically, evidence suggests that identity style or processing orientation influences the way in which adolescents cope with potential stressors and make decisions. It should be reiterated that by late adolescence or earlier, all normal adolescents should be *capable* of utilizing all three of the orientations. The particular approach that is employed, therefore, may depend on situational influences as well as personal preferences: Flexible processes, rather than fixed personality traits or states, are involved. Also, structural consolidation of self-beliefs, attitudes, and values may affect the way in which subsequent information is processed and utilized. For instance, information-oriented individuals who have "achieved" a well-integrated sense of self-identity may then begin to operate in a more restricted, normative manner. This would provide a possible explanation of some of the theoretically inconsistent changes reported in longitudinal studies of identity development: for example, achiever-to-foreclosure or moratorium-to-foreclosure regressions (see Adams & Fitch, 1982; Marcia, 1976). Of course, a characteristic preference to continually process and be open to novel information may dispose some individuals to recurring identity "crises" over the life span (Vaillant, 1977).

It is important to emphasize that identity develops within a given cultural context and cannot be divorced from environmental constraints and interpersonal influences. The adaptiveness of a particular processing orientation may depend on the socio-historical circumstances within which it is instantiated: There may be nothing inherently advantageous about an information orientation. Identity Style × Environmental Context interactions need to be investigated.

Finally, process is inextricably confounded with other aspects of identity: A person is an integrated whole who is different from the sum of separate components. While componential analyses may be useful for investigating identity and stress management (and other specific issues), they necessarily fail to capture the complexities of individuals as they function in real-life contexts. A more complete understanding of identity development requires consideration of the reciprocal and interdependent relationships among identity components: process, structure, content, function, and context.

REFERENCES

Adams, G. R., & Fitch, S. A. (1982). Ego stage and identity status development: A cross-sequential analysis. *Journal of Personality and Social Psychology, 43*, 574-583.

Adams, G. R., Ryan, J. H., Hoffman, J. J., Dobson, W. R., & Nielsen, E. C. (1985). Ego identity status, conformity behavior, and personality in late adolescence. *Journal of Personality and Social Psychology, 47*, 1091-1104.

Adams, G. R., Shea, J., & Fitch, S. A. (1979). Toward the development of an objective assessment of ego-identity status. *Journal of Youth and Adolescence, 8*, 223-237.

Alpert, R., & Haber, R. N. (1960). Anxiety in academic achievement situations. *Journal of Abnormal and Social Psychology, 61*, 207-215.

Bandura, A. (1964). The stormy decade: Fact or fiction? *Psychology in the Schools, 1*, 224-231.

Berzonsky, M. D. (1982). Inter- and intra-individual differences in adolescent storm and stress: A life-span developmental view. *Journal of Early Adolescence, 2*, 211-217.

Berzonsky, M. D. (1986a). Discovery versus constructivist interpretations of identity formation: Consideration of additional implications. *Journal of Early Adolescence, 6*, 111-117.

Berzonsky, M. D. (1986b). Identity formation, metaphors, and values: A rejoinder to Waterman. *Journal of Early Adolescence, 6*, 123-126.

Berzonsky, M. D. (1988). Self-theorists, identity status, and social cognition. In D. K. Lapsley & F. C. Power (Eds.), *Self, ego, and identity: Integrative approaches* (pp. 243-262). New York: Springer-Verlag.

Berzonsky, M. D. (1989a). The self as a theorist: Individual differences in identity formation. *International Journal of Personal Construct Psychology, 2*, 363-376.

Berzonsky, M. D. (1989b). Identity style: Conceptualization and measurement. *Journal of Adolescent Research, 4*, 268-282.

Berzonsky, M. D. (1990). Self-construction over the life-span: A process perspective on identity formation. In G. J. Neimeyer & R. A. Neimeyer (Eds.), *Advances in personal construct theory* (Vol. 1, pp. 155-186). Greenwich, CT: JAI Press.

Berzonsky, M. D. (in press). Identity style and stress management: A process view of identity development. *Journal of Personality*.

Berzonsky, M. D., & Neimeyer, G. J. (1988). Identity status and personal construct systems. *Journal of Adolescence, 11*, 195-204.

Berzonsky, M. D., & Neimeyer, G. J. (1990). *Identity status and identity style*. Unpublished data.

Berzonsky, M. D., Rice, K. G., & Neimeyer, G. J. (1990). Identity status and self-construct systems: Process × Structure interactions. *Journal of Adolescence, 13*, 251-263.

Berzonsky, M. D., Schlenker, B. R., & McKillop, K. (1987, April). *Identity status, self-presentations, and self-conceptions*. Paper presented at the biennial meeting of the Society for Research in Child Development, Baltimore, MD.

Berzonsky, M. D., Trudeau, J. V., & Brenna, F. (1988, March). *Social-cognitive correlates of identity status*. Paper presented at the meeting of the Society for Research in Adolescence, Alexandria, VA.

Blasi, A. (1988). Identity and the development of the self. In D. K. Lapsley & F. C. Power (Eds.), *Self, ego, and identity: Integrative approaches* (pp. 226-242). New York: Springer-Verlag.

Blos, P. (1962). *On adolescence: A psychoanalytic interpretation.* New York: Free Press.

Block, J. (1982). Assimilation, accommodation, and the dynamics of personality development. *Child Development, 52,* 281-295.

Blustein, D. L., & Strohmer, D. C. (1987). Vocational hypothesis testing in career decision making. *Journal of Vocational Behavior, 31,* 45-62.

Bourne, E. (1978). The state of research on ego identity: A review and appraisal. Part II. Journal of Youth and Adolescence, 7, 371-392.

Carver, C. S., Scheier, M. F., & Weintraub, J. K. (1989). Assessing coping strategies: A theoretically based approach. *Journal of Personality and Social Psychology, 56,* 267-283.

Cheek, J. M., & Briggs, S. R. (1982). Self-consciousness and aspects of identity. *Journal of Research in Personality, 16,* 401-408.

Coleman, J. C. (1978). Current contradictions in adolescent theory. *Journal of Youth and Adolescence, 7,* 1-11.

Compas, B. E. (1987). Coping with stress during childhood and adolescence. *Psychological Bulletin, 101,* 393-403.

Cote, J. E., & Levin, C. (1988). A critical examination of the ego identity status paradigm. *Developmental Review, 8,* 147-184.

Douvan, E., & Adelson, J. (1966). *The adolescent experience.* New York: John Wiley.

Epstein, S. (1973). The self-concept revisited: Or a theory of a theory. *American Psychologist, 28,* 404-416.

Erikson, E. H. (1968). *Identity: Youth and crisis.* New York: Norton.

Folkman, S. (1984). Personal control and stress and coping processes: A theoretical analysis. *Journal of Personality and Social Psychology, 46,* 839-852.

Folkman, S., & Lazarus, R. S. (1980). An analysis of coping in a middle-aged community sample. *Journal of Health and Social Behavior, 21,* 219-239.

Folkman, S., & Lazarus, R. S. (1985). If it changes it must be a process: Study of emotion and coping during three stages of a college examination. *Journal of Personality and Social Psychology, 48,* 150-170.

Grotevant, H. D. (1987). Toward a process model of identity formation. *Journal of Adolescent Research, 2,* 203-222.

Grotevant, H. D., & Adams, G. R. (1984). Development of an objective measure to assess ego identity in adolescence: Validation and replication. *Journal of Youth and Adolescence, 13,* 419-438.

Hansen, R. D. (1985). Cognitive economy and commonsense attribution processing. In J. H. Harvey & G. Weary (Eds.), *Attribution in contemporary psychology* (pp. 65-85). New York: Academic Press.

Heider, F. (1958). *The psychology of interpersonal relations.* New York: John Wiley.

Jorgensen, R. S., & Dusek, J. B. (in press). Adolescent adjustment and coping strategies. *Journal of Personality.*

Kelly, G. A. (1955). *The psychology of personal constructs.* New York: Norton.

Kihlstrom, J. F., & Cantor, N. (1984). Mental representations of the self. In L. Berkowitz (Ed.), *Advances in experimental social psychology* (Vol. 17) (pp. 1-47). New York: Academic Press.

Langer, E. J., Blank, A., & Chanowitz, B. (1978). The mindlessness of ostensibly thoughtful action: The role of "placebic" information in interpersonal interaction. *Journal of Personality and Social Psychology, 36,* 635-642.

Lazarus, R. S. (1966). *Psychological stress and the coping process.* New York: McGraw-Hill.

Lazarus, R. S., & Folkman, S. (1984). *Stress, appraisal, and coping.* New York: Springer-Verlag.

Lobel, T. E., & Gilat, I. (1987). Type A behavior pattern, ego identity, and gender. *Journal of Research in Personality, 21,* 389-394.

Marcia, J. E. (1966). Development and validation of ego identity status. *Journal of Personality and Social Psychology, 3,* 551-558.

Marcia, J. E. (1967). Ego identity status: Relationship to change in self-esteem, "general maladjustment" and authoritarianism. *Journal of Personality, 35,* 118-133.

Marcia, J. E. (1976). Identity six years after: A follow-up study. *Journal of Youth and Adolescence, 5,* 145-160.

Marcia, J. E. (1980). Identity in adolescence. In J. Adelson (Ed.), *Handbook of adolescent psychology* (pp. 159-187). New York: John Wiley.

Marcia, J. E. (1988). Common processes underlying ego identity, cognitive/moral development, and individuation. In D. K. Lapsley & F. C. Power (Eds.), *Self, ego, and identity: Integrative approaches* (pp. 211-225). New York: Springer-Verlag.

Markus, H. (1977). Self-schemata and processing information about the self. *Journal of Personality and Social Psychology, 35,* 63-78.

Melgosa, J. (1985). *Occupational identity assessment among middle and late adolescents.* Unpublished dissertation, Andrews University.

Neimeyer, G. J., Prichard, S., Berzonsky, M. D., & Metzler, A. (1990). Vocational hypothesis testing: The role of occupational relevance and identity orientation. Manuscript submitted for publication.

Neisser, U. (1976). *Cognition and reality.* San Francisco: Freeman.

Offer, D. (1969). *The psychological world of the teenager.* New York: Basic Books.

Petty, R. E., Cacioppo, J. T., & Goldman, R. (1981). Personal involvement as a determinant of argument-based persuasion. *Journal of Personality and Social Psychology, 41,* 847-855.

Piaget, J. (1950). *Psychology of intelligence.* London: Kegan Paul.

Read, D., Adams, G. R., & Dobson, W. R. (1984). Ego-identity, personality and social influence style. *Journal of Personality and Social Psychology, 46,* 169-177.

Reischl, T. M., & Hirsch, B. J. (1989). Identity commitments and coping with a difficult developmental transition. *Journal of Youth and Adolescence, 18,* 55-69.

Schank, R. C., & Abelson, R. P. (1977). *Scripts, plans, goals, and understanding: An inquiry into human knowledge structures.* Hillsdale, NJ: Lawrence Erlbaum.

Schenkel, S., & Marcia, J. E. (1972). Attitudes toward premarital intercourse in determining ego identity status in women. *Journal of Personality, 40,* 472-482.

Shiffrin, R. M., & Schneider, W. (1977). Controlled and automatic human information processing: II. Perceptual learning, automatic attending, and general theory. *Psychological Review, 84,* 127-190.

Showers, C., & Cantor, N. (1985). Social cognition: A look at motivated strategies. *Annual Review of Psychology, 36,* 275-305.

Slugoski, B. R., Marcia, J. E., & Koopman, R. F. (1984). Cognitive and social interactional characteristics of ego identity status in college males. *Journal of Personality and Social Psychology, 47,* 646-661.

Snyder, M. (1974). Self-monitoring of expressive behavior. *Journal of Personality and Social Psychology, 30,* 526-537.

Tetlock, P. E., Skitka, L., & Boettger, R. (1989). Social and cognitive strategies for coping with accountability: Conformity, complexity, and bolstering. *Journal of Personality and Social Psychology, 57,* 632-640.

Vaillant, G. (1977). *Adaptation to life.* Boston: Little, Brown.

Waterman, A. S. (1982). Identity development from adolescence to adulthood: An extension of theory and a review of research. *Developmental Psychology, 18*, 341-358.

Waterman, A. S. (1986). Identity formation, metaphors, and values: A rejoinder to Berzonsky. *Journal of Early Adolescence, 6*, 119-121.

Wicklund, R. A., & Brehm, J. W. (1976). *Perspectives on cognitive dissonance.* Hillsdale, NJ: Lawrence Erlbaum.

11. Ego Identity and Adolescent Problem Behavior

Randall M. Jones
Utah State University

INTRODUCTION

Increasing national concern about substance abuse and a variety of adolescent problems has fostered a plethora of prevention/ intervention activities in recent years. Unfortunately, few of these efforts have yielded measurable decreases in substance-related behaviors (e.g., Botvin, 1983; Mauss, Hopkins, Weisheit, & Kearney, 1988; Moskowitz, 1983; Schaps, DiBartolo, Moskowitz, Palley, & Churgin, 1981). Tobler (1986) performed a meta-analysis on evaluation results from 143 adolescent prevention programs and concluded that her analysis "seriously challenges the concept that knowledge changes will lead to attitude changes with corresponding behavioral changes" (p. 560). Nevertheless, knowledge-based prevention programs continue to flourish despite mounting evidence that contraindicates continuation.

Why haven't these prevention programs been successful to date? A probable explanation is related to the fact that the "theoretical" underpinnings of most are difficult to identify, and when they do exist, they are typically a major source of weakness. For example, the "theory" that drives knowledge-based prevention approaches postulates that participants, when exposed to information and fact concerning the possibility of legal sanctions, known health risks, and so on, will be less likely to consume illicit substances when given a choice. To the contrary, many information-based prevention programs have actually been shown to increase substance use among participants (the "boomerang" effect).

The knowledge-attitude-behavior relationship has been and continues to be elusive. And yet, information-oriented attempts to prevent substance use and abuse are based entirely upon the unsubstantiated assumption that a change in knowledge will prevent or produce a change in undesirable behavior consistently and predictably. Unfortunately, many contemporary approaches to substance abuse prevention are based upon general assumptions with little or no empirical support. For example, the basis for information-based prevention approaches is "If people knew better, then . . . "; the basis for affective prevention approaches is "If people felt better about themselves, then . . . "; and the basis for the alternative strategy approach is "If people were aware of substance-free recreational activities, then . . ." Somewhat confusing is the fact that all of these approaches implicitly assume that people use and abuse substances for identical reasons, but these reasons vary from one prevention package to the next.

Clearly, the failure of previous prevention efforts is directly related to missing, illogical, and weak theoretical bases for prevention programming. This deficiency is quite disturbing, given that numerous theories of human learning, development, and behavior have been employed to explain (quite successfully) substance use/abuse and related behaviors. The work of Richard Jessor (problem behavior theory) and colleagues is but one example that has essentially been ignored in contemporary prevention curricula and programming.

PSYCHOSOCIAL EXPLANATIONS FOR SUBSTANCE USE AND ABUSE

According to Jessor (1987), "The most basic tenet of a psychosocial perspective on drinking behavior is that—like all other learned behavior—it is functional, purposive, and instrumental towards the attainment of goals" (p. 331). Moreover, goals change as one develops throughout the life span. During adolescence "problem behavior may be an instrumental effort to attain goals that are blocked or that seem otherwise unattainable. Thus, [problem behavior] may be a way of attaining independence from parental authority and taking control of one's life . . . [it] may serve as an expression of opposition to the norms and values of conventional society . . . [it] may serve as a coping mechanism . . . [it] may also function to express solidarity with peers or to demonstrate identification with the youth culture . . . and [it] may also serve to confirm personal identity" (Jessor, 1987; pp. 334-335). Baumrind (1987), too, acknowledges that "risk taking behavior characterizes normal adolescent development" (p. 98). So much for the unidimensional argument—*everybody does it for the same reason.*

Psychosocial explanations of substance use and related behaviors have proven to be quite robust (Chase & Donovan, 1980; Jessor, 1987; Jessor & Jessor, 1977, 1984), combining with environmental and behavioral constructs to explain more than 50% of the variability in composite measures of problem behavior, including substance use/abuse.

PSYCHOSOCIAL DEVELOPMENT, "RISKY BEHAVIOR," AND "RESILIENCY"

In a similar vein, the notion of "at risk" (similar to "problem behavior proneness") has generated a tremendous quantity of attention and research over the past decade. This approach has focused upon identifying risk factors associated with low socioeconomic status (SES), alcoholic and/or psychotic parents, maternal employment, troubled family relationships, separation and/or divorce. These factors are assumed to influence adolescents who, for example, exit the educational system prior to graduation; engage in substance use and abuse (Jessor, Chase, & Donovan, 1980; Newcomb & Bentler, 1988); participate in unprotected sexual relations; or develop problems with the legal system. Conversely, a more optimistic approach has evolved among a small group of scholars who have opted to view at-risk conditions somewhat differently by examining groups of vulnerable children and documenting ("resiliency") factors that appear to waylay seemingly probable doom.

The literature on "resilient children," that is, those who "recover from or adjust easily to misfortune or sustained life stress" (Werner, 1984, p. 68) echoes Erikson's (1963, 1968) theoretical notions regarding the eight stages of human psychosocial development. Researchers studying resilient children have observed and documented resiliency factors that parallel Erikson's description of healthy progression through the early stages of psychosocial development. For example, Erikson (1959, 1963, 1968) emphasizes the importance of maternal care during the first years for establishing a basic sense of trust versus mistrust; whereas, Werner (1986), in describing characteristics of the resilient children in her study, noted that "more of the resilient children had received a great deal of attention from their primary caretakers during the first year of life" (p. 37). Resilient children had "at least one caregiver from whom they received lots of attention during the first year of life" (Werner, 1984, p. 69). The resilient children described by Werner were in situations that were conducive to successful resolution of stage 1 in Erikson's paradigm.

Likewise, resilient children are known to exhibit pronounced autonomy (autonomy is associated with stage 2 in Erikson's model); they "seek out novel experiences, lack fear, and are quite self-reliant" (Werner, 1984, p. 69); they "often find a refuge and a source of self-esteem in hobbies and creative interests (initiative is the crisis of stage 3 in Erikson's model); ". . . such activities . . . gave them a reason to feel proud. Their hobbies, and their lively sense of humor, became a solace when things fell apart in their lives" (Werner, 1984, p. 69). As Werner further noted:

> [I]n middle childhood and adolescence resilient children are often engaged in acts of required helpfulness . . . many adolescents took care of their younger siblings. Some managed the household when a parent was ill or hospitalized; others worked part time after school to support the family. Resilient children are apt to like school and to do well in school, not exclusively in academics, but also in sports, drama, or music. (p. 70)

Clearly, the characteristics of the resilient children described by Werner and others parallel Erikson's writings regarding healthy psychosocial development.

Erikson (1959, 1963) asserted that successful resolution of the first four developmental stages facilitates resolution of stage 5 (identity versus role confusion) during adolescence and young adulthood. Conversely, inadequate or faulty resolution of the earlier stages will hinder identity development as well as successful resolution of stages that follow (stage 6—intimacy versus isolation; stage 7—generativity versus stagnation; and stage 8—integrity versus despair).

ADOLESCENT IDENTITY

The bulk of existing research concerned with identity formation has employed the identity status paradigm developed by Marcia (1966) which dichotomizes "crisis" (exploration) and "commitment." Briefly, individuals who commit to various ideologies and behavioral styles following an active period of exploration (crisis) are viewed as identity achievers; those who formulate commitments in the absence of exploration are viewed as foreclosures; those who are currently engaged in the process of exploring options but haven't solidified their commitments are viewed as moratoriums; and individuals void of commitments and exploration are classified as diffusions. Debates as to the utility of Marcia's (1966) identity statuses for evaluating Erikson's theoretical propositions are ongoing (see for example, Cote & Levine, 1987, 1988; Waterman, 1988). Nevertheless, the identity status paradigm has generated a wealth of research, most of which supports Erikson's theoretical premises.

Several studies have demonstrated that advanced stages of identity development (i.e., achievement and moratorium) are: (a) positively related to socioeconomic status (SES) (Archer, 1982; Raphael, 1978; St. Clair & Day, 1979); (b) positively related to age (Adams & Fitch, 1982; Marcia, 1976; Meilman, 1979; Munro & Adams, 1977); (c) mediated by certain family characteristics and childrearing styles (Adams & Jones, 1981, 1983; Conger, 1973); and (d) associated with documented gender differences (Adams & Fitch, 1982; Adams & Shea, 1979; LaVoie, 1976). Interestingly, these same correlates have been related to adolescent substance use and abuse (for SES, see Braucht, Brakarsch, Follingsted, & Berry, 1973; Winburn & Hayes, 1974; for age, see Brook, Lukoff, & Whiteman, 1977; Weschsler & McFadden, 1976; for family characteristics, see Currie, Perlman, & Walker, 1977; Jessor & Jessor, 1977; Rees & Wilborn, 1983).

The robustness of various psychosocial models for explaining substance use and abuse (cf. Baumrind & Moselle, 1985; Jessor et al., 1980), combined with documented correlates that are common to both identity development and substance use/abuse, and the similarities between resiliency and healthy psychosocial development all point to the utility of examining substance use in the context of identity formation. The remainder of this chapter will summarize four studies that address this issue.

EGO IDENTITY AND ADOLESCENT SUBSTANCE USE

Initially, substance use experience was examined in the context of the identity status paradigm (Jones & Hartmann, 1988). A total of 12,988 7th-grade through 12th-grade students attending 19 private and public schools in the state of Arizona completed the Young People Survey (Jones, 1986) during the 1985–1986 school year as part of an Arizona statewide needs assessment to determine the extent of youth involvement with both licit and illicit substances. The Young People Survey contains 9 demographic questions, 49 questions designed to elicit information regarding past and present involvement with alcohol and a variety of drugs, and 3 separate scales that measure Self-Esteem (Rosenberg, 1965), Social Desirability (Reynolds, 1982), and Ego Identity Status (Grotevant & Adams, 1984; Objective Measure of Ego-Identity Status, OMEIS).

A random sample of 6,975 students was selected and, using the procedures outlined by Grotevant and Adams (1984), classified into one of the four identity statuses: achievement, moratorium, foreclosure, and diffusion. Next, dichotomous (yes/no) responses to questions concerning lifetime experience ("Have you ever tried . . . ?") with cigarettes, alcohol, inhalants, marijuana, and cocaine were compared across the identity statuses, using a separate but identical discriminant analysis for each grade level (7th through 12th). The criterion variable in each analysis consisted of identity status classifications (achieved, moratorium, foreclosed, diffused, and "unclassified"), and six predictor variables consisted of the binary responses to questions regarding lifetime substance experience.

Not surprisingly, each (grade) analysis yielded a significant discrimination function, and in all instances, diffused respondents reported greater frequencies of substance-use experience, regardless of substance type, when compared to their cohorts who were classified as achieved, moratorium, or foreclosed. Conversely, foreclosed respondents reported the lowest frequencies of experience; while respondents classified as either moratorium or achieved reported experience levels that fell between the two extremes.

Although these data are summarized in detail elsewhere (Jones & Hartmann, 1988), the marijuana and cocaine comparisons are worth repeating here, particularly for foreclosed and diffused respondents. Among 7th-grade respondents, 36.8% of the diffused and 7.4% of the foreclosed respondents reported experience with marijuana. For the 8th-grade students these estimates had increased to 52.5% and 15.0%, respectively; and by 12th grade, 75% of the diffused and 33.3% of the foreclosed students had tried marijuana. As mentioned above, experience with marijuana for moratorium and achieved students fell between that of the foreclosed and diffused respondents (see Figure 11.1). Clearly, diffusions—at all grade levels—are at greater risk for substance use/abuse than their achieved, moratorium, and foreclosed agemates.

The patterns for cocaine experience parallel those for marijuana. More than 12% of the diffused 7th-grade respondents had tried cocaine, whereas experience estimates among foreclosed respondents were substantially lower (2.1%). By 10th grade, experience with cocaine had increased to 30.6% (diffused) and 7.4% (foreclosed); and at 12th grade, one-third (33.8%) of the diffused students and 15.5% of those classified as foreclosed had tried cocaine. Again, experience estimates for the achieved and moratorium respondents were sandwiched between the two extremes (foreclosure and diffusion).

Generally, diffused 7th-grade through 12th-grade respondents were about twice as likely to have tried cigarettes and alcohol, three times as likely to have tried marijuana, four times as likely to have tried inhalants, and five times as likely to have tried cocaine than their foreclosed agemates.

EGO IDENTITY AND ADOLESCENT
MOTIVATIONS FOR SUBSTANCE USE

Using the same sample (n = 12,988), Christopherson, Jones, and Sales (1988) randomly selected 1,691 adolescents (approximately 200 for each of the ideological and interpersonal classifications of achievement, moratorium, foreclosure, and diffusion) to see if reported motivations for substance use varied systematically across

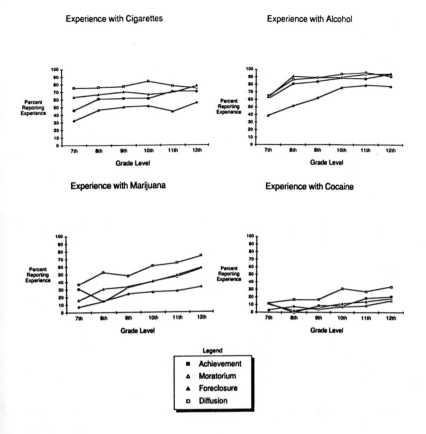

Figure 11.1
SOURCE: Adapted from Jones and Hartmann (1988). Ego Identity: Developmental differences and experimental substance use among adolescents. *Journal of Adolescence.*

the identity classifications. For this study, two multiple-response, forced-choice questions assessed motivation for chemical use and nonuse: "In your opinion, why do people your age use alcohol and drugs?" and, "If you have never experimented with alcohol, what has stopped you from trying it?" (Jones, 1986, p. 80). For both, respondents were instructed to circle all response options that applied. These options were generated during an earlier (1984) pilot test of the Young People Survey, and the most common of these were included in the final version. The final set of response options for the first question were *Peer Pressure, Recreational Purposes, Stress, Curiosity, Boredom,* and *Holidays (Christmas, New Year's Eve, and such).* Response options for the second question were: *Fear of Alcohol, No Interest, Religion, Friends, Fear of Arrest, Fear of Parents Finding Out,* and *Health.* To test for differences, univariate analyses of variance were computed, using the binary variables (the dichotomous response generated for each possible motivation) as dependent measures, and the identity classifications as independent variables.

Cited motivations for use were notably discrepant across the identity statuses. Comparisons across the ideological identity classifications indicated that achieved (51.6%) and moratorium (45.3%) youths—both groups previously or currently experiencing crisis—were much more likely to cite *Curiosity* as a motivation for substance use than their foreclosed (20.7%) and diffused (38.8%) agemates. *Recreation* (39.5% achieved, 45.7% moratorium, 27.6% foreclosed, and 36.5% diffused) and *Peers* (52.9%, 52.3%, 51.2%, and 36.5%, respectively) also yielded significant variance ratios across the ideological identity classifications.

For interpersonal comparisons, all but one (*Peers*) of the motivational response options were significantly different across the identity classifications. From the achieved, moratorium, foreclosed, and diffused respondents, response frequencies were as follows: *Recreation* 42.2%, 35.3%, 29.7%, 37.5%; *Curiosity* 43.6%, 49.3%, 34.0%, 36.6%; *Boredom* 23.2%, 21.6%, 16.0%, 36.0%; *Holidays* 26.1%, 27.5%, 20.0%, 19.3%; and *Stress* 37.3%, 35.9%, 33.3%, 30.5%.

For the question "What has stopped you from trying alcohol?" *Religion, No Interest,* and *Fear of Arrest* were significantly different across the identity classifications regardless of domain (interpersonal and ideological). Within the ideological domain, 10.5% of the achieved and 10.6% of the foreclosed respondents (both committed statuses) cited religion as a reason for abstinence—compared to 3.0% and 2.0% of the moratorium and diffused respondents. As for the interpersonal identity statuses, the largest differences emerged for *No Interest* (achieved 24.0%, moratorium 22.9%, foreclosed 37.3%, and diffused 14.9%) and *Fear of Arrest* (achieved 4.9%, moratorium 6.5%, foreclosed 9.3%, and diffused 9.5%).

These data demonstrate that motivations for substance use, as well as abstention from alcohol, differ across the identity statuses in a theoretically (identity status theory) consistent manner. The achieved and moratorium respondents, both groups (by definition) having experienced a period of exploration, cited *Curiosity* as a reason for experimenting with substances more frequently than their foreclosed and diffused agemates. Likewise, achieved and foreclosed respondents, both groups (by definition) having solidified various commitments, cited *Religion* as a reason for abstaining from alcohol more frequently than their agemates classified as moratoriums or diffusions. These differences were evident regardless of whether the respondents had actually tried these licit and/or illicit substances.

ADOLESCENT SUBSTANCE ABUSERS
VERSUS ADOLESCENTS IN SCHOOL:
A COMPARISON OF IDENTITY PROFILES

Given the variation in use rates (Jones & Hartmann, 1988) and the differences in motivations for use that were observed across the identity statuses (Christopherson, Jones, & Sales, 1988), a third study was designed to contrast the identity profiles of adolescents in a residential treatment center against adolescents attending Arizona schools (Jones, Hartmann, Grochowski, & Glider, 1989). Initially, all 27 adolescents in a Southwest Arizona residential treatment center, age 18 or younger, completed the Young People Survey in a group setting on the same day. Each question was read aloud by a member of the treatment staff, who also collected the completed questionnaires and coded the number of days in residence for each respondent.

The nonclinical (i.e., in school) group was extracted from a larger data base (n = 26,764), consisting of junior high and senior high school students who completed the Young People Survey during the fall of 1987. For purposes of this study, the nonclinical sample was randomly selected from a cohort that was intentionally matched (age, gender, ethnicity, grade, religious preference, and church attendance) to the clinical sample. This process yielded a matched random sample (n = 54) of adolescents attending school (n = 27) or residential treatment (n = 27).

To contrast the identity profiles of both groups, a stepwise discriminant analysis was employed, where group membership (clinical versus school) was entered as the criterion variable, and scores from the eight EOM-EIS subscales (ideological and interpersonal achievement, moratorium, foreclosure, and diffusion) were entered as discriminating variables. Four of the eight subscales (namely interpersonal achievement and foreclosure, and ideological achievement and moratorium) combined to form a significant function, which explained 75.7% of the variability in group membership.

Group means for these subscales revealed that the student group was more psychosocially "sophisticated" than the clinical group, as evidenced by higher scores on interpersonal achievement (34.16 versus 21.00), ideological achievement (32.11 versus 24.33), and ideological moratorium (29.78 versus 28.33); whereas adolescents in treatment registered higher scores on the interpersonal foreclosure subscale (34.89 versus 22.74). The classification function based upon this analysis was able to identify actual group membership for 53 of the 54 respondents: 100% of the clinical group was placed correctly and 96.3% (all but one) of the student group was identified. Ninety-eight percent of the sample was classified correctly, using only their identity profiles. Even treatment duration (an obvious "red flag"), *when forced* into the function during the last step, was unable to add additional explanatory power to the analysis.

The finding that known substance abusers obtained higher foreclosure scores than the comparison group contradicted our expectations. Previous research (Jones & Hartmann, 1988) had shown that foreclosures were *less likely* to get involved with substances, and yet, known substance abusers obtained foreclosure scores that were almost twice those of the comparison group. Perhaps aspects of the treatment process were inflating foreclosure scores? Bivariate correlations between days in treatment and both ideological ($r = -.33$) and interpersonal foreclosure ($r = -.26$) contradicted this argument. Obviously, data from this investigation raised at least as many questions as it answered, but the utility of using the EOM-EIS with adolescents in treatment had been demonstrated. Longitudinal data were needed to further define the relationship between the identity statuses and substance use.

Given that resilient children seem to possess the very same qualities that Erikson deemed necessary for successful resolution of the identity crisis (namely trust, autonomy, initiative, and industry), and given that adolescents who are having difficulty resolving identity issues (diffusion) also report higher levels of substance use, the central question reduces to one of which came first. In other words, the literature on resilient children clearly suggests that psychosocially healthy children may be inoculated against the pressures involved with substance use and associated at-risk behaviors; and our own research on identity and substance use also indicated that psychosocially advanced adolescents are less likely to use substances. Moreover, when they do, they do for reasons that are quite discrepant from those of their diffused peers. Does substance use/abuse impede normal psychosocial development? Or is abnormal psychosocial development conducive to heightened frequencies of substance use? The final study to be summarized in this chapter was designed to address this issue.

A SHORT-TERM LONGITUDINAL INVESTIGATION OF PSYCHOSOCIAL DEVELOPMENT AND SUBSTANCE USE

For this study, 509 3rd-grade and 4th-grade children were assessed on Erikson's first five stages of development in January of 1988, and again the following May. Additionally, these children were asked whether they had ever tried various substances (cigarettes, smokeless tobacco, alcohol, marijuana, inhalants, and cocaine), and if not, whether they expect to try them in the future (behavioral intentions).

Erikson's stages of development were assessed, using a modified version of the Rosenthal, Gurney, and Moore (1981) "Erikson Psychosocial Inventory Scale" (EPSI). The original instrument was developed to measure the first six stages in Erikson's paradigm (trust, autonomy, initiative, industry, identity, and intimacy) among "respondents of about 13 years of age or above" (Rosenthal et al., 1981, p. 528). Our revisions to the EPSI were guided by feedback provided by several 3rd-grade and 4th-grade teachers, one elementary school principal, and two volunteer parents (who, at the time, had children in either the 3rd or 4th grade). All 12 of the intimacy items were deemed inappropriate for 3rd- and 4th-grade students, so were not included in the revision. Also, of the 60 original items corresponding to the first five stages, 38 were reproduced verbatim, 16 underwent slight revision, and 6 were replaced completely. The response format was also changed from a 5-point Likert scale to an "Almost Always"—"Almost Never" dichotomy. Groups were formed on the basis of whether experience with any of the six substances had increased over the 5-month interval, or remained the same. In other words, all respondents who reported having tried at least one new substance between January and May were combined to form an "increase in experience" group (n = 131), and respondents who reported identical substance use experiences in both January and May constituted the "no change" group (n = 378).

To examine the relationship between psychosocial development and substance-use experience, a 2 × 2 × 2 multivariate analysis of variance was computed, where all five EPSI subscales were entered as dependent measures, and grade (3rd versus 4th), experience with substances (increase versus no change), and gender (male versus female) constituted the independent variables. Results from this analysis yielded significant multivariate F ratios for the main effects of gender and experience with substances, but grade effects were not significant. All 2- and 3-way interactions were nonsignificant as well.

Univariate analyses of covariance (2-gender × 2-substance experience × 2-grade) using time 2 scale scores as dependent measures in separate analyses (covarying time 1 scores) revealed that the main effect of substance experience was significant for measures of trust, industry, and identity. Cell means indicated that for trust, respondents in the "increased" experience group (mean = 8.30) scored significantly lower than their peers who reported identical experiences with substances in January and May (mean = 8.69). The adjusted means (adjusted for all three independent variables and time 1 trust scores) were even more discrepant (8.25 versus 8.69). Likewise, for industry scale scores, respondents who reported "increased" substance-use experience (mean = 8.00) scored significantly lower than those who remained stable (mean = 8.62). And a similar pattern was evident in identity scores ("increased," mean = 8.00; "stable," mean = 9.49).

In all instances, students who increased their experience with substances during the 5-month interval also scored lower on measures of psychosocial development. While these differences were not significant for the measures of autonomy and initiative, comparisons for trust, industry, and identity were quite discrepant. Students who increased their substance-use experience netted small gains in trust (+1.1%), autonomy (+3.9%), and initiative (+1.2%); but their industry (−2.2%) and identity (−0.1%) scores decreased. Conversely, students who did not increase their substance-use experience gained on all measures: trust +7.9%; autonomy +6.4%; initiative +5.0%; industry +5.8%; and identity +4.9%.

Clearly, these data indicate that early involvement with various substances may impede normal psychosocial development. Hence, the fact that diffused adolescents report greater frequencies of substance use (Jones & Hartmann, 1988) is partially attributable to the fact that early involvement with substances may hamper successful resolution of the developmental tasks (trust, autonomy, initiative, and industry) that are necessary for healthy identity formation, therefore inflating the likelihood of diffusion during adolescence. Baumrind and others (Baumrind, 1987; Baumrind & Moselle, 1985) have speculated that early substance use/abuse may impede adolescent development: "including impairment of attention and memory; developmental lag in cognitive, moral and psychosocial domains, motivational syndrome; consolidation of diffuse or negative identity; and social alienation and estrangement" (Baumrind, 1987, p. 103). Findings from this study on preadolescents indicate that the negative effects of substance use/abuse on adolescent development (at least with respect to psychosocial development) may be a function of earlier developmental problems.

FOSTERING PSYCHOSOCIAL DEVELOPMENT AS AN ALTERNATIVE TO TRADITIONAL PREVENTION/INTERVENTION APPROACHES

In a recent survey of all 222 school districts in the state of Arizona (Robinson, 1988), 77 identified (by "brand name") the substance abuse prevention programs being used in their districts. And even though a majority of these districts listed two or three different programs (typically varying by elementary school, junior high/middle school, and high school), almost 50 (n = 47) different "brand names" were listed by the 77 responding districts. Fewer than one-fifth (18.5%) of the districts had conducted an evaluation of their programs.

Aside from imparting information concerning alcohol, cigarettes, marijuana, narcotics, cocaine, and other drugs, most of the identified programs also emphasize decision-making skills, refusal skills, and strategies for resisting peer pressure. This was generally the case, regardless of whether the targeted populations were elementary school, junior high/middle school, or high school.

Collectively, the research on psychosocial maturity, substance use/abuse, and related problem behavior offers important insights as to why our previous unidimensional approaches to prevention/intervention have not been successful. By assuming that similar behavior serves an identical purpose for all who choose to emit that behavior, we have failed to acknowledge individual differences. This oversight may be analogous to a surgeon who performs appendectomies on all patients, regardless of their symptoms; to a financial planner who recommends stocks to all clients, regardless of their financial status; or to a statistical consultant who recommends analysis of variance to all clients, regardless of their hypotheses, design, level of measurement, and so forth. Prevention "professionals" who are ignorant of individual differences, similar to a century's worth of substance use and abuse prevention/intervention approaches, are destined to fail.

The fact that substance use (and related problem behavior) is mediated by psychosocial development creates some interesting possibilities for prevention and intervention. Awareness of an individual's identity status provides insight regarding (a) motivation for initial and continued use; (b) the probability that an individual will experiment with various licit and illicit substances; and (c) the probability that an individual, having experimented with various substances, will eventually develop addictive problems. Prevention/intervention recipients may benefit if various efforts are designed and delivered on the basis of preidentified (and matched) target populations.

REFERENCES

Adams, G. R., & Fitch, S. A. (1982). Ego stage and identity status development: A cross-sequential analysis. *Journal of Personality and Social Psychology, 43,* 574-583.

Adams, G. R., & Jones, R. M. (1981). Female adolescent's ego development: Age comparisons and child rearing perceptions. *Journal of Early Adolescence, 1*, 423-426.

Adams, G. R., & Shea, J. A. (1979). The relationship between identity status, locus of control, and ego development. *Journal of Youth and Adolescence, 8*, 81-89.

Archer, S. L. (1982). The lower age boundaries of identity development. *Child Development, 53*, 1551-1556.

Baumrind, D. (1987). A developmental perspective on adolescent risk taking in contemporary America. In C. E. Irwin (Ed.), *New directions for child development: No. 37. Adolescent social behavior and health*. San Francisco: Jossey-Bass.

Baumrind, D., & Moselle, K. (1985). A developmental perspective on adolescent drug use. *Advances in Alcohol and Substance Abuse, 4*, 41-67.

Botvin, G. J. (1983). Prevention of adolescent substance abuse through development of personal and social competence. In T. J. Glynn, C. G. Leukefeld, & J. P. Ludford (Eds.), *Preventing adolescent drug abuse: Intervention strategies*. Rockville, MD: National Institute on Drug Abuse (NIDA) Monograph #47.

Braucht, G. N., Brakarsch, D., Follingsted, D., & Berry, K. L. (1973). Deviant drug use in adolescence: A review of psychosocial correlates. *Psychological Bulletin, 79*, 92-106.

Brook, J. S., Lukoff, L. F., & Whitman, M. (1977). Correlates of marijuana use as related to age, sex, and ethnicity. *Yale Journal of Biological Medicine, 50*, 383-390.

Christopherson, B. B., Jones, R. M., & Sales, A. P. (1988). Diversity in reported motivations for substance use as a function of ego-identity development. *Journal of Adolescent Research, 3*, 141-152.

Conger, J. J. (1973). *Adolescence and youth*. New York: Harper & Row.

Cote, J. E., & Levine, C. (1987). A formulation of Erikson's theory of ego identity formation. *Developmental Review, 7*, 273-325.

Cote, J. E., & Levine, C. (1988). A critical examination of the ego identity status paradigm. *Developmental Review, 8*, 147-184.

Currie, R. F., Perlman, D., & Walker, L. (1977). Marijuana use among Calgary youths as a function of sampling and locus of control. *British Journal of Addiction, 72*, 159-165.

Erikson, E. H. (1959). Growth and crisis of the healthy personality. In G. S. Klein (Ed.), *Psychological issues*. New York: International Universities Press.

Erikson, E. H. (1963). *Childhood and Society* (2nd ed). New York: Norton.

Erikson, E. H. (1968). *Identity: Youth and crisis*. New York: Norton.

Grotevant, H. D., & Adams, G. R. (1984). Development of an objective measure to assess ego identity in adolescence: Validation and replication. *Journal of Youth and Adolescence, 13*, 419-438.

Jessor, R. (1987). Problem-behavior theory, psychosocial development, and adolescent problem drinking. *British Journal of Addiction, 82*, 331-342.

Jessor, R., Chase, J. A., & Donovan, J. E. (1980). Psychosocial correlates of marijuana use and problem drinking in a national sample of adolescents. *American Journal of Public Health, 70*, 604-613.

Jessor, R., & Jessor, S. L. (1977). *Problem behavior and psycho-social development: A longitudinal study of youth*. New York: Academic Press.

Jessor, R., & Jessor, S. L. (1984). Adolescence to young adulthood: A 12-year prospective study of problem behavior and psychosocial development. In S. A. Mednick, M. Harway, & K. M. Finello (Eds.), *Handbook of longitudinal research: Teenage and adult cohorts*. New York: Praeger.

Jones, R. M. (1986). *Young People Survey results for school 16*. Unpublished manuscript.

Jones, R. M. (submitted). Psychosocial development and substance use in third and fourth grade students: A longitudinal assessment.

Jones, R. M., & Hartmann, B. R. (1988). Ego identity: Developmental differences and experimental substance use among adolescents. *Journal of Adolescence, 11*, 347-360.

Jones, R. M., Hartmann, B. R., Grochowski, C. O., & Glider, P. (1989). Ego identity and substance abuse: A comparison of adolescents in residential treatment with adolescents in school. *Personality and Individual Differences, 10*, 625-631.

LaVoie, J. C. (1976). Ego identity formation in middle adolescence. *Journal of Youth and Adolescence, 5*, 371-385.

Marcia, J. E. (1966). Development and validation of ego identity status. *Journal of Personality and Social Psychology, 3*, 551-558.

Marcia, J. E. (1976). Identity six years after: A follow-up study. *Journal of Youth and Adolescence, 5*, 145-160.

Mauss, A. L., Hopkins, R. H., Weisheit, R. A., & Kearney, K. A. (1988). Prevention in the classroom: Do alcohol education programs reduce drinking? *Brown University Digest of Addiction Theory and Application, 7*, 62-65.

Meilman, P. W. (1979). Cross-sectional age changes in ego identity status during adolescence. *Developmental Psychology, 18*, 230-231.

Moskowitz, J. M. (1983). Preventing adolescent substance abuse through drug education. In T. J. Glynn, C. G. Leukefeld, & J. P. Ludford (Eds.), *Preventing adolescent drug abuse: Intervention strategies*. Rockville, MD: NIDA Monograph #47.

Munro, G., & Adams, G. R. (1977). Ego identity formation in college students and working youth. *Developmental Psychology, 13*, 523-524.

Newcomb, M. D., & Bentler, P. M. (1988). *Consequences of adolescent drug use: Impact on the lives of young adults*. Newbury Park, CA: Sage.

Raphael, D. (1978). Identity status in high school females. *Adolescence, 13*, 627-642.

Rees, C. D., & Wilborn, B. L. (1983). Correlates of drug abuse in adolescents: A comparison of families of drug abusers with families of non-drug abusers. *Journal of Youth and Adolescence, 12*, 55-63.

Reynolds, W. M. (1982). Development of reliable and valid short forms of the Marlowe-Crowne social desirability scale. *Journal of Clinical Psychology, 38*, 119-125.

Robinson, S. E. (1988). *Substance abuse prevention programs in Arizona schools*. Unpublished document, Arizona State University.

Rosenberg, M. (1965). *Society and the Adolescent Self Image*. Princeton, NJ: Princeton University Press.

Rosenthal, D. A., Gurney, R. R., & Moore, S. M. (1981). From trust to intimacy: A new inventory for examining Erikson's stages of psychosocial development. *Journal of Youth and Adolescence, 10*, 525-537.

Schaps, E., DiBartolo, R., Moskowitz, J. M., Palley, C. S., & Churgin, S. (1981). A review of 127 drug abuse prevention program evaluations. *Journal of Drug Issues, 11*, 27-43.

St. Clair, A., & Day, H. D. (1979). Ego identity status and values among high school females. *Journal of Youth and Adolescence, 8*, 317-326.

Tobler, N. S. (1986). Meta-analysis of 143 adolescent drug prevention programs: Quantitative outcome results of program participants compared to a control or comparison group. *Journal of Drug Issues, 16*, 537-567.

Waterman, A. S. (1988). Identity status theory and Erikson's theory: Communalities and differences. *Developmental Review, 8*, 185-208.

Werner, E. E. (1984). Resilient children. *Young Children, 40*, 68-72.

Werner, E. E. (1986). Resilient offspring of alcoholics: A longitudinal study from birth to age 18. *Journal of Studies on Alcohol, 47*, 34-40.

Weschler, H., & McFadden, M. (1976). Sex differences in adolescent alcohol and drug use: A disappearing phenomenon. *Journal of Studies on Alcohol, 37*, 1291-1301.

Winburn, G. M., & Hayes, J. R. (1974). Dropouts: A study of drug use. *Journal of Drug Education, 4*, 249-254.

Index

About the Editors

Gerald R. Adams is a Professor in the Department of Family Studies at the University of Guelph. He is a Fellow of the American Psychological Association and has been awarded the James D. Moran Research Award from the American Home Economics Association. Currently he has editorial assignments with the *Journal of Adolescence*, *Journal of Primary Prevention*, *Journal of Early Adolescence*, and *Social Psychology Quarterly*.

Thomas P. Gullotta is Executive Director of the Child and Family Agency of Southeastern Connecticut. Holding academic appointments at several state colleges in Connecticut, he is a nationally recognized expert in the field of primary prevention and adolescence. In addition to being the founding editor of the *Journal of Primary Prevention*, he currently serves on the editorial boards of *Family Relations*, the *Journal of Early Adolescence*, and the *Journal of Adolescence*.

Raymond Montemayor is Associate Professor of Psychology at The Ohio State University. His research interests include parent-adolescent relations, conduct disorders, behavioral approaches to the study of adolescence, peer relations during adolescence, and adolescent substance abuse. He is Associate Editor for the *Journal of Early Adolescence* and is an editorial board member for the *Journal of Adolescent Research*.

About the Contributors

Sally L. Archer is an Associate Professor of Psychology at Trenton State College. A developmental psychologist, she received her master's degree from Tulane University in 1973 and her Ph.D. from the University of Pennsylvania in 1980. Her research interests include adolescent development, identity and intimacy formation across the life-span, and gender-role socialization. She is a co-author of the forthcoming book, *Ego-Identity: A Handbook for Psychosocial Research.*

Michael D. Berzonsky is Professor of Psychology at the State University of New York at Cortland. He received his Ph.D. from the University of Toronto in 1969. His current research interests include adolescent identity formation, social-cognitive processes, and self-construction across the life span.

Harke A. Bosma (1946) graduated in 1972 at the State University of Groningen, the Netherlands, with a major in developmental psychology. In 1985 he completed his doctoral dissertation on identity development in adolescence. In 1972 he was appointed Lecturer at the Department of Psychology of the University of Groningen, and in 1985 he was appointed Senior Lecturer in Adolescent Psychology.

Harold D. Grotevant is Professor and Head of the Department of Family Social Science, and Adjunct Professor of Child Psychology, at the University of Minnesota. His research concerns human development within the context of the family, parent-adolescent relationships, and relationships in adoptive families. He is a Fellow of the American Psychological Association and recipient of the James D. Moran Research Award for his research on adolescents and their families.

Randall M. Jones received his Ph.D. in Educational Psychology (1984) from The University of Arizona. He presently holds positions in Family and Human Development and Psychology (adjunct) at Utah State University. Teaching and research interests address adolescent development and problem behavior, with emphasis upon psychosocial indicators of risk. He is currently designing interventions to address psychosocial difficulties with the intent of decreasing adolescent problem behavior.

Jane Kroger is Associate Professor of Human Development and Counseling in the Education Department, Victoria University at Wellington, Wellington, New

Zealand. She has published widely in the area of adolescent identity development, including a book and more than 30 journal articles. Her current research examines interrelationships among different structural developmental measures of identity during late adolescence.

James E. Marcia is a professor at Simon Fraser University. He received his Ph.D. in clinical psychology from The Ohio State University and has directed psychological clinics at both SUNY/Buffalo and Simon Fraser University. He has a private practice in psychotherapy; his research interests are in construct validation of psychosocial developmental theory.

Carol Markstrom-Adams is an Assistant Professor in the Department of Family Studies at the University of Guelph in Guelph, Ontario. Her publications and presentations have centered on identity formation among ethnic minority adolescents, interventions designed to enhance identity formation, social relationships between religious minority and majority adolescents, and sex roles in adolescence.

Serena J. Patterson is a psychology instructor at North Island College in Campbell River, B.C. She received her Ph.D. in clinical psychology from Simon Fraser University. Her research interests are in feminist psychodynamic theory and ego development in women.

Jean S. Phinney is a professor of psychology at California State University, Los Angeles. She received her B.A. from Wellesley College, and her Ph.D. from the University of California at Los Angeles. Her primary interest is in social development. Her research focuses on ethnic identity, ethnic attitudes, and intergroup relations in adolescence.

Doreen A. Rosenthal is a Reader in Psychology at The University of Melbourne, Australia. She received her Ph.D. from that university in 1975. Her research interests include the adaptation and acculturation of ethnic minorities. She is currently investigating the predictors of adolescent sexual risk-taking behavior in the context of HIV/AIDS.

Ingrid Sochting has studied psychology at the University of Copenhagen and is currently a doctoral student in clinical psychology at Simon Fraser University. Her research interests include identity development in women and the influence of gender and sex-role orientation on moral reasoning and prosocial behavior.

Alan S. Waterman earned his Ph.D. in clinical psychology from SUNY/Buffalo. He is Professor of Psychology at Trenton State College. His scholarly interests include the philosophical foundations of personality theories, the nature of optimal psychological functioning, and identity formation from adolescence to adulthood. His books include *The Psychology of Individualism* (Praeger) and *Identity in Adolescence: Processes and Contents* (Jossey-Bass). He is serving as the North American Editor for the *Journal of Adolescence*.